Ukuaq
A WOMAN'S ARCTIC MEMOIR

Dorothee Komangapik

crowecreations.ca
Ottawa Canada

Ukuaq, A Woman's Arctic Memoir © 2022 by Dorothee Komangapik

All rights reserved. No part of this book may be reproduced or transmitted in any form or by any means, electronic or mechanical, including photocopying, recording, electronic transmission, or by any storage and retrieval system, without written permission from the author except for the purposes of study or review.

First Crowe Creations print edition October 2022

Designed by Crowe Creations
Text set in Times New Roman; headings in Gill Sans MT Condensed

Cover photo © Jeeteetah Merkosak
Cover design © 2022 by Crowe Creations

Crowe Creations
ISBN: 978-1-927058-99-2

To my family in memory of
those we loved, now passed away,
and all we had to leave behind.

And still, I rise. — Maya Angelou

Foreword

Here I present the events that led to my going to Pond Inlet, called Mittimatalik by Inuit, on the northern coast of Baffin Island on the northeast coast of Canada, my leaving, returning, and then staying as ukuaq (a daughter-in-law or relative in-law). And, later, how and why I left.

I have been asked this question: "Why would a decent-looking, well-educated young woman throw her life away like this?" I hope to explore this in this memoir.

Although there are scenes from earlier times, the main events occur between 1973 and 1986, a period during which Inuit emerged from being called "uncivilized Eskimos", but still long before the establishment of the Nunavut Territory as one of the Inuit homelands in 1991. Much has changed since then.

Part I
1973–75

One

It all began with an ending as all adventures do.

This particular spring day had been sunny, full of promise. I felt unreasonably hopeful all day, but now the sun had gone down and it was time. I climbed the stairs and opened the door. I knew it was never locked when Michael was in his studio. He sat at his drawing table in the large, mostly empty room. Some panels leaned against a wall, random shapes of pink plastic. The electric router and jigsaw stood against the far wall. They showed signs of use. There was a little mound of pink, acrylic sawdust neatly swept together onto a dustpan. He was always so careful and organized, even in the throes of artistic inventiveness. I was glad this had not changed. At least he appreciated and used the equipment I had given him for his birthday the previous year.

It had been a few months since we had last set eyes on each other. Since our breakup, he always avoided me if he could and refused to talk to me when I tried to speak with him. I was surprised that he had agreed to see me when I happened to bump into him on the street this morning. For me, our meeting tonight was to clear the air between us so we could either take up where we had left off in our marriage, or go on our separate ways. Our mutual friends reported they had not been able to get him to talk about me or our marriage. He was not a verbally expressive person and did not like to share his private life, I knew. When sober, he was not known to speak much. But he spoke passionate volumes on impersonal topics like philosophy or politics when he was drunk or high. Now he was cold-sober and silent.

I stood near the door, while across the studio before the window he sat bent over his drawing table. We kept our distance, each of us probably wary of expectations. First, our initial monosyllabic hellos, then a long silence. He had said on the street that he had an answer for me and invited me here this evening. Finally, I broke the silence.

"So, what's the answer? Are we still a married couple, or not?"

"Um. That. Yes." Pause. "Well, actually …"

He took another pause, took a deep breath, and looked up so I could see his face, his blue eyes. He knows that I don't usually hear well when I cannot see the face.

"We're not," he said. "We're not married anymore."

He spoke in clear final tones. There was no mistaking their meaning, no chance for misinterpretation.

"Thank you for telling me," I mumbled. "I know it was hard for you to speak."

I turned and somehow stumbled down the stairs to the street. I let my tears flow down my cheeks when I reached the sidewalk. The love of my life said we are not married anymore. The empty future without him loomed in front of me. How could he reject me? He, who cared so little about my flaws when he had married me. I began to remember our shared past. Perhaps the answer to the question why this had happened would come to me.

❊

The first time I met Michael we were both twelve years old, his birthday a little over a month before mine in the summer of the same year. We were at the mayor's office where they presented prizes to the winners of the county logo design contest held in area elementary schools. I won first prize, a boy in my class, Cornelius, won second prize, and Michael, from another school, won third prize. I was tall and pudgy; in contrast, Michael was short and skinny. The top of his head just reached my chin. I was given a big ornate plaque to be displayed at my school. My parents and his mother were there but his father did not attend. My parents had brought me and were very proud of me. Photos were taken of the mayor and the contest winners for the next edition of the local newspaper.

Michael in 1974.

The previous school year, after I had visited Germany during school holidays, I was fitted with glasses. I went suddenly from being the class dummy to smart person almost overnight. And I gained the attention of a teacher who believed in my artistic talent. I suppose that helped me to win this contest. From class dummy to winning an arts prize was to my Papa a sign that I did possess a smidgen of intelligence after all, as Mama had always claimed.

The next time I met Michael was in the second year of high school when we attended classes in the refurbished old folks' home while our new high school was being built. The old people had been moved into their new retirement home up the road. By this time, Michael had grown taller and had caught up with me in height, but he was still quite skinny. By this time, I had developed breasts which offset some of the excess weight I carried. I thought I looked better than I had at twelve. We recognized each other as artistic rivals but soon became friends. On breaks, we used to cross the street to smoke at the new drive-in restaurant and

Class 10B in 1959, me far left in 1st row and Michael second left in 2nd row.

talk. We talked about becoming artists and even shared an art class. I was so happy to have a friend who was a boy, even if he was not my boyfriend. But this came to an abrupt end by peer pressure.

"Hey, Mike, come on. What are you doing, anyways, hanging around with that dog?"

The "dog", I knew, was me. This was Michael's best friend speaking. I saw Michael turn bright red in shame, smile crookedly at me, shrug his shoulders and turn away to go with his friends. After that, he did not speak to me again, not even in art class. I heard later that the art teacher had arranged for him to go to the Ontario College of Art in Toronto the year he graduated. I missed my Michael, my friend, but was happy that he could start on his arts career in the face of his father's objections.

Oh well, I could not blame him, I thought. I was, after all, just some overweight, sad, teenage girl. And friends come and go, don't they? The year before, my one and only girl friend had suddenly moved away to Chicago and we lost touch.

Making friends was not easy for me. I was a German immigrant and that did not wear well with those of English or of other European country origins or descent. This remained a problem, even a decade after the end of World War II, even though I dressed like the other girls and spoke English without an accent, not like poor Mama with her Germanized English pronunciation.

My life skidded along without Michael. I tried having boyfriends, but Papa's interrogations scared them away. I spent my free time writing poetry and painting pictures. Summers were spent learning to sail boats at the yacht club arranged by Papa as he was moving up in the world of business. I participated in a school-arranged student exchange trip to Trois Rivières, Quebec, to practise my spoken French and started a correspondence with a boy I met there. Unfortunately, the last letter I got was from his mother. She wrote that he had entered a Catholic seminary school and would no longer be writing to me. These things happen, I thought, as I moved to another high school for my last grade.

In my last year at high school, I had just won an inter-school poetry contest, but had failed my final English examination. That had been a great disappointment. I had always been good at English and had dreamed of becoming a writer. When the elderly teacher heard that I had won the contest, she offered to re-mark my examination to give me a better mark, no doubt to protect her reputation. Feeling somewhat vengeful, I refused. I had struggled with her all year and I was not going to let her off that easy. I had nothing to lose at this point. I was not doing well in my other classes. My home life was a constant battle with my critical, controlling Papa. I had no friends. It was hard for me to feel hopeful about anything. And now this.

Ursula, Mama, me, and Irmgard on the right, 1960.

At the awards reception at the local Historical Society

someone spoke to me, "So now you have a future in writing. What mark did you achieve in your English examination?"

"I failed the exam" I replied. "You can ask my English teacher. She's right over there."

Mama attended the awards ceremony with me. She thought I had lost my mind. When we returned home, she scolded me for my vindictiveness.

"That was so unkind to your old English teacher, so humiliating. I am so ashamed of you."

That shook me because I always valued Mama's faith in me and my talents in the face of Papa's constant criticisms. Her good opinion of me meant a lot. I regretted having disappointed her. Her shame became my shame, not only for this unkind act but also for failing at school generally. It was not only English that troubled me there.

Not long after that incident, my life began to fall apart. I had a major fight with my controlling Papa, this time more serious than ever before. I knew I had to leave and said so.

"In that case, you can't live in my house anymore," he yelled after me as I stepped out of the house with my travel bag.

I had made a friend at school whose large friendly family took me in and I tried to continue at school. At home, I was used to having my own room and valued my privacy. I missed that. It all became too much for me among all those strange people and all that noise. I finally dropped out of school, took a coffee shop waitress job and rented a room of my own.

With only a bit of money left after paying the rent, and lacking Mama's meals and Papa's edict to eat everything she put on my plate, as well as having to walk everywhere, I soon lost a fair bit of body fat. That helped to lift my spirits a little.

I did soon get a break. I was able quit the waitress job and start working writing advertising copy for the local radio station. Their copywriter had signed up to become a flight attendant and was leaving them. I was to fill in until they found a new permanent copywriter. After being shown how to do it, I loved the work writing three-minute and five-minute blurbs to advertise local businesses and their products. It showed me that I could work at writing even without formal education.

I often spent time in the municipal park that had vivid green lawns and large oak, walnut and chestnut trees. Dominating the park was a large, roofed pavilion and a gazebo big enough to hold a chamber music ensemble for summer Sunday afternoon performances. When the weather was good, I read on a bench in the rose garden behind the pavilion. I often felt too lonely in my rented room.

One sunny Saturday afternoon that summer, I sat in the rose garden absorbed in my book. Someone sat down on the bench beside me. I glanced up. For a moment I could not believe my eyes. Was my mind playing tricks on me? No, it really was Michael, the friend I had missed for so long, but now no longer the boy he had been in Grade 10.

"Hi," he said, like we saw each other every day.

I could not speak right away. But that passed quickly as the joy of seeing him again lifted me. I closed my book.

"Oh. Hi," I said.

We talked. He told me he had dropped out of the art college in Toronto and had come home to St. Catharines after a few months of hitchhiking all the way out to Vancouver and back. He had found art college boring and pretentious. He said he needed to be free, that he needed to find himself. I could understand that. It's what I thought I needed, too.

I gave him the telephone number at the rooming house where I could be reached. From then on, we spent nearly every evening together, he speaking about his experiences on the road and me listening. We went to movies and sat in the dark theatre drinking wine I had smuggled in my bag. We visited the local arts centre to look at paintings and sculptures. We walked all over town. We sat long hours in all-night restaurants. We laughed a lot. At one point, he tried to make love to me but, bless his heart, he became embarrassed and too flustered to proceed.

Perhaps he was still a virgin. I guessed I was more experienced than he. I could let this pass, I thought. I did not hear from him the next few days.

When I finally called him at his home, "Oh," his mother said, "He's gone. I thought you knew."

I was shocked. I didn't know what to think. This really hurt. That was when I knew I loved Michael more than just as a friend.

Not too long after, the radio station replaced me with a woman copywriter who had eleven years of experience plus a university degree. This job had only been temporary. I was just a high-school drop out and knew this would happen.

There was nothing left for me here in this town, so I moved to Toronto in the vain and unreasonable hope that I would somehow bump into Michael there. After all, Toronto was where he had hung out for years. But that did not happen even though I hung around all the art galleries, artsy cafes, coffee houses and bars that he had mentioned as places he liked.

It was the mid-1960s when long hair and being "hip" and "bohemian" was the great "in" thing, especially in Toronto. I had long hair, so fitting into the hippy crowd was easy when I was homeless for a few months and even after I finally found a job. I made some eccentric friends, a group of experienced hippies and a gay couple who kept an eye out for my safety. I had never met any gay men before and was well aware that being gay was still very much against the law. I was lucky to have had their protection.

I tried out intoxicating substances but after numerous bad experiences, I found I did not actually enjoy the sensations of being high or inebriated. Alcohol destroyed my sense of balance, causing me to fall down a lot. Cannabis and hashish had me vomiting and breaking out in skin rashes. I had a hard time explaining these reactions to my new hippy buddies. We remained acquainted, but we did not have much in common after that. I was too "straight" for them, I guess, not to mention that I worked whenever I could. That meant I spent a lot of time exploring the city on my own. It was a big, noisy, dirty, impersonal and lonely place, a place where you could lose yourself. I wondered how I would find myself here. I will never find Michael here, I thought.

After two years in Toronto, I had finally found a steady travel agent job on Queen Street that paid minimum wage, and, also, an affordable little suite of rooms near the university. I still missed Michael, but being so lonely, I had become involved with a man who said he was single. I had some trouble breaking up with this man after I discovered that he was married. I needed a break from him and Toronto.

On one Thanksgiving long weekend, I took the bus from Toronto back home to my parents' house in St. Catharines. Papa had forbidden me to visit when I had left home, but finally he relented. Mama and my sisters were so happy to see me after all this time. My youngest sister had just dropped out of high school and had started an apprenticeship with a local jeweller. We made plans to meet each other in town on her lunch break the next day. We were having lunch at a popular downtown restaurant, when Stephen, Michael's youngest brother whom we both knew, came to sit across from my sister.

"Have you heard from or seen Michael lately?" I asked Stephen.

"Ask him yourself," and got up.

I thought he was just being rude. And then Michael sat down and smiled at me like he had never been away. I smiled back at him.

That evening, Michael and I went on our first formal date. He had taken his dad's car without permission knowing that his father would be too drunk to notice. We had a lengthy dinner at a fancy restaurant and he took me back to my parent's house. It was quite late, yet Papa was up, waiting for my return. He interrogated me about this date. The interrogation did not bother me too much anymore. Michael was back.

I returned to Toronto after that amazing weekend. Michael had said he was working layout for a local printing company but that his contract would soon be over. Before long, Michael moved in with me in my Toronto apartment. The married man came by one time and saw that he had been replaced, and, thankfully, moved on.

By this time Michael was no longer a virgin, I noted. In fact, women liked him, I saw. That made me a bit jealous but I was just overjoyed that Michael was back in my life. He painted a silver Indiana "Love" symbol on the wall above the head end of our bed and worked on collages and sculptures. I met his artist friends and quite enjoyed their company. They accepted that I did not smoke up or drink much, probably because I was obviously Michael's woman.

In those days, I felt vaguely uncomfortable about "living in sin" with him. Living together as an unmarried couple was still not as socially acceptable as it is now. But then, he was an artist and normal rules of society did not apply, I thought.

One day in the summer of 1968, he said, "It's time for me to hitchhike to Vancouver." He had gone hitchhiking the summer before and had been gone for two months.

"This time I'd like to come along." I was curious about Michael's fascination with hitchhiking.

"You won't like it," he said.

Somehow, I got him to agree to take me hitchhiking for my upcoming summer holiday from work. We took the bus from Toronto to Barrie and hitchhiked across the country from there to Vancouver and back to Toronto. It was not at all as romantic as I had imagined. Rather, it was a misery from start to finish but, somehow, I was able to keep up my good spirits for both of us and we got home okay. Michael was in awe of me that I could not only survive such a trip but could also laugh about it all.

We married a month later with the understanding that we both did not wish to have children. I had had a miserable childhood being abused by Papa and Michael had no wish "to procreate a hapless child into this miserable world", as he said. Both of us were in our early twenties and there was no room for children in our lives.

Nearly a decade later, that changed for me and I began to think, now and then, about having just one child. I guess my body clock had begun to tick. I knew that if I were to get pregnant, Michael would definitely leave me. I continued to take my birth control pills.

Our lives gradually changed as they must after the honeymoon was over. I continued to work as a travel agent and Michael did whatever artists do. He took me to art gallery openings and we walked about Toronto together on weekends. My income was decidedly modest so we could afford very little beyond the rent and food. Michael and I often joined his artist friends in the evenings. I often felt out of place because I had given up painting. After all, Michael was a *real* artist, not like me, a mere amateur. I stuck to writing poetry and songs which I did not share with anyone.

I was still so ashamed of having dropped out of high school. On one occasion, a travel client, an official at the Royal Ontario Museum, took me out for a martini lunch after her successful trip through the mountains of Bulgaria that I had arranged for her. She convinced me that I could attend university and realize my dream of becoming a writer after all. Everyone had told me I would never be able to attend university without having first completed high school. This woman told me that this was not true, that I could write York University's adult entrance exam. Having passed this exam, I could pay down my course fee and be enrolled. That easy. I did not hesitate and soon had five part-time university credits. I applied for full-time university and was accepted at Brock University in St. Catharines, home town to Michael and me.

In February 1971, before Michael and I moved away from Toronto, we travelled to Germany so he could meet my grandparents. That was a mixed experience. We visited in Bavaria, where I was born, and then in northern Germany. We shopped and did tourist things, exploring museums and churches. We visited relatives, which was cheaper than paying for hotels. My mother's father predicted that our marriage would not last, which was disappointing. And my father's mother, Omi, shocked us with her mistreatment of her husband, my Opa, who had cancer and had been sent home to die. Michael was absolutely disgusted with her. We were able to escape to my uncle's house in Trier where we recuperated.

At the Frankfurt airport ready to leave Germany, I was suddenly held by police for several hours, suspected of murder, of all things. The infamous terrorist group, the Baader-Meinhoff Gang, had been active in Germany at this time. The police suspected I was part of this group based on my long hair and how I was dressed. This bizarre experience frightened both me and Michael. I was finally released after a call was made to my maternal grandfather, a well-known professor who attested to our visit to him in Erlangen during the time that the murder had taken place. Michael and I were relieved to get back to Canada. That's what I get, I thought, for trying to show off my artist husband to my family.

Two

In spite of my incomplete high school, I was going to university. I was overjoyed. Michael left Toronto first in spring 1971 to set up his artist studio where we would live in St. Catharines so I could attend Brock University which had accepted me. He had somehow agreed to work a short-term contract for my Papa. Papa had hired Michael for a few months to make precisely layered wood contour map models of arctic regions from satellite photos. I believed that Papa was finally beginning to accept Michael as my husband. Michael was curious about his father-in-law, too, I guessed. As it turned out, Michael was not at all happy working for Papa, learning how manipulative and controlling he could be, but he did welcome the money he needed for the rent deposit for his studio.

In his non-working hours, Michael discovered a vibrant local artist community in our old home town. In the summer, I moved into Michael's artist studio and arranged for full-time classes at Brock University for the fall. Our future seemed to be shaping up nicely.

At Brock, I enrolled as an English major, fully intending to become a writer when I grew up and graduated. I also signed up for advanced German Literature courses. I already had five credits, so could choose additional courses to make up my course load. Looking around for extracurricular activities, I found that the university poetry magazine needed an editor/manager. I had a few years of world experience on my fellow students which I knew would stand me in good stead. I was also not afraid of those who thought themselves in power. Creative solutions to problems came easily to me, especially needed for managing the poetry magazine that was deep in debt at this point. I stepped forward to rectify that and got the job.

This, of course, drew the attention of the English department. Perhaps I offended them by being an adult student who had just transferred from York University part-time studies to full time at Brock as an English major. I think this because just after I took on the management of the poetry magazine, I had a clash with the head of the English department, my first-year English professor. He demanded that I drop the advanced German Literature courses I was taking. He gave me no valid reason for this. I checked with the registrar's office and my student advisor and we could find nothing wrong with my taking advanced courses in first year. German was my first language and I had felt honoured that the German department allowed me into their advanced courses. I did not want to drop my German courses as this English professor wished just because he had the power to order his will on me as his student. I refused and I switched to a double major, Psychology plus the German Literature. but still continued to edit the university's poetry magazine for another year.

I maintained high grades for all my classes and finally succeeded in being promoted to the fourth-year Psychology honours program in the spring, 1974. I put my writing ambitions on ice for the meantime. Psychology interested me because my maternal grandfather was a psychology professor at a university in Germany as well as the fact that there had been suicides and evidence of mental illness in our family. I knew that if I did not wish to do therapeutic practice or social work after university, there was a strong possibility that I could teach at university level after attaining a graduate degree or, perhaps, do research.

I suppose one reason for pursuing psychology studies was to help me understand incest and sexual abuse along with mental illness and suicide as these had affected my family and me. While the incest and sexual abuse were topics still very much taboo and not generally talked about, I did encounter the Freudian take on these topics in most of the learned literature. It was all the woman's or girl's fault according to Freud. Either she manipulated the male family member who then succumbed to her wiles, or she imagined the incidents as wishful thinking. This repelled me and left me very much out of love with Freudian theory. The world was not yet ready to tackle such tricky subjects, I thought, and concentrated my efforts in other areas, like cognition.

My university's psychology department was in the process of developing a new innovative daycare centre, an educational model for daycares to come. I knew that if I ever changed my mind and wished to have a child without Michael there would be ways to manage childcare on my own and still pursue a career. Even in those days, mothers still took care of their children at home while the father worked away from home at a job to support himself and his family. It was still quite rare for women to have careers like men, but this was rapidly changing. The Feminine Liberation movement, or Fem Lib as we called it, was already in full swing, led locally by university students. There were more and more women university instructors being hired, albeit at a lower rate of pay, and under short-term contracts. These women had childcare needs which the university met with the agreement that the children in their care could be studied by the psychology department, satisfying the department's need for child subjects. More and more adult students attending classes also availed themselves of this cutting-edge but affordable childcare centre.

At the time I entered university, I was convinced that my educational plans were very much compatible with my husband's artistic career. Each of us required solo time in which to work. What I had not counted on was how estranged we would become with me going to classes, researching, writing papers, and holding down my cocktail waitress job evenings to help pay our living expenses while my husband did whatever he did with his artist colleagues. We barely saw each other.

At one point, he disappeared without notice, leaving me to guess if he had actually left me or if he was coming back. Maybe he had gone hitchhiking again? He reappeared quite suddenly after three months, a bit sheepish about not letting me know that he was going or where to. He and his friend had driven to Cape Canaveral in Florida to watch a NASA space launch. The reason for taking so long to return was that they had run out of money. They even sold their blood at one point so they could eat, he said. What could I say? At this point it looked to me like we had become such strangers to each other in spite of being married.

By this time, I had handed the management of the poetry magazine to an English-department-approved scholar. In order to fill time during my husband's long absence, I had joined the university fencing club as well as the parachute jumping club as extracurricular activities. I dropped out of fencing after our first tournament as I had no talent for this sport, being somewhat graceless on my feet, I thought. Instead, I focused on learning how to "drop and roll", the parachute landing method required before being allowed to do the first jump. Learning to meticulously pack my parachute was simple for me. But the physical bit about throwing myself off a four-foot height to roll onto my shoulder and thereby avoid broken arms or legs, well, that was a bit hard for me. It took me about six weeks to achieve this through many bouts of shoul-

After my 1st parachute jump 1973.

der injuries. I did my first parachute jump and then followed with three more. Then a fellow parachute jumper, a good friend, had his chute blown into hydro wires and was fatally electrocuted. That was it. I quit.

My husband had just shaken his head at my new sports obsessions while my parents had been so worried about me during this time that they took out accident insurance on me. I think, now, that my taking such risks was a barely disguised expression of my anger and frustration at my non-existent marriage.

Michael and I, in fact, were not the friends we had been in high school. As far as I could see, he had changed. I know, I had, too. We no longer had those long soul-searching conversations that we'd had during the first years of our marriage when we were so very much in love. He probably found the acceptance and support he needed among his local artist friends while I was immersed in university life. We seemed to be now on different life paths.

My parents were away from home more and more each year since I returned to our home town. They were shifting their business to focus on arctic logistical support and research at this point and were in the process of training young Inuit, then still called Eskimo, to do local research in Pond Inlet, now known as Mittimatalik, on the northern shore of Baffin Island. Papa was able to host Brock University's geology department chair and graduates for a convocation ceremony on the sea ice in Pond Inlet after they had gathered samples of rare spores from local glaciers on Bylot Island, to the north of Mittimatalik across Eclipse Sound. While my parents were away, they asked me to look after things for them at their home office.

In the spring of 1973, Papa's mother, my Omi, whom Michael had met on our trip to Germany, was to visit and attend my sister's graduation ceremony. She was graduating with a Bachelor of Science in Geology. In order to attend with Omi, Papa had left Mama in charge of the training and construction of his laboratory in Pond Inlet. The original plan was that Omi was to live with my sister for the duration of her week's visit in St. Catharines. That did not work out. My sister and Omi had a falling out at the airport on her arrival. Papa was due to return immediately to Pond Inlet after my sister's graduation ceremony. Suddenly there was the problem of who was to look after our grandmother, Omi. Since our grandfather, my Opa, had died a few years earlier, she was suffering from bouts of dementia as well as severe diabetes and her hampered mobility due to obesity.

Michael had witnessed how Omi had abused my dying Opa on our trip to Germany and reminded me that he had no love for her or my father. He did not want me living at my Papa's house to take care of her. Still, I felt I had no choice. She was, after all, my grandmother. I reluctantly agreed to take care of her to release my Papa. It was mainly to help Mama who I knew needed Papa beside her in Pond Inlet. After that week at Papa's house, I was more than happy to see Omi off at the airport and return home to Michael's studio. But that turned sour when I discovered a stranger's toothbrush and feminine underwear in our washroom.

When I confronted him, Michael shrugged and mumbled something to the effect that someone had filled the space I'd left. I felt as if a part of me had been stripped away. I strongly identified with being the artist's wife supporting her husband while he produced art and I had taken some pride in that. Now I was merely an older woman psychology student, a rejected woman replaced by a younger woman. My self-esteem took a nosedive.

I could do nothing else except move away from the studio into a house together with a few other students with whom I had made friends, but I was not up for socializing with them. I even lost my enthusiasm for my studies and found myself wondering why I was pursuing higher education. The study of psychology had turned out to be a definite disappointment. I found no answers there for the pain I carried in my heart. I had no idea where my studies would lead. German literature was at least interesting, but somewhat irrelevant to my life in Canada. Still, I persisted. What else was there for me to do?

I had been so hopeful that spring day in 1974 when Michael had invited me up to his studio to talk. I thought perhaps we could reconcile and repair our marriage. I had faced disappointment and grief before, but now Michael's final rejection left me completely undone.

Alcohol was abused by both university students and artists, but I, ever the outsider, did not participate much with them because of my adverse sensitivities. Still, I could dull the pain with alcohol and after my marriage ended, I began to seriously overdrink at times enduring the consequences. Somehow, the months after Michael and I separated were a blur of grief and drunkenness outside of my university classes. I often had hangovers when I participated in my seminars, handed in my assignments, and wrote my exams. In spite of feeling so down and strung-out, I was able to maintain my scholastic honours' standing. I continued to work late shifts as a cocktail waitress at the night club. I recall often waking in strange bedrooms with men I did not know. I felt as if a rational part of me had been amputated. I was scrambling to reconnect with some lost part of myself. I did not recognize myself without a shred of self-esteem.

I could not excuse my bad behaviour and judged myself harshly. I hated myself for sleeping with just anyone at all and getting so very drunk and disorderly. But no one seemed to notice or care. Those were the days of "free love", uninhibited hippies and eccentric lifestyles. I was an artist's wife, after all, and everyone knew that artists drank too much, did lots of drugs, had sex with everyone, and were otherwise generally decidedly odd.

Of course, everyone expected me to be like that, too. I did not, as a psychology student, fit in very well with the other wives of artists with whom I had absolutely nothing in common. Of course, my marriage had failed. I was such an outsider, as I have always been, as a child immigrant, as an overgrown, abused adolescent, and now as an artist's ex-wife. I even questioned my role as a psychology student. I felt utterly unattractive and worthless. What could the future hold for me?

Three

Now my marriage to the love of my life was over and done. This hit me hard. I was almost twenty-nine years old and nothing about my life made sense to me anymore. I felt my sanity slipping. I tried to act normal, struggling to keep my despair at bay while I continued my classes at the university and my part-time job.

Late one night when my nightclub waitress work shift was over, I stepped out of the Leonard Hotel onto St. Paul Street. My feet hurt and I wanted to go home. A gravelly voice called out to me. I turned to look. There sat the burly gang member named "Mother" on his heavy Harley-Davidson motorcycle under a street light. I knew Mother from the time I had waitressed out at that gang hangout place on the bluffs above the lakeshore. Mother had protected me from the other drunken gang members while I worked my shifts. He took a shine to me, he said, because I was working my way through university and that I did not mind serving what he termed as "low-life", like himself.

"Hey. I heard you split up with your old man and why. Do you want me to pound him?" he asked.

"No," I said. "Not worth it. But thanks." It comforted me that someone wanted to stick up for me, even if it was only Mother, the motorcycle gang member.

I had a few women acquaintances in town, but I did not feel up to any expressions of sympathy or criticism of my new erratic lifestyle. My Mama was the only one that I did not totally avoid. I needed her comfort. She and I had become friends as I grew to adulthood in spite of my troubles with Papa. Papa, meanwhile, did not say much, but I knew he was more than happy that his son-in-law was no longer with me.

Nearly a decade earlier, Papa and I had had that huge estrangement. I discovered later, when Michael and I got together, he had Michael followed by a private detective. When I confronted him about this, Papa said that this surveillance of family members and their partners was necessary because he was doing top secret work for the Canadian and United States governments. When Michael and I married in Toronto, he forbade Mama to come to my wedding, but she did manage to send my sister with modest wedding presents and flowers.

Papa's attitude toward me changed when I began to take part-time courses at York University in Toronto as an adult student. Mama yearned to also apply as an adult student to Brock University in St. Catharines and I encouraged her. She did and was accepted into the Classics and Linguistic programs the year before I was accepted there for full-time studies. In Germany, before the war, she had been good in her ancient Greek and Latin classes and had always longed to take linguistics at university. She was amazed at how easy it was now to fulfill her desire. She often gave me a lift to the university in her car when she drove to her classes. She and I became even closer friends than we had been before.

Both my parents had been deprived of their university studies in

Germany with the onset of World War II. Yet, Papa was a true autodidact. Through self-discipline and dedicated study, Papa was able to teach himself all he needed to know in order to function as a professional naval architect and marine engineer and, later, as an oceanographer. Mama, meanwhile, had been busy raising her children and helping Papa.

Mama had become Papa's official business partner when she was able to provide for the business start-up funds through her family connections. Besides that, she functioned as proposal writer and accountant. She had taken English as a Second Language courses as well as the expensive Famous Writers correspondence courses to practise her English writing.

Now, at this point of my parent's business development, they were able to retain a secretary. Their business operated from their home office in the extension Papa had built onto their house. They had been focusing on oceanography for some time, especially in oil reclamation from tanker spills. But, for the past few years, they began to look north. Their most recent move was making connections in the arctic to support the new efforts of international scientific exploration involved with oil and gas extraction and transportation for refining and world markets.

By now, Papa and I had mostly mended that rift between us, I thought. I was happy about that mainly because I could once again freely visit and talk with Mama. She and I had always supported each other, staying in touch even when Papa forbade it. She had never been against my marriage to Michael, not like Papa. She knew how heartbroken I was.

Later in spring 1974, Mama had asked me, "So what will you do this summer?"

"Oh, take a German Literature summer course, work at my cocktail waitress job, and lie on the beach, I guess," I said.

"Do you really like working at that night club?" Mama paused. "I ask you this because Papa is looking to hire a person to help me with the logistics and training end of our new arctic project. I suggested you. It would only be for the summer and would not interfere with your studies. We would pay you well. Are you interested?"

"I don't mind working for you, but for Papa? I don't think so. I'll just carry on as I am, with my summer school classes and the night club."

I was not convinced that Papa would accept me without trying to control my every move as he did when I was still living at home.

"Papa has definitely changed," said Mama, "especially since your separation from Michael. He will treat you well. You will be pleasantly surprised."

Mama kept at me, begged me to help her, hoping that I would agree to care for the young women Inuit trainees staying at their house planned for the early part of summer. Then I would go north with her in mid-July to help her care for the two guest foreign research scientists until the end of September.

"I will even pay for your divorce. I know both you and Michael have no money for that."

I laughed. "Okay. Okay, I'll do it. You've convinced me. But I don't think that the divorce will be happening within the foreseeable future."

I smiled. I loved and respected Mama. I thought she had my best interests at heart.

My parents must have discussed hiring me for several months as their project developed. I could just picture them speaking.

Mama says, "What are we going to do about our troubled eldest daughter? You know I was so worried about her when she did those parachute jumps. I just know she's suicidal."

Papa says, "She picked that no-good artist for her husband. It's her own fault for not listening to me. I'm glad he broke up with her. Maybe we can help her come to her senses. Let's find a place for her with us when we go back to Pond Inlet. We can work on her there."

While my parents were away in Pond Inlet in late spring 1973, I stayed at their house caring for the young Inuit women trainees. They came separately, first Jeeteeta came in late May escorted by Papa, and then Naomi came in June. They were to experience and learn office practice and what life is like in southern Canada. They took training during the daytime from Papa's secretary in basic business practice, filing, and basic bookkeeping while I attended my university summer classes. In the evenings, we would prepare supper together and review our day. Weekends would be time to go shopping, go to a movie theatre, or go for a drive to Niagara Falls and the surrounding farmland. Niagara Falls became a favourite destination for Jeeteeta after my parents had taken her there to enjoy the sights when she first arrived. I learned a little about some of the misconceptions I had about Inuit generally. I was especially amazed at how well these young Inuit women spoke English and the fact that Pond Inlet had a new public school. At that time, I also met one of the Jeeteeta's brothers, who had hitchhiked from Montreal to see Papa before my parents departed for their summer in Pond Inlet.

Papa was very pleased with the care I had given his trainees. His approval of me worked like a tonic after all the years he had criticized me. In our conversations, he wisely did not comment on my newly defunct marital state. We limited our discussions to his plans and the observations he had made dealing with the Inuit of Pond Inlet.

In 1974, environmental pollution, especially in the north, was a popular topic at the university. The acclaimed 1962 book, *Silent Spring* by Rachel Carson, one of my heroes, actually a renowned marine biologist, explained the cost to birds resulting from pesticide use and environmental destruction which sparked interest in environmental protection. I'd attended several public presentations at the university over the previous months about preserving the arctic tundra from the damage done by heavy equipment used in arctic exploration, as well as lectures by a handsome young David Suzuki, at that time still just a bug scientist, the rising star popularizer of environmental issues.

I became so excited about the arctic that I did a little library research about Inuit life, but there was not very much about Canadian Inuit or Inuit psychology except for Greenland Inughuit and Alaskan natives which, I thought, may be similar. Papa gave me Peter Freuchen's 1961 *Book of the Eskimos* that I found especially interesting because Freuchen had actually married a Greenlandic Inughuit woman. I found that fascinating. The more I thought about going to Pond Inlet, the more I liked the idea of going there. It would be a definite change of scenery and an adventure.

The few weeks before departure to Pond Inlet in mid-July 1974 were very busy for me. I quit my night-club job and returned the skimpy-skirted red and black uniform and gave away the fishnet stockings and high heels. I hastily moved into an apartment with another student because the house I had been living in was being demolished to make way for a new highway. I arranged with my psychology professors for me to do a summer project of collecting Inuit children's drawings. I planned to write my fourth-year honours thesis about children's art using the Inuit children's drawings as comparative research on my return from Pond Inlet. I was surprised that I had done so well in my Psychology studies considering my toxic mental state throughout this time.

As Mama had promised, Papa kept whatever negative thoughts he had about me to himself and even praised how I helped her, making lists of supplies and locating businesses that could fill our orders at short notice and making the necessary arrangements. I enjoyed the work, managing the logistics of food and equipment to go along with us, completing long checklists and packing it all in Papa's aluminum travel trunks. This could work out, I thought. I began to feel much better about myself.

My parents had come home from Pond Inlet wearing Inuit-made parkas consisting of an inner wool duffel coat trimmed with wolf fur around the hood, with a wind-proof cotton outer coat, all embroidered at the hem and at the cuffs with braiding. I was instantly smitten by this attractive and practical style. Until I could get my own, I had to settle for a navy-blue utilitarian army-surplus expedition parka for my trip up. I actually began to look forward to this trip. I went off to buy myself a set of long underwear for under my jeans and a plaid lumber shirt.

It was a little over a year after the love of my life told me our marriage was done. My personal life had been a mess and now I was a working guest at my parents' house here in St. Catharines and in Pond Inlet for the summer to help Mama. And, not only that, I had a plan to collect Inuit children's drawings for my fourth-year honours psychology project at Brock University after my return in September. I looked forward to discovering Inuit contemporary life and to taking a break from my personal troubles.

Four

Finally, all was ready to Papa's exacting satisfaction for our departure on July 13, 1974. The luggage and boxes had been sent on ahead by truck and Papa, Mama and I headed off by car to the airport in Toronto. We flew to Montreal and there boarded the Nordair flight to Frobisher Bay, located in the south of Baffin Island, now known as Iqaluit, the capital of Nunavut Territory. At that time, it was the capital of the Eastern Arctic sector of the Northwest Territories which included what is known today as Nunavut Territory. The flight was long, almost as long as flying to Germany, but we were blessed with clear good weather for our trip.

As we descended to land in Frobisher Bay, I noticed no trees at all on the landscape below us from the airplane window. There were only dark mountains draped in sparkling-white glaciers interspersed with rounded ultramarine or turquoise lakes circled by tiny patches of green vegetation and white snow. I saw dark-blue rivers snaking down to the emerald-green sea where ice pans floated off the coast, looking like tiny white paper sailboats tossed by waves. What enchanted me most was the clear azure sky holding a few fluffy clouds. Sunlight flashed and glinted everywhere off the lakes, sea, snow and glaciers. To me, it looked like a new world, clean and pristine, untouched by humans.

On landing, we were taken by truck to the Frobisher Inn Hotel for our first overnight in the arctic. A lot of jovial middle-aged white men staying at the hotel came to eat with us in the dining room. The only Inuit I saw were employed by the hotel: waiters, busboys and cleaners. My mother and I were the only white women in the dining room that evening. Most of the men we met were government officials or scientists and their attendant crews on their way to other points north or on their way back home.

In my hotel room that night, I could not get to sleep right away. I pulled aside the blackout curtains and looked out of my hotel window. I was fascinated by the endless long daylight, the lingering twilight after midnight bathed all of what I could see, the buildings and landscape, in a deep rose-pink glow. Utterly exhausted, I did finally fall asleep. Suddenly, it seemed, my mother was at the door calling me to get up. I had only slept a few hours.

After an early breakfast, we boarded another Nordair plane and flew off to Hall Beach, a fuel stop, then on to Resolute Bay on Cornwallis Island, north of Baffin Island.

Here, we were taken for a quick lunch at the local air crew centre while the ground crew off-loaded our gear. Then we boarded a little dual-engine Twin Otter airplane, painted orange and white with a black stripe on its sides. It looked so puny next to the big blue and white Nordair plane on the runway. Our little plane sported two multi-purpose pontoons fitted with landing wheels underneath to let it land on water or gravel, I was told. There were about twelve small seats inside, some folded up to make space for our baggage and boxes. Somehow, we got all our things on board. I noted that there was no onboard washroom and hoped the flight would not take too long. We all applauded when our pilot introduced himself as Markoosie, one of the first Inuit commercial pilots. This pleased Papa. This was evidence that Inuit could be taught technical skills, just as he was doing in his Pond Inlet project.

Since the Twin Otter flew closer to the ground, I was able to see the green plants and the black, grey and orange lichen, like flung carpets, covering the rocks. Most of the snow had already melted at ground level and on the south sides of the mountains, I saw, leaving snow mostly on their north sides, just as Papa had pointed out. He told me the heat of the day came from the south side during the arctic summer. I was to discover that the sun circled to the north during the time generally known to us as night.

As we circled Pond Inlet, I could make out Bylot Island to the north with its two glaciers flowing into Eclipse Sound and a mountain, a near perfect isosceles triangle, lodged between them like part of a crown. Toward the east on the south side stood the stepped silhouette of Mount Herodier, like a stairway down to the sea. I had seen these views in photographs, but to see them in this panoramic view was breathtaking.

Our Twin Otter landed and bumped along the long, gravel runway.

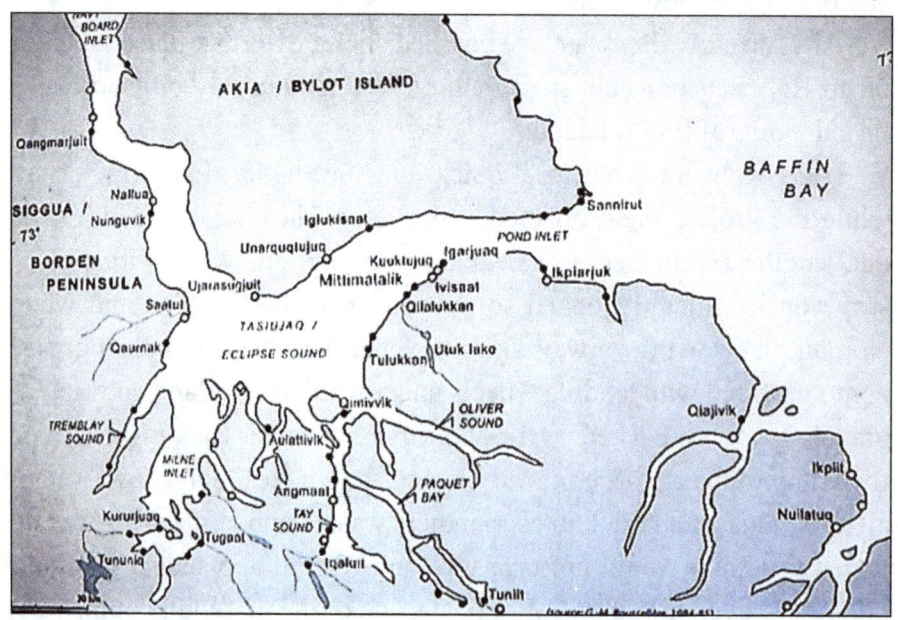

Area map of Pond Inlet/Mittimatalik.

The little plane's wheels in their pontoons threw up a wave of tiny pebbles on each side and a huge grey dust plume welled up behind us. We taxied up to a small, orange-painted, black-roofed building with oddly indented side walls that served as a landing office and passenger waiting room where outgoing mail bags and freight were stored for shipment.

The fine weather, warm and sunny with no wind, surprised me. I had expected it to be much colder. I was dressed in my heavy, navy-blue expedition parka and had to remove it as soon as we landed, I was sweating so much. I noticed that most of the people crowded around us wore light jackets or windbreakers. We were met by a group of Inuit, and some Qallunaat (white people). There were also a few trucks from the Hudson's Bay Company (HBC), the Royal Canadian Mounted Police (RCMP), and the settlement administrator's office. The mail bags destined for recipients in Pond Inlet, and other unloaded goods, were quickly taken away by trucks.

Our goods were loaded into a truck with an extended cab, room enough for us all to sit. We were driven down the hill from the airstrip on a dirt road, past the power plant, identified to me by Mama when I asked, to the three-way crossroad where we turned left onto the beach road. We stopped at my parents' new house and laboratory with attached garage located beside the HBC property on the east side with the Anglican mission house and church on the west side, right across from the tiny Catholic mission and church. The HBC buildings were painted white with red trim and roofed in black. Neat gravel paths bordered with white-washed stones led up to the road and surrounded each HBC building. I was enchanted with all the green I saw, so much grass, so many tiny plants and flowers in white, purple and yellow. A large, brilliantly white crucifix holding a white almost-life-sized figure of Christ stood on top of the hill behind the small white Catholic mission and church. Getting out of the truck I looked up and saw the words "Pond Inlet" picked out in large, white-washed stones on the sloping side of the bluff overlooking the beach road.

Papa had had the pine siding of the new house oiled to keep the wood from drying out so now the house looked golden. Papa's buildings had been erected with the help of his Inuit building crew. It sat right on the beach overlooking Eclipse Sound with Bylot Island to the north on the farther shore with a spectacular view of glaciers and snow-capped mountains. The sea ice had broken up and the dark-blue water of the sound was flecked with white floes.

A small reception committee of Inuit, the trainees and others, awaited us at the house. After a quick hello, Papa went out to see his Inuit building crew still working on the laboratory and garage located between the house and the road. Mama greeted everyone inside and introduced me to them. I did not catch their, to me, strange-sounding Inuit names. They were hard for me to hear, but I guessed I would get to know them as we got to know each other better. I shook everyone's hands in greeting as this seemed to be the custom here. Everyone smiled and nodded a lot, self-conscious and awkward, especially me.

Mama organized supper after someone connected and lit the large kitchen propane stove for her. There were two stoves in her kitchen. She told me that an electric stove was only used during an emergency shortage of propane because it used too much electricity and put a drain on the local limited power supply produced by a diesel generator in the power plant up the hill.

She warned about being frugal with water because water was delivered by truck and stored in a water tank. One never knew, she said, when the water truck would break down or the road become impassable or the lake's water level would fall too low. This occurred usually in summer, like now, and there could be extremely long waits between municipal water deliveries. Papa's new house did not sport a flush toilet. Instead, there was what was known as the "honey bucket", lined with heavy

View of Papa's house (left) below the Crucifix, photo by Norman Koonoo.

plastic bags. Disinfectant was poured into the honey bucket after each use. Mama said the honey bucket was to be emptied when half-full. Okay, then. So, it was nice to see running hot and cold water in the washroom as well as a small shower stall. Mama had posted signs about not letting the water run too much, about using only what you absolutely need. She said to use the plug in the sink when brushing my teeth. In the shower, she said to stand in a tub to collect the shower water. One rinse, one soaping, and another rinse. That was the shower and allowed once a week. This would take some getting used to.

"That empty little room beside the radio room is yours for the duration of your stay," Mama told me.

The radio room was used for daily transmissions to the home office in St. Catharines, Ontario, because direct long-distance telephone was not yet available even though local telephone connected every house in Pond Inlet. The telephone system was expected to be patched through the new Anik communications satellite later that summer.

Mama gave me a foldout army cot, a heavy-duty sleeping bag and a pillow with pillowcase. She had sewn liners from cotton bedsheets for use inside the sleeping bag. These liners were like long pillowcases with an open top and one open side that acted as one-piece top and bottom sheets inside the sleeping bag and could be easily removed for laundering.

"The beauty of these is that they can be rolled up and taken along with the sleeping bag when camping," she pointed out.

Mama was in charge of feeding everyone. The visiting scientists accompanied us at table for daily meals when they were in town but they slept at the transient centre, like a hostel, located up the beach road. She also provided the trainees' mid-morning and mid-afternoon "coffee times" complete with baked goods. She had arranged for local Inuit women to bake pies, bread and other baked items. She had been amazed, she said, at how well these women baked but found later that they had learned while serving Qallunaq employers, the RCMP, government officials and Hudson's Bay managers. Mama bought caribou meat and fish — mostly arctic char — from Inuit hunters for our meals.

She had brought along a small supply of root and fresh vegetables on the plane with us as a relief from canned and dried goods that had to be served when the fresh supply ran out. The Bay (HBC) Store, at the time, stocked only canned vegetables until their annual supply ran out, like now in July. Mama said she was told that Inuit did not like canned vegetables and preferred canned fruit when they could afford it. This was way before frozen foods became popular and available at the Bay store.

Mama told me it would soon be the once-a-year sea-lift time, when the re-supply ships delivered dry and canned goods, building supplies, equipment and vehicles. Government officials, schoolteachers, the missionaries, and now my parents, who had placed their sea-lift orders the year before, would also receive their supplies. Mama looked forward to receiving hers. She told me how the local Qallunaat schoolteachers had shown her how to complete a sea-lift order and advised on what she would need. She showed me her copy of the *Northern Cookbook* by Eleanor Ellis in which were listed things "to be remembered" by white women planning to live on the arctic fare to be brought up from southern supermarkets. She made sure, too, that Papa, who smoked constantly, had his supply of favourite cigarettes.

Meanwhile, I considered my little bedroom. I liked that it had a window with colourful blackout curtains. The view was to the south and limited to the gap beside the Catholic mission hill and the next rise. My cot was set up with my lined sleeping bag and I stacked a few cartons for shelving some clothes and books. Now I just needed a worktable.

I looked around outside and found two wooden sawhorses and an old door with a plain front. I asked Papa if I could use them, and he allowed me to take them. The door was a bit grimy so, with salt water from the beach, I washed it off outside before bringing it inside. I set up the sawhorses in my room and put the door flat on top with the door handle opposite from where I would sit on a folding chair. I found a small empty jar, filled it with water and stuck in some yellow arctic poppies I had picked from the side of the house. I liked my worktable and spread out my papers and things on it.

While I looked around outside, I spotted some vines with purple flowers growing at the tideline on the beach in front of Papa's new house. I found them so special that I dug a few up and replanted them in front of the house. These were flowering arctic beach pea, I learned years later. They were somewhat delicate, I guess, because when I looked the next day the replanted beach pea plants had died overnight. Mama was collecting wildflowers on her walks and used a drying press for her specimens. She was making an arctic wildflower catalogue with her drawings complete with descriptions and other details.

My psychology project was to collect Inuit children's drawings to later compare with children's drawings of other cultures. I had brought a supply of paper, lead and coloured pencils, and crayons. It was my aim to collect as many drawings as I could get. I had already spoken with some of Papa's trainees who said they would be happy to help me arrange drawing sessions with their younger brothers, sisters and cousins.

A few days later, I had already collected a fair number of Inuit children's drawings. I noticed that very young children of about two or three years of age produced the same dot and fan markings that children of other cultures and ethnicities used at that age. Children a little older, produced images of big heads with stick bodies, also in line with study findings. In my research, I had read these motifs were universal, across all world cultures and races, but I knew that Inuit children's art had not yet been studied.

The older Inuit school-age children drew houses with upside-down "V" gabled roofs, doors with round handles, and square windows divided into four panes by a cross. These features were unexpected because most of houses I saw in this town had shallow or flat roofs, except for the HBC, RCMP and the mission buildings. Only a few of those had old-style four-paned windows.

When some of the older children drew women, they identified them as such by showing them in skirts although most women wore long pants topped by tunics or blouses. Only the elderly Inuit women wore dresses or skirts over their long pants. A few of the older children were especially talented and identified a woman by showing her wearing a child on her back in amautik, in the carrying parka. Some children drew pictures of their fathers hunting, and some of their tents in their summer camp.

I felt happy that my project had begun well. By the time I left in September, I would have more than enough drawings for my research project.

Five

Mama soon introduced me to Father Guy Mary-Rouselière, known as Ataata Mari in Inuktitut to the people of Pond Inlet. He lived across the road in the small mission house attached to the tiny, white church. He was tall and thin, with abundant white hair and wore thick dark-framed glasses. He spoke English with a heavy French accent. Mama had told me that he was an eminent anthropologist in addition to being a Catholic missionary. He had been living in the areas of Igloolik, Arctic Bay and Pond Inlet since 1948. This was 1974 so that would make his arctic stay then about thirty-six years. This elderly man, tall, thin, and white-haired, dressed in ordinary clothing except for his black shirt with the white unbroken collar and his plain crucifix that spoke of his calling.

Fr. Guy Mary-Rouselière, aka Ataata Mari.

Mama said Ataata Mari was perfectly fluent in spoken Inuktitut as well as able to read and write in Inuktitut syllabics. These are symbols used for each Inuktitut word syllable developed by missionaries several generations ago. Ataata Mari explained his verbal proficiency saying he needed to understand what his Inuit parishioners wanted to tell him, especially during confession. He learned from them while living with them in their camps. This was before Inuit were moved into settlement in 1968 and 1969 for their children to attend the newly built school in Pond Inlet.

When he was not busy with mission work, Ataata Mari did physical anthropological field research in several areas around Pond Inlet, conducting digs, and collecting Inuit elders' oral stories. He had conducted an exchange program with the Inuit of Pond Inlet with their relatives in Qaanaq, Greenland, the year before and was writing a book about the history of these connections. I later discovered that he also edited the *Eskimo* periodical for the Arctic Catholic Diocese. I found him humble, self-effacing, and full of kindness and humour. I knew I would like him right away.

Through Ataata Mari, Mama had been introduced to Inuuja, a local Inuit woman elder. Her adopted daughter Apphia worked at the local nursing station as a medical translator and also served as the old woman's translator when she had English-speaking visitors like Mama. Papa thought it important to pay respect to this elder. He believed she held the power in the Inuit community and could sway their opinion in his favour. He sought her approval of his project thinking this would keep his Inuit workers and trainees content.

After dinner one evening just after we arrived, Papa spoke about how I should relate to Inuit as a visitor from southern Canada.

"Many white people succumb to a kind of arctic madness. It could be because of the twenty-four-hour daylight, the thin air or whatever. For this reason, I will be watching you for signs of mental disturbance."

I was somewhat puzzled. This was new to me. I could see such "arctic madness", as he called it, occurring to those who suffered long isolation or from extreme cold or lack of food. But this was the height of summer, the weather was pleasant, even warm, and all of us were well-fed. I wondered what he meant. I did not dare to question him about it because I thought he might think I was opposing him, the way he often did when I was a child. I could not help but wonder about why Papa would tell me this.

Soon after our arrival, a short, thin, scruffy, bald, elderly Inuit man appeared for morning coffee, and grimaced with an almost toothless smile. To me, he looked a little comical.

Mama introduced him as Simon Anaviapik. His fingers were severely gnarled by arthritis, I noticed. With such afflicted hands I could see that he was no longer able to hunt. Mama told me this man had been teaching her and Papa how to speak Inuktitut. Mama had more time during the workday, so she had progressed more rapidly than Papa. Of course, my mother had studied linguistics, Greek, Latin, and French, so she had an easier time learning a new language. She told me that Inuktitut was linguistically similar to Sanskrit, and Ataata Mari, in his authority as anthropologist, had agreed.

Papa's Inuit young women trainees, Jeeteeta, Naomi and Sarahme, whom I already knew, gave me snippets of information

Simon Anaviapik and my Mama, Sophie.

about life in Pond Inlet. At that time, there were about seven hundred and fifty people living in the settlement. It was now summer so most of the people were out at their summer camps. Only those who could not leave were in the settlement during July and August, like the elderly, the sick, those who had no boat, and, of course, those who were employed. Those with jobs in the settlement tried to get away on weekends to their families in the summer camps.

To me, Pond Inlet looked empty on weekends, a little like a ghost town. Those left behind seemed to greatly appreciate summer visitors to relieve their relative solitude and, perhaps, as something new to talk about. For those young people who were left in the settlement, movies were shown on weeknights and dances were held every weekend. The settlement still lacked a community centre, so the movies were shown in the new Takijualuk School gymnasium and the dances were held in a decrepit little portable school building. Even though I was older than my new Inuit friends, I enjoyed being with them and going to these events.

A few days after my arrival, I visited Caleb Ootoova and his wife Regilee in their tiny two-room house. Caleb (I knew him as "Calipee") was the trainee Jeeteeta's brother whom I had met the year before when he visited us in St. Catharines. His little house was somewhat crowded with all their children. His wife, Regilee, said it was even more crowded right now since Caleb Sanguya was staying with them for a while. He, too, was one of Papa's trainees, like Jeeteeta.

Caleb Sanguya told me he was sleeping on Regilee's couch because his grandmother had made him give up his room in her house. This room was now needed for his grandmother's son (his uncle), and his new Qallunaq common-law wife who was pregnant. His uncle had just returned from college in south Canada and now he, Caleb Sanguya, was suddenly homeless. There was no housing for single Inuit men in Pond Inlet. In fact, there was a distinct general lack of housing as far as I could see, and what Inuit housing existed was sub-standard, inadequate and definitely overcrowded. I felt so sorry for him.

But the mention of that pregnant Qallunaq common-law wife of Caleb Sanguya's uncle interested me. A white woman was brave enough to go against convention to live with a local Inuk. Curious.

After my visit, Caleb Sanguya walked me home down to Papa's house. The next day I heard that he had quit Papa's training and left Pond Inlet. Papa said Caleb had not given a reason for quitting. I thought that he did not enjoy couch-surfing and being homeless, but I kept my thoughts to myself. I hoped that Caleb had found a good place to stay with his relatives in Arctic Bay, where, as I heard from the trainees, he had gone.

The weather continued sunny and warm, and then the temperature reached an unheard of 87 degrees Fahrenheit, 30 degrees Celsius. We still measured temperature in Fahrenheit in those days. Metric conversion had just begun to be implemented in Canada under the Pierre Elliot Trudeau Liberal government and had not yet been widely adopted. I could not imagine more glorious summer weather.

At about this time, Papa hired on two very strong local men to move a heavy fuel tank over the tundra to the building site of his garage attached to the laboratory. From the radio room window, I watched how two handsome young Inuit men sweated and strained, exerting all their strength to the point of exhaustion, inching this enormously heavy tank along. They often had to take breaks, but finally got that tank into place. The trainees and I applauded them when they succeeded. I overheard their names: Sheattie and Mikiseetee. I, at that time, could not have pronounced these names but I could recognize them. Later Jeeteeta told me that Mikiseetee was her youngest uncle, a few years older than she was.

On his own initiative, Papa had begun building his weather station up the hill near the Pond Inlet airstrip. This was his attempt to facilitate more frequent and better flight communications for this small community. The outer walls and roof were already done, the windows and doors had been installed and the floors laid. Most of the weather-recording instruments were already working: the Stevenson screens outside containing wet and dry bulb thermometers, the anemometer, and barometer, the sunshine recorder and precipitation gauge. Papa had secured the services of an official of the Canadian Atmospheric and Meteorological Services (CAMS) to train some of Papa's trainees to become weather observers.

Papa thought I should learn along with them. I was interested and so I learned basic cloud formations, estimating cloud height and identifying meteorological phenomena, reading the instruments and how to record the findings. A daily radio report was read by radio to the Resolute Bay weather station and was made available to incoming pilots before taking off for Pond Inlet. Along with the meteorological training, I was also included in the two-way radio operator's training, preparing for our oral radio license tests. I memorized the Morse Code for this. We all passed the test and were awarded our radio licenses.

The CAMS trainer was not happy with Papa's weather station building, probably because it was not being built by CAMS, and not even according to Canadian building standards, we later learned. Papa had begun building without CAMS approval and this caused future problems. My parents had invited this CAMS trainer to stay at their house at no cost, but he, in chagrin, elected to stay at the local transient centre, which was like a youth hostel with bunk beds, and took his meals there as well.

Years earlier, during the early 1960s, Papa had read in a report that the Canadian meteorological services considered Inuit "un-trainable" based on their one attempt at training Inuit in Cape Dorset that had failed miserably. He thought that the lack of proper training was at fault, not some lack within the Inuit themselves. Papa thought that training exercise had been a racist set-up to discredit Inuit. He said, that with proper adult training principles, he could do much better. This was his motivation to start the Inuit sea-ice technician training project in Pond Inlet. And it meant that Papa was passionate about the weather observers' training project as well. He meant it to succeed, especially since the number of flights into Pond Inlet had recently increased to once a week with the now-reliable, on-the-ground meteorological reports to pilots. Prior to the daily official weather reports, aircraft came only once or twice a month, weather permitting. This was a definite improvement for all the people of Pond Inlet.

By this time, Papa was fifty years of age. He was still as tall, handsome, and charismatic as he had been as a young man, but now his powerful shoulders were beginning to be overshadowed by the beginnings of a belly.

He had interrupted his university education in Germany when he was drafted for war service from which he returned physically and emotionally damaged. My uncle told me he had been a war hero, but for the losing side, so his heroism had never been acknowledged.

After World War II, he attempted various ways to make a living in war-torn Germany, without success. There were simply too many damaged returning German soldiers, as well as displaced people in Germany during that time. He decided to bring his family to

Steltner family in 1951, me at 5 years old in front.

At my grandfather's house in Germany 1951, we are at the lower left.

Canada on an agricultural worker immigration scheme in 1951.

In Canada, Papa began in farming with dreams of owning his own farm but soon learned the futility of that in Ontario where all the choice farmland had already been taken by 1951. Tiring of the back-breaking farm-work and plagued by his war wounds, he gravitated to marine engineering and naval architecture, the work his own father was engaged in back in Germany. As I mentioned before, Papa was a superb autodidact, self-taught. He did not have the means or the time to attend university formally. From books and manuals, he taught himself all the necessary higher mathematics, physics and chemistry as well as mechanics and various branches of the budding science of oceanography. Owning his business with Mama's help, he invented marine measuring instruments and, later, oil-reclamation equipment, among other things, and now he had this project in Pond Inlet.

Papa learned to maintain his independence at all costs the hard way. He did a contract for the Canadian government for which he was never paid because of an election reshuffle of government ministers. He tried to sue the government during the late 1950s, using lawyers who had actually won such a case but, unfortunately, that did not work out for Papa. Ever since those days, he had a problem dealing with Canadian government officialdom. Being a sensitive German immigrant did not help matters in those days of active post-war discrimination. But it did make him aware of injustices and racism that he noted in the way Canadian government officials had dealt, and were dealing, with Inuit.

I was sure he was not prepared to run the gauntlet of political wrangling and government delays in getting a functioning weather station built for Pond Inlet. Of course, he would do it on his own.

Papa had been able to impress Dr. Jan Terasme of the Brock University Geology department, whom he had met through my sister, at this time completing her degree in geology. In 1973, he arranged for Dr. Terasme and the graduating geology class to travel to Pond Inlet to take pollen samples from the ice of the Sermilik Glacier on Bylot Island across from the settlement and to hold a graduation ceremony there on the ice. The local government and settlement officials, the HBC

My grandfather's house in Erlangen, Germany, 1951.

personnel, the RCMP constables, everyone, including the Inuit, welcomed these visitors.

Papa made up his mind to put Pond Inlet on the map for scientific research by providing training for Inuit to become competent sea-ice technicians and weather observers, thereby giving them steady employment in his laboratory and weather station. His hope was that eventually the research station could in the future become Inuit-owned and operated. It was a grand dream that even I, who had reason to distrust Papa, bought into. I even began to think I could be part of this venture.

In addition to my training at the weather station. I helped Mama when she needed it in the new house and collected children's drawings. In my free time, I walked around in the settlement. Many Inuit women came out of their houses as I walked by along the road and indicated with hand gestures, broken English, and wide smiles that I should come in, drink tea with them. I shook my head and they nodded, still smiling. I felt a little exotic, like I was a celebrity to them. I knew Inuit were curious about me, but I was not yet ready to satisfy their curiosity. I wanted to find my way around the settlement first, like the tourist I was.

One sunny afternoon, Mama took me up the hill to a house past the nursing station. The house was painted in light baby blue with white trim outside and had the number 69 on a board beside the white entrance door. It all looked a little worn and shabby. We were to visit Inuuja Komangapik, Jeeteeta's grandmother, for afternoon tea. Mama had arranged with the settlement nurse for Apphia to take an hour off work to act as translator at home. In her early twenties, Apphia worked at the nursing station as the official medical translator.

"We don't have to knock," said Mama. "We just walk in, like everyone does here." She explained that doors here were never locked unless the family was away for a long time, like out camping. Theft was not yet a problem in Pond Inlet because Inuit still respected each others' property.

The first thing I saw when we opened the door was a battered brown space heater with a shiny metal chimney pipe up through the ceiling. Behind it, the walls of the room were painted a faded yellow. The room was L shaped, the kitchen area forming the shorter part and the longer part serving as dining and living room area. In the kitchen area there was a large, ornate, old-style wood stove, converted to burn diesel fuel I was told later, dominating the right-hand wall. It was mostly black with white porcelain and chrome trim and had a warming oven, a shelf above the heating surface, a hot-water well on the right side, as well as a baking oven. Opposite the stove was a long laminate-topped kitchen counter with stainless steel sink without faucets and cupboards above it. All the woodwork was painted a faded light blue.

It seemed odd to me that the house would appear so worn. As I understood it, Inuit were moved in off the land from their home camps in 1968, only six years earlier. Did this mean that the prefabricated houses the government erected for the Inuit families had been in use in other parts of Canada before they arrived here?

Against the south wall beside the back door stood a large new avocado-green-coloured refrigerator with a separate top door for the freezer compartment. Seeing this modern refrigerator, I had to smile thinking of the current catch-phrase "able to sell refrigerators to Eskimos" used in southern Canada to describe top salesmanship skills. Across from the refrigerator at the rear kitchen door and blocking part of the window beside the cook stove, stood a large translucent plastic tank with a spigot at the bottom. I could see the water level stood at about halfway up the tank that was covered with a lid. There were rigid copper pipes, about one-inch in diameter, suspended over the stove that were not connected to a water supply as far as I could make out. These pipes struck me as odd.

Under the window beside the stove stood a well-used couch covered with a rumpled plaid bedspread and a colourful knitted throw. The furniture I saw looked like donated items from a thrift shop. In spite of their worn condition, everything, including the linoleum floor, was clean, although there was a pervasive smell that I could not identify. The room was bright with two windows above the dining table against the wall looking north over the rooftops of other houses, the open waters of Eclipse Sound, and Bylot Island with its snow-topped mountains and glaciers glistening in the distance.

In the corner stood a very new large brown console television set like the ones then found in upscale southern Canadian living rooms. I was aware that the satellite reception was not yet working, so I knew that this one was not yet in use. I had heard that the HBC had imported and sold these televisions in anticipation of the new communication services soon to be available in the settlement, perhaps later that summer, or the next.

There was a black dial telephone mounted on the wall beside the space heater opposite the table. Telephone service was only available locally within the settlement, I was told. Long distance still needed to be patched through by two-way radio dispatch. Long-distance conversations needed to be "2-way radio"-style, that is, one speaker said "over" when he or she wanted the other to speak, taking turns, alternating speaking and listening. That made long-distance telephone calls quite awkward and very expensive. And this would hopefully soon change as the local satellite communications were being refined to provide direct long distance that summer via satellite.

Apphia welcomed us while the old woman, Inuuja, her "grandmother", as she called her adoptive mother, gave us a wide smile showing off a set of ill-fitting false teeth. She was seated on a kitchen chair beside the table under the front window, a pillow covering her chair seat. After introductions and the customary shaking of hands, Mama and I sat down on worn chromed tubular steel chairs with cracked yellow plastic seats. The matching table had a scratched-up yellow and white mottled laminate surface that showed years of constant wear. Mama and I pulled down the front zippers of the jackets we were wearing but kept them on. We were only making a quick visit as Apphia needed to get back to the nursing station soon.

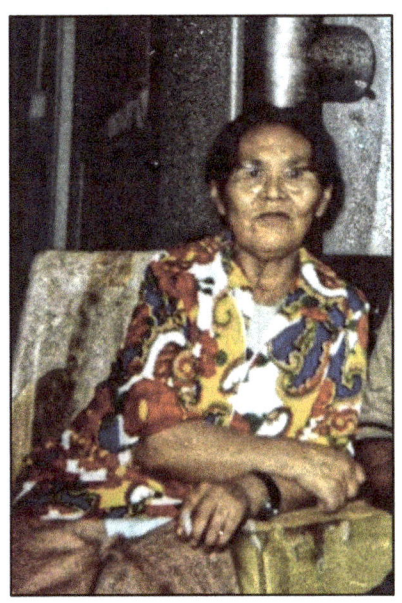
Inuuja Komangapik.

The old woman had one leg folded under her buttocks while the other hung down showing a well-worn white kamik, boot, made from some kind of white fabric topped with a bright blue fabric cuff. The foot portion showed a white fabric top surrounded by intricately pleated black seal leather that covered the side and bottom of the foot. Turned over her kamik top was a cream-coloured duffel sock embroidered with tiny red and blue flowers. She was dressed in worn beige pants and a bright-yellow cardigan sweater over a white flower-patterned tunic. She had wispy black hair pulled together behind her neck in a thin knot. Her face was dark and wrinkled and these wrinkles deepened as she smiled. She wore brown plastic-framed glasses with thick lenses giving her a vaguely owlish, wise look. I noticed a few lines of faint, dark-blue dots from both sides of her chin to her bottom lip. Even though she was seated, I could tell she was very short. Mama had said that she was probably in her late sixties but she looked older to me.

There was a large aluminum tea kettle as well as a large aluminum pot with a lid, simmering on the back of the stovetop. Apphia brought out some enamel mugs and teaspoons and set them before us on the table, followed by a freshly opened tin of evaporated milk and a full sugar bowl. She got the tea kettle from the stove and poured out dark orange tea into the mugs. I saw the old woman put two large teaspoons of sugar and a generous splash of milk into her mug. I took a sip of mine and discovered the tea strong and very bitter. I had to add sugar and milk, too, so I could drink it. The old woman caught my facial expression and nodded as if she knew how to make her tea palatable to Qallunaat tastes. I saw Mama, who usually did not take milk and sugar in her tea, had also succumbed.

Joshua Komangapik.

An elderly man wearing black-rimmed glasses, his scruffy salt-and-pepper-grey hair standing up about his head as if he had just got out of bed, shuffled in from a back room, a dark tobacco pipe clamped between his teeth. He wore a rumpled red and black plaid shirt over dark trousers and I could see the top of his long johns at the open shirt collar. He wore grey wool socks on his feet. Apphia gave up her chair for him and pulled up another one for herself from beside the stove. She brought him a mug of tea and he served himself, adding milk and lots of sugar. As Apphia introduced us, we each shook his right hand while he held his pipe in his left hand. He smiled broadly, revealing stumpy worn-down, tobacco-stained teeth beneath his moustache. He seemed genuinely happy to see us. This was Inuuja's husband, Apphia's "grandfather", Joshua Komangapik.

Then Mikiseetee came out of his room beside the space heater to say a shy, quick hello and instantly disappeared again without shaking hands. I had forgotten that he lived here, that he was Inuuja's son. I had seen him earlier that week when he helped to move and install that tank at Papa's new laboratory. I was surprised at his shyness, because his cousins and other Inuit in his age group were so open and friendly and spoke English fairly well.

The conversation went very slowly with back-and-forth translations from English to Inuktitut and back again. Mama tried out a few of the words she had learned from her Inuktitut tutor, Anaviapik, and the old couple applauded her for her efforts. We discussed the new television and prospects of when it could be used, the nice weather, and other such small talk, while we all accustomed ourselves to each other. Mama spoke a few words about the Inuit training and Papa's building progress.

Before this visit, Mama had told me to stuff my jacket pockets with tissues in case I needed to use the washroom. I am glad I did because that strong tea soon made me need to pee. Apphia directed me to their washroom across from Mikiseetee's bedroom door. She brought a dipper of hot water from the simmering large pot at the back of the stove and poured it into the blue plastic bowl in the little sink so I could wash my hands, and showed me the soap and hand towel. The washroom was a small narrow room with a bare window facing the front of the house. It held a sink without hot and cold spigots, only the holes where they would be and a drain leading out through the wall. Of course, there was no running water here, hot or cold.

There was no flush toilet, but there was a honey bucket, like at Papa's house. I lifted the seat cover and did my business. There was a metal can of strong-smelling pine disinfectant, Pine-Sol, beside it on the floor to splash over whatever I left in the bucket. As Mama had predicted, there was no toilet paper, so I used the tissues from my jacket pocket, thankful she had warned me. I washed my hands, and dried them with the hand towel. I really appreciated Apphia's thoughtfulness. She'd learned hygiene at the nursing station, of course. The open honey bucket was nearing half full and accounted for some of the unfamiliar smell I had noted earlier.

Mama and I soon left the Komangapik house and Apphia went back to work at the nursing station. Walking down the road to Mama's house, we were called to from many of the houses along the way to come in, have tea. We smiled our thanks, shook our heads and made walking signs with our fingers. Mama said the first time she went visiting alone in the settlement, she had not taken along extra facial tissues in her pockets and learned fast that all the strong tea drinking can become a problem. She said now she visits only one house per outing and comes equipped.

We talked about our visit to the old Komangapiks. We both knew what it was to live poor in the south of Canada in the 1950s as immigrants from Germany, with no running water and an outhouse for our toilet behind the house, when we first arrived from Germany. The visit reminded us how fortunate we were these days to have modern facilities in our homes in southern Canada as well as the ability to pay for it all.

I noted that the Inuit of Pond Inlet seemed to be about a decade or so behind us in all things in spite of the refrigerators, telephones, and new, unconnected television sets. The young local Inuit had caught only the tail end of the "hippy" years of "flower power" and had had only sporadic exposure to Qallunaat living in the south of Canada. The current youthful interpretation and expression of southern style was in longer hair and biker style of dress for the young men and hair-sprayed bouffant hairdos, make-up, and matching outfits for the young women. It seemed to me the sources of the modern style of local Inuit youth came from their interpretation of Qallunaat ways of living as shown them by imported schoolteachers, the religious ministers and their wives, settlement officials, and HBC managers. This seemed further influenced by modern movies, and the reports of Inuit who had visited or gone to school in the south. Mama and I talked about how we could help our Inuit friends learn a bit more about the rest of Canada, not just the white Anglo-Saxon Protestants who had influenced them so far. I told Mama that I felt totally accepted and valued by the Inuit I had met so far. This was much different from how I usually felt meeting people anywhere else, in Canada or in Europe.

Mama and I had been good friends since before I reached adolescence. She had always been my ally in the face of Papa's angry outbursts, his more-outrageous restrictions and edicts. In retrospect, I must believe that Papa suffered from post traumatic stress disorder from his war experiences and, perhaps, borderline personality disorder. Both these psychological disorders did not exist in the Diagnostic and Statistical Manual of Mental Disorders at the time I had encountered it in my psychology studies. Over the years, she had been able to deflect and redirect much of Papa's physical violence. There were, of course, times when she could not do much. The prevailing times were such that the man of the house was also its ruler. Papa, for a long time, used to take Mama for granted, but gradually over the years he learned that she was a person of intelligence, determination, and talents that he could use to further his business. These positive changes had taken place after I left home. Maybe Papa really was changing from what I had known after all. And now I was happy to spend time with Mama this summer when my heart was sore from losing my husband. I needed her comfort as well as her nonjudgmental ear.

Six

Papa, in all earnestness, had warned me that white people coming to the arctic for the first time usually suffer from "arctic madness", becoming a little crazy because of the sheer amount of sunlight, the long days unbroken by night, and the resultant lack of sleep. I noticed some difficulty in getting to sleep during those overly light nighttime hours the first few nights, but found that this soon passed. Other than that, I felt energized and happy in the arctic summer sunshine, sometimes even euphoric. If this was "arctic madness", I quite liked it.

After supper on a Saturday about a week later, when the others had left the table, I announced that I was going to go see a movie just to let my parents know where I would be.

Papa spoke up, "You should go with Billy. He's lonely."

I was surprised. Billy had been brought up to Pond Inlet by Papa to serve as the project's small engine mechanic. We barely tolerated each other, that is to say, we were civil to each other but nothing more. After all, he was Papa's employee and a very good mechanic. I knew and liked his wife and children.

"No," I said, "I will not. I am meeting some friends and afterwards we are going to the dance."

I could see anger reddening Papa's face, but I just ignored him. I left the house before he could say anything.

Times had changed a lot from when my parents were young. It was now well into the "free love" era, after the discovery and widespread use of reliable birth-control measures. These were the days of rising feminism and women's liberation. Sexual mores had loosened and women's power over the use of their bodies had strengthened. Did Papa not know that? I was no longer a child, but a grown woman, an almost divorced woman, even though I was again living in Papa's house. Did he really believe that I had reverted to earlier times, compelled to do whatever he demanded as if he owned me just because I was living there?

We had had some difficult times, Papa and I, when I was a child and adolescent, but a decade and a half had passed since I had freed myself from all that. Before that, he had been a very strict and critical parent, given to verbal and physical abuse, not to mention control. I thought that whatever had not worked well between us had been put to rest, especially with my recent marital breakup since he had not approved of my marriage to Michael. Perhaps Papa thought, because I was friendly and willing to help him and Mama with their project here in Pond Inlet, that I was back under his control, again at his beck and call in all things. I had actually thought he had changed for the better, had lost his need to control me and my life.

This was the first time since we began to discuss my coming here that he had showed signs of his former controlling self. Maybe it was Papa who was suffering from the "arctic madness" that he warned me about? I was certain Mama would help to calm him down as she usually was able to do.

At the movie in the school gym, I met up with several of the young Inuit trainees and Mikiseetee, Jeeteeta's young uncle, joined us. He sat beside me and together we watched the movie, some action adventure involving young men and motorcycles. The movie's sound was not very good, so I missed a lot of the dialogue.

After the movie, we all walked over to the portable school dance hall where the windows had been covered with plywood sheets to darken the interior for the sake of atmosphere, with limited success. Gaps around the windows let in brilliant slivers of sunlight. Battered wood and steel tube assembly chairs were lined up around the walls and a record player with big speakers stood on a folding table at the end of the room. A young Inuk served as disc jockey. At the back of this dance hall was a tiny room with a door designated as the honey bucket room, I saw.

At the dance, Mikiseetee again sat beside me. I saw him as a handsome young man, bronze skinned and black haired, with pronounced slanty eyes, an aquiline nose and a radiant smile. I was quite flattered that he wanted to be close to me. We danced a little and then sat together. He pulled a small flat bottle of vodka out of his jacket pocket and offered me a sip. I said I did not want a drink. He appeared a bit shy, a little anxious and seemed to need the drink in order to talk to me. After a while, he relaxed and loosened up. He tried to get me to pronounce his name properly. I had great difficulty with that. I kept saying "Mee-see-kee-tee" or "Mik-ee-sa-tee-tee" until I got it right: Mikiseetee "Mik-ee-si-tee", emphasis on the second and fourth syllables. He said he did not like the nickname, "Mickey", Papa called him. It was too much like Mickey Mouse, the Disney cartoon character, which he thought childish. We danced a little more and then left to walk along the beach until it was time for me to go back to Papa's house for the night.

The next day, on Sunday after the service at the Anglican Church I attended with Mama, I went with Apphia and Mikiseetee, to visit at their home. Later, Mikiseetee took me to see his brother, Joseph Koonoo, who was called Josepee. He looked like a Qallunaq, with light-brown hair, light, freckled skin and a long neck with a prominent Adam's apple, but he could not speak English at all. This was Mikiseetee's brother?

"Different father," said Mikiseetee with a shrug of his shoulders.

Josepee was sobbing and crying, tears streaming down both his cheeks. Mikiseetee told me Josepee had just received news that his best friend had been accidentally shot and killed in Clyde River, located halfway down the eastern coast of Baffin Island. We sat with Josepee while he grieved. I was fascinated by the fact that he could show such raw emotions in front of me, a strange Qallunaq woman. This was truly freedom of expression, I thought. I took this as a sign of my being accepted.

The next Saturday morning when I had no training scheduled at the weather station, Papa called me to walk with him on the beach. He said he wanted to talk with me in private. He appeared friendly, as if he had gotten over his anger with me last week. This was when I did not do as he wanted, for me to go to the movies with Billy, the lonely mechanic. I was certain this was Mama's doing. She had always been good at calming Papa's anger.

It was another beautiful summer day. The brilliant sun shone in the clear blue sky. All seemed well with the world, peaceful. Papa and I walked along the shore, past the Anglican Church and mission house toward the west. As we walked along, our boots crunched on the beach gravel. The sun was already quite hot but there was a refreshing light breeze from across the water from the Bylot Island glaciers to the north. I noticed strange cloud formations in the distance over Eclipse Sound to the west that looked like upside-down mountains where I knew no actual mountains existed. Papa was pleased to tell me that this was called "fata morgana", a mirage, an optical phenomenon that often occurred over the open sea.

"Such mirages once famously frightened many sailors in the past," he said. "Other sailors mistook them as evidence of land and recorded them on their navigation maps, but nothing was there when others tried to find this land."

We walked on. I breathed in deeply, enjoying the clean air, and this new camaraderie with my Papa.

Mama had told me that when Papa heard in 1943 that he would probably not be able to father children as a result of his massive war wounds, especially the groin shot, she saw how he just gave up. She had then made it her business to produce a child for him and I was their first live-born child after a few miscarriages and one stillbirth. She even volunteered for a controversial experimental hormone therapy to maintain her pregnancies. Mama often said that I saved my Papa's life by my birth for which she was always so grateful. At times, when things became so very difficult between Papa and me, I regretted that I was responsible for his existence, that it was my own fault. This, along with his constant criticisms and his abuses, added to my burden of regret and obliterated any good opinion I had of myself. But when Papa approved of me, my good opinion of myself was instantly restored and I could achieve anything, I believed.

Papa and I came to some large boulders about halfway to Salmon River where we sat down to rest, facing the open water. The glaciers of Bylot Island over the dark blue waters seemed to loom so much closer than usual.

"Another trick of the arctic atmosphere," said Papa. We sat silent for some time.

I wondered why Papa wanted to speak to me in private, out of the hearing of Mama.

Then Papa turned to me and said without preamble, "Now that your marriage is broken up, as an adult formerly married woman, I realize that you are used to having regular sex. You must miss it."

I was stunned to silence.

He continued, "I don't want you consorting with Inuit men. I forbid it. And now I have thought up the perfect solution to your problem. I will arrange for you to sleep with Billy."

I could not believe the words Papa had spoken. I had already turned Billy down as a movie date. How could Papa think I was desperate enough to sleep with him?

The year before, back at home, when Papa was away, Billy and I had had a dispute over his pay cheque which I had signed. He punched me in the nose in the heat of anger. Oh, Billy later apologized to me and, of course, I forgave him.

But, Billy, the mechanic? As a lover for me?

The Inuit trainees had nick-named him "Billy Bazoo" because he so often lost his temper, cursing and swearing at the broken machines, and sometimes even at them. His job was to repair snowmobiles and motor vehicles as well as pass on his skills to the male trainees. He had already been in Pond Inlet for three months and made it no secret that he sorely missed his wife. I know Papa had forbidden him to seek comfort among the local Inuit women of Pond Inlet. So, this was how Papa wanted to solve the problem of his unhappy mechanic and at the same time ensure that I did not get involved with Inuit men?

"Billy Bazoo? No! Never!" I yelled and was suddenly aware that no one could hear me except Papa.

"Okay, then. Not Billy. You know I love your Mama more than anyone, even more than I love you." He paused, "But, I am prepared to make this sacrifice. I will sleep with you again to keep you away from Inuit men."

Papa had dared to refer to how he had taken advantage of me sexually from when I was nine years old until I was sixteen when I finally gained enough inner strength to refuse. I had believed everything he told me when I was still a child. He was, after all, my beloved Papa. As I grew, I gradually realized his words were lies to manipulate me. I had scared him into stopping the abuse when I was sixteen by going to a psychiatrist.

That was a shocking and disappointing experience for me. I was appalled that the psychiatrist accused me of seducing my father. I felt helpless and alone. I thought this sort of thing did not happen to other people. Those were the days when child sexual abuse was not openly acknowledged or ever talked about. Somehow, I had to cope, to carry on. After a while, coming to terms with having been abused seemed a little like trying to repair a broken egg. I resigned myself and finally accepted that it was just something I had to live with. After the sexual abuse stopped, it was my love for Mama that had kept me at home and in school. I managed that for another two years until I was eighteen when I dropped out of school and left home.

I took a deep breath. "No! Absolutely not!" I screamed.

I'd had enough. I began to run back up the beach, stumbling at times, all the way back to my parents' house. Mama saw how upset I was and I told her about Papa's proposal about Billy, but did not mention the offer of himself. Still, her face showed she was as stunned and amazed as I was.

I left the house before Papa returned.

I walked east along the sandy beach in front of the HBC buildings to calm myself. I knew that Mama would speak with Papa after lunch when he and she were alone. I stayed away until just before suppertime and went in to talk to Mama. I asked if I had to move out. She said I did not, that Papa saw that he had made a big mistake. She said, also, that he would not apologize to me because I had defied him, but begged me to be civil to him to avoid further upset. I did not have another place to live here in Pond Inlet, in any case, so I agreed to keep the peace.

I was glad when Monday came and I could go to the weather station for my training. I now made it my practice not to linger about my parent's house, to leave right after supper and stay out until bedtime. I visited among the people I had become acquainted with, Inuit and Qallunaat.

I also spent more and more time with Mikiseetee. He had a way about him that had me laughing and enjoying myself. With him, I forgot my sorrows and worries, which was such a relief. He was shy and I liked that. He told me a little about his life, how he had gone to the local school but had to stop after grade eight because there was no high school here. His mother did not want him to go to residential high school and college for higher learning like some of the other local young men.

Mikiseetee took what jobs he could, he said. His last job was away working in a cafeteria kitchen in Resolute Bay. He said he did not enjoy that much. In Pond Inlet, he said, a project was getting under way to establish a local lending library of English language books. Some generous Qallunaq donor had sent up a collection of books on the last sea-lift. He said he would be the librarian once the town had received the proposed government funding. That seemed to me a wonderful job for him. A seal-hunting librarian. I could just picture it in my mind. Lovely.

"I love books. I love reading," I told him as he showed me the many boxes of books in the library rooms in one of the three black-roofed pink-and-grey government buildings on the road to the school.

One evening, we walked along the beach to Salmon River past the place where Papa had propositioned me. I tried to put that out of my mind to focus on Mikiseetee.

At Salmon River where the river flows into Eclipse Sound, we found a great, thick length of rope — a hawser — washed up on shore between the stranded ice floes left by the outgoing tide. The diameter of this hawser must have been about a foot. We talked about the possible origin of this immense fragment of water-logged rope, torn away from some ice breaker or delivery ship during a storm, maybe. Mikiseetee picked up the loop end, hauled it over his shoulder and dragged it along the beach, like some ancient hero of myth and legend. We laughed and talked nonsense. I was enchanted by his playfulness and sense of humour. But there were serious moments, instants of silent reflection, too.

On the way back, we walked up along the bluff over the beach and he showed me the grave of Robert Janes, marked by a broken, bleached, wooden headboard surrounded by long grasses. Mikiseetee told me a short version of how the RCMP and the Canadian law court came to Pond Inlet during the 1920s, how Inuit were accused of murder when they had only been defending themselves, according to their traditional ways, from this crazed Qallunaq trader who had gone wild. It was a bleak story, but I began to see a little of the love-hate relationship that Mikiseetee, and perhaps other Inuit, might generally have with the dominant Qallunaat, those now in charge of Inuit, backed up by the power of the RCMP. It made me sad to think of the freedom Inuit had lost to govern themselves.

When I arrived in Pond Inlet, I confess I actually wore a Mickey Mouse watch on my left wrist. I had bought this cheap little watch during the late 1960s when I got my first job in Toronto after leaving home to remind me not to take life and its challenges too seriously. After Mikiseetee told me he did not like to be called "Mickey", I wondered what he thought of my watch. Then, when my thirtieth birthday arrived in August, Mikiseetee gave me a small box carefully wrapped in white paper and tied with a blue ribbon.

"I hope you like it," he said shyly. "Happy birthday."

I unwrapped the little parcel and found a stylish stainless-steel watch with a luminous royal-blue dial face. He took off my Mickey Mouse watch and replaced it with my new watch, his gift. He pocketed my old watch and I never saw it again. I did not think to ask him what he would do with it. I saw this gift as a sign of change for the better, that someone cared for me.

It did not take long before the whole settlement knew that Mikiseetee and I were an "item". We even held hands openly on the settlement roads and beaches. We often played card games at his mother's house. His parents greeted me when I came and did not seem to mind my presence, as I had feared they would. I felt totally at ease and accepted by his relatives as well. A little over a month passed before Mikiseetee and I became lovers. I did not think ahead at all. I only enjoyed each day, each moment, as it unfolded. We were careful, though, not to make a show of our mutual admiration in front of my parents, but as Mikiseetee was not employed by them, they rarely saw us together. I did not want to stir up Papa's anger, as he had forbidden me to "fraternize with the natives", a rule which I chose to ignore. I was, after all, a modern adult woman who could make up her own mind about such things.

One evening at supper, Papa told a story about a Qallunaq schoolteacher, a man, who had been stationed in Pond Inlet to teach at the newly built school. That teacher fell in love with a local Inuit woman and they had an affair soon discovered by the government settlement manager. At that time, it was the official rule that no public employee was allowed to "fraternize with the natives", a hangover from the British colonial regulations practised in their foreign territories. To me, this was ridiculous because we were Canadians in Canada. Pond Inlet and its inhabitants were Canadians, not foreigners in a strange land. Unfortunately, this rule was enforced in Canada until the late 1960s. That young teacher lost his job and he and his Inuit wife, whom he had married, were forced to leave the settlement in disgrace.

I found this story sad, but I did not believe the rule about not "fraternizing with the natives" would apply to me. After all, I was not employed by the government. I was employed by Papa, a private businessman. And, I recalled Caleb Sangoya recently losing his room in his grandmother's house to his uncle and his pregnant Qallunaq common-law wife. Racially mixed unions were totally accepted by the Inuit, I knew, as many of them were products of Qallunaq-Inuit unions of long ago. I began to dream, envision how such a union might work for me, given the opportunity.

Seven

A few days after my thirtieth birthday, Mikiseetee took me down the road to the east side of Pond Inlet. We looked over the bay to the southeast at Mount Herodier that Mikiseetee called Igarjuaq, Inuktitut meaning "big fireplace or oven", the name of his family's home camp at the base of this mountain.

"I was born at Igarjuaq and grew up there," he said. "We moved to Mittimatalik, as Pond Inlet is called in my language, after the school was finished. The RCMP wanted all the children to go to school and our parents were too lonely in camp without us. They worried about us, too."

Mikiseetee told me that Mittimatalik was named after a sea gull sitting on a partly submerged rock near the shore. It was also known as Mittima's Grave, where the ancestral Mittima was buried. I attempted to pronounce Mittimatalik several times until I got it right. I began to think of this place as Mittimatalik instead of Pond Inlet.

He sounded very nostalgic about his home camp, Igarjuaq. He said it was just a small place, two houses on gravel above the beach at the foot of the mountain.

We were walking hand in hand back up the hill to his parents' house from the east beach when suddenly my parents appeared coming down toward us over the rise of the hill. I snatched my hand away from Mikiseetee's, but Papa had seen our clasped hands. He immediately grabbed Mama's arm, turned her around and walked rapidly away from us, almost dragging Mama along. I think she had not seen us and was confused by this sudden change of direction.

To delay having to face Papa's anger, I stayed at the Komangapik house with Mikiseetee for a few hours and then ventured back to my parents' house. Papa met me at the door. He was pale but struggled to keep his emotions under control.

"I have contacted the RCMP constable and filed an official complaint against you on the grounds that you are disrupting the conduct of my business and disturbing the local people," he said. "The day after tomorrow the RCMP will escort you to the airplane because you are being expelled from Pond Inlet, as a "persona non grata", a legal term meaning an undesirable foreign person unwelcomed by the local settlement government."

Papa shook his head. "You have truly fallen into arctic madness, haven't you?" He sighed. "I warned you."

I remained silent. Mama looked on with tears in her eyes. It hurt me to think that I was causing her trouble with Papa. I knew I had forced the issue. I was sorry, but also suddenly very angry.

I was not a member of the Feminist Liberation movement, but I did believe that a grown woman should be in charge of her own life, neither controlled by her father nor her husband. I had no regard, either, for the small-mindedness of government officials ready to call people names when they did not toe the official line. I was not afraid of being considered a "slut", a woman of low moral character. Clearly, the issue here was that I was "fraternizing" with an Inuit man. That is what troubled Papa, the idea of a racially mixed union. Was it possible that some of the Nazi teachings he had been exposed to in the "Hitler-Jugend", the Nazi youth organization, as a teenager and young adult had rubbed off on him?

Oh, yes, I thought, Papa can befriend Inuit, even champion their right to learn technical skills, but that did not mean he wanted an Inuit consorting with his daughter. Just a little hypocritical.

I spent a restless night in my room, unhappy that I had to leave this wonderful place so abruptly. I had even met a person in Mikiseetee who made me laugh and forget that I was an aging divorcee. Now I must leave him behind and go back to my broken life in disgrace.

At least I had collected a fair number of Inuit children's drawings for my psychology research project, I said to myself.

The next day, I went up the hill to the Komangapik house and told them that I was being forced to leave by the RCMP through an order arranged by Papa..

Mikiseetee was shocked and upset.

"You can't go," he wailed, crying real tears. He kept carrying on, distraught, saying how much he would miss me, how he could not live without me.

I shrugged, "You could come with me if you want."

"But I have no money. I cannot go with you."

"I have some savings. I can pay for you to come with me."

His face lit up. Then and there he decided to come with me.

This was unexpected. I remembered the Qallunaq woman who had come to Pond Inlet, that is Mittimatalik, with her Inuk. It could work the other way, too, I thought. This man wanted to be with me so much, he was willing and unafraid to face the unknown with me in southern Canada.

Mikiseetee went to tell his parents in their bedroom. I did not see or hear how his parents reacted to the news of his leaving Mittimatalik, the next day, so suddenly.

And so, I was busy planning this new adventure with Mikiseetee, thinking of what I should do next: the flight arrangements, the hotels, transportation from Toronto to my apartment in St. Catharines. I made a to-do list. I used the Komangapik telephone to arrange Mikiseetee's flight ticket with the local air agent. I already had my return ticket, so I only had to change my return date. Luckily, the air agent had found space for us together on the flights south. All was settled when I later left Mikiseetee's house.

I returned to my parents' house and packed up my things and the children's drawings I had collected. Papa had gone out and Mama stayed to speak to me as I packed.

"It's not too late to apologize to your Papa and promise to break it off with Mikiseetee," she said.

"Mama, it's too late for that now. Mikiseetee is coming with me tomorrow on the plane. We are leaving together."

She had been weeping but now she dried her eyes. She knew that with this announcement I was declaring war against Papa's relentless attempts to control me and my life. Mama knew that I had absolutely no idea what I was doing, that I had not thought out the implications of this whole thing, Mikiseetee's coming with me, nor of my plans for continuing my university studies, or anything else.

She also knew that deep down I was also afraid of what would happen but, now that this course of action had been set in motion, I would not abandon it. She knew I was reacting in hurt and panic at being trapped once again by Papa as I had been during my childhood and adolescence. She understood that this struggle for independence I had with Papa was very important to me, about who I was as a woman. My first marriage was history and I wanted a future without the constant interference from Papa's manipulations and schemes. I respected his work and what he was trying to do here in Mittimatalik with the Inuit, but I had to make a break from him once and for all. Of this I was most certain.

Mama knew that I was in no state to listen to reason. She gave me a final hug.

"My dear child," she said, "you must do what you must do. God bless you both."

It was a comfort to me that Mama was not against me, even if she did not agree that I was doing the right thing.

I went back to the Komangapik house and spent the last night in Mittimatalik with Mikiseetee in his parents' house.

Eight

The next morning, on the day I was to leave Pond Inlet with Mikiseetee, I went early to my parents' house. Mama served me breakfast. I did not see Papa. Mama said he would be away until suppertime by which time I would be long gone. I helped Mama with housekeeping until it was time for me to leave. Mama hugged me goodbye. I gathered up my things and the settlement manager took me to the airstrip in his truck. The RCMP constable met me there to ensure my departure. There was a small crowd of Inuit who had come to see the plane leave, some of them Mikiseetee's relatives, but none of the Inuit trainees I had come to know through my work with Papa.

At that point, I was not at all certain that Mikiseetee would actually come with me after all. Then suddenly he was there beside me, all smiles, loaded down with his travel bag, boarding the plane. The little plane flew us to Resolute Bay. We overnighted at the air crew quarters where we shared a bed. The next morning, we boarded the Nordair plane for the long direct flight to Montreal where we transferred to an Air Canada flight to Toronto. In Toronto we took a bus to St. Catharines. Finally, we arrived, exhausted, at my apartment on Glendale Avenue. It was a long trip.

When I left St. Catharines in mid-July, I had been sharing my apartment with John, a university student. He had briefly been my lover but that had ended some months before I left on my trip north. We had agreed not to continue with the apartment share before I left. He promised to find another place to live and to move out before I arrived back at the end of September. Of course, I came back earlier than expected, and so I found that he was still there. It could be that he thought that we could somehow re-establish our former relationship.

"John, you said you would move out. What are you still doing here?" I demanded.

I was utterly weary from the long trip and disappointed he had not kept his promise. When he saw Mikiseetee, he understood there was no hope for a reconciliation between us. It took John a few phone calls to find another place to stay. In about an hour, he had moved out. How awkward. Good riddance and not soon enough, I thought.

Mikiseetee and I were alone at last. He was not happy. I had to deal with his not understanding why John was living in my apartment and his jealousy about that. It took some doing to explain about how university students often lived together, in separate bedrooms, sharing the apartment costs. I don't think he was fully convinced but let it pass. I realized that he, too, was tired from the long trip, not to mention being a bit disoriented.

A week later, a new student, an African, came to rent our back room. This arrangement worked for a while, but soon, Mikiseetee wanted him to leave. He was put off by the tiny circles of hair that always graced our bathroom sink and shower after this student had used the bathroom.

"Those hair circles creep me out," he said. I had to find another way to help pay the rent.

It had been my plan to continue my university studies and so I applied for my annual student loan. Even with this boost of cash, it was difficult to meet ongoing expenses. I started back to classes, but soon found that Mikiseetee did not do at all well being left alone on his own in the apartment during my class time.

My Uncle Hermann tried to help Mikiseetee get a job, but that did not work out. He worked a few days and then quit. He was not interested in working at a job and was too shy to admit this to my uncle. I tried getting him to talk to me. All he expressed was that he just wanted to go back home. I could think that he found it hard to accept my university-student lifestyle, that it was not one long party-time, but that I would have to go to classes, do research, and do my assignments, all of which I had to do without him.

My other usual sources of income, such as posing as a life-model for the local high school art course and the Rodman Hall Arts Centre life-drawing classes were no longer options. Mikiseetee definitely did not want me to be nude in front of arts students. He could not see the students being only interested in drawing or painting line and form.

My nightclub waitress job, which had paid so well in tips, was also becoming out of the question. Mikiseetee would come to the nightclub while I was on the job, over-drink and become noisy, lamenting his homesickness. After the second such incident, I was fired. Desperate for income, I finally found another waitressing job in a sleazy beer hall where they tolerated First Nations people, then still called "Indians". No one there seemed to care how Mikiseetee acted. At this place, I earned the minimum wage like I had at the nightclub, but here I did not get tips from the impoverished clientele who were, most of them, just up from homeless. Still, in this way, I was able to meet most of our expenses. Luckily, I had the use of Mama's old Chevrolet car to

My uncle Hermann, 1974.

get about to my distant workplaces and the university, as well as to take Mikiseetee on outings on weekends.

Feeding Mikiseetee was definitely a problem. He wanted to eat lots of red meat, of course, but meat has always been so expensive. Fish was cheaper but he would not accept any other fish but the arctic char. Salmon was similar, but he refused that too. It also did not help that he drank up a fair bit of my income. It was becoming clear that keeping Mikiseetee in southern Canada was too challenging for me without his cooperation.

The only solution I could come up with was to somehow take Mikiseetee back home to Pond Inlet. I felt he could not find his way back on his own and would most likely succumb to abject homelessness, or worse, in Ontario. He had come with me to southern Canada for love of me and now I felt I could not abandon him, no matter how hard it got.

The first step to improve things for Mikiseetee in St. Catharines was for me to quit university. I gave my collected Inuit children's drawings to my favourite psychology professor specializing in children's art as research material.

"I am sad that you are leaving the honours year program, but do understand that your life has got in the way, as it sometimes does," he said.

I had completed my necessary three years for a pass degree already, so in October I attended my graduation with my class and received my Bachelor degree in Psychology and German Literature. Now I was free to stay with Mikiseetee during the day and take him to my sleazy bar job in the evenings. Mikiseetee showed some signs of improving. One evening, my estranged husband, Michael, took him off my hands and took him out drinking with his artist friends while I worked. I suppose he was curious about this Inuk who had caught my fancy.

"I feel sorry for him, so far away from home with no way back. It's not his fault, is it?" Michael commented when I came to take Mikiseetee home.

I was fully aware of my responsibilities and did not need Michael to point that out to me. It was my fault to have allowed Mikiseetee to come here where he felt so alien. I had made assumptions about how Mikiseetee was just like other people and therefore able to adjust to new surroundings. I was so wrong. Now I had to find a way out of this problem, to get him home safely. I considered accompanying Mikiseetee to Resolute Bay and sending him off to Pond Inlet from there. But that was far too expensive. Besides, I was not at all eager to part from him just yet. What other way could there be?

I remembered the young Inuit man who had been made homeless by his uncle returning from southern Canada with his pregnant Qallunaq wife. A "mixed-race" union could work, I thought. Then I recalled how Mama had mentioned that she was prepared to pay for my divorce from Michael as part of the deal of my accompanying her to Pond Inlet. This may be the solution to ensuring that Mikiseetee and I could return. If I were legally married to him, we could somehow overcome my being banned from his home town, I thought.

My mother's lawyer was also our family friend and I called him. He said he would contact Mama. He got back to me saying that she agreed to pay for my divorce from Michael. So, we went ahead and I sued for a no-contest divorce. My lawyer and I were able to get it all done without Michael having to be present at court. It was all unusually quick, thankfully. Mama, true to her word, transferred money to my bank account to be able to pay the lawyer. She must have believed that getting married to Mikiseetee might be a productive move. Or, perhaps she feared that I was pregnant.

At the end of the divorce proceedings, the judge waived the Decree Nisi, the document finalizing the divorce, usually issued months after a divorce.

"This is to allow the divorcing couple the time to reconcile, which sometimes happens," my lawyer explained.

We argued in court for the need for speed in completing the divorce in order that Mikiseetee and I could return to Pond Inlet in time for him to participate in the annual winter caribou hunt.

"This is the first time I have waived a Decree Nisi in a divorce to accommodate Eskimo caribou hunting season," the judge commented.

The divorce done, Mikiseetee and I could now legally get married.

"This raises some new questions," said my lawyer. "The main one is, would you lose any of your personal rights by marrying an Eskimo? Your mother wanted me to look into this," he told me.

"Contrary to marrying a native Canadian Indian, you would legally have your Canadian citizen status in addition to Eskimo status, that is, dual status. You are not giving up any rights by marrying Mikiseetee. You are adding to them," he concluded.

This was good to know. I knew that, at that time, a non-native woman married into the First Nations reservation system lost her rights, while a native woman lost her treaty rights when she married a non-native man. This smacked to me of the colonialist way to discourage inter-racial marriage. I was relieved that it did not affect me and my Inuk.

My first marriage to Michael had been a civil service at Toronto City Hall and I did not want to repeat that. Mikiseetee and I agreed that a church wedding would be better for us.

To that end, we visited the local Anglican Church and were told that we would have to submit a petition to the church governance because I was divorced, a procedure that could take years and was not always successful. Mikiseetee was Anglican, as was his mother and most of the people of Mittimatalik, except for his father and one family who were Roman Catholic. I was raised Lutheran, Mama's religion, while Papa was Roman Catholic. Having had parents of mixed religions, differing Christian religions was not a real issue for me. I had left the Lutheran church when I was sixteen, had not attended church for decades, and had no local connection for arranging a Lutheran wedding.

To Mikiseetee, though, it seemed as if his religion would not allow us to marry and he began to lose heart.

In the end, as a compromise, we approached the St. James United Church, a classic brick church with stained-glass windows and a proper steeple in downtown St. Catharines. The minister there told us kindly that as long as we were allowed legally to marry under Canadian law, he would happily perform the ceremony. He told us that many of his congregation were Anglicans, Lutherans and other Protestant denominations.

"The United Church believes that Christian couples should marry rather than just live together. We do not follow antiquated rules and procedures," he said.

With our church date set, Mikiseetee seemed to regain hope and began to behave himself like someone about to get married. He was pleased that we could marry in a proper Christian church. He told me that he now felt sure that being married was how we would be able to go home again. I was not that sure that everything would work out that way, but I kept that thought to myself. I took it one step at a time.

Amazingly, Mikiseetee even went to work with my uncle for a few weeks so he could buy a wedding ring and a dark suit. My aunt helped me sew a light-blue, long-sleeved plain wedding gown trimmed in white lace.

In mid-November, in front of a few friends, my sister and her boy-

Gathered outside the church after the wedding ceremony, 1974.

In the church: Sheila, me, Mikiseetee, Glen and Ron, 1974.

friend, as well as my uncle and his family, Mikiseetee and I exchanged wedding vows before the United Church minister. My uncle walked me down the aisle and my friend Sheila from university served as my maid of honour. A friend, member of my former university fencing club, served as Mikiseetee's best man. I carried a small, white-leather-covered Anglican prayer book with flowers on top instead of a bouquet in solidarity with Mikiseetee's Anglicanism. After the church service, we held a small reception at my apartment with food, cake, and some bubbly wine. My ex-husband, Michael, declined the wedding invitation but did send our

At our wedding reception, 1974.

mutual friend, John Moffatt, to record the proceedings by taking wedding photographs for us.

There we were, Mikiseetee and I, married.

Nine

Our plan for the evening of our wedding after our guests had left the apartment was for Mikiseetee and I to go out dancing to celebrate on our own. That afternoon we had eaten well, shared out the wedding cake and drank the toasts. I had not kept track of how much Mikiseetee drank. After all, it was our wedding reception and I knew he would behave himself in company. By the time it came to go out dancing after everyone had left, the picture had changed. I found my new spouse was simply too drunk. Our plan cancelled itself.

This time Mikiseetee's drunkenness was very different, something I had not seen with him before. Mikiseetee's face twisted in revulsion when he looked at me, became darker, sharper, and his eyes narrowed to hard black slits. He began to rage and shout. I was shocked. This was our wedding night. We were newlyweds. This, our happy time, now flipped into a nightmare.

"You're sleeping with those guys! The ones you call your friends, those who came to our wedding!" he shouted.

"That's ridiculous!" I yelled back.

This was our very first argument. We had usually been able to compromise our differences when we disagreed, but this time, now that we were married, all that changed.

I could not believe what I saw and heard. Of course, I had been drinking, too, and did not notice how everything had slipped and escalated out of control with Mikiseetee.

Suddenly he struck me. That was the first strike of many. It all happened so fast, I did not defend myself. I mean, this was Mikiseetee, the person I loved and whom I married this day. I was absolutely stupefied, unable to move. Just as suddenly, he stopped and simply passed out on the living room floor. The effort of beating me up seemed to have worn him out. I was actually happy that he had lost consciousness.

Instead of a joyful wedding night with dancing, I had bruises about my head and ears, not to mention other parts of my body. I left him passed out on the living room floor and I went to bed to think over what I had gotten myself into. And soon I passed into troubled sleep myself.

The next day, I awoke about noon and considered the situation as I surveyed my bruises in the bathroom mirror. I now knew that I was married to someone who would beat his wife when he was drunk. This was devastating. This had never happened before we married. It was as if Mikiseetee had turned into another person this time. When drunk he now looked and sounded completely different. Like a Jekyll and Hyde personality switch, he became the opposite of how I knew him. By getting married to him, he must have thought he now owned me, that I was his possession and could relax his careful control over himself. I had to find a way to fix that.

Mikiseetee took this photo of me the day after our wedding, 1974.

❄

I knew that wives were often abused by their husbands. I had seen Papa do this on one occasion to Mama when I was about seven years old. It was in our second year in Canada. Papa came home drunk one night and hit Mama. She fell down in front of him, apparently in a faint. Papa was immediately alarmed and sorry. To him, she appeared unconscious. He did not see me hiding at the top of the stairs. Mama opened her eyes and saw me there, and knew how worried I was about her. She winked at me and closed her eyes again without Papa noticing. I knew she was all right, but Papa did not. He carried her carefully up the stairs to their bedroom while I quickly disappeared into my bed. He apologized to Mama over and over for the next few days and, of course, Mama graciously forgave him. He was so relieved, he never did that again. Mama had found a way. Perhaps I could find a way, too.

The next day, Mikiseetee was his usual self again and apologized over and over to me. Of course, I forgave him. He was my new husband and I loved him, I told him. He spent much time on long distance telephone talking with his mother, confessing his sins, telling her how terrible he had been to me and what a bad person he was. By this time, the Anik-A1 Satellite enabled regular long-distance telephone connections between Pond Inlet and southern Canada. His mother, my new mother-in-law, was able to calm him down after a while with her words over the telephone.

This is how we began our married life. Although I was dazed and dismayed, I had noticed one important thing about Mikiseetee. There was one point in his overdrinking at which he underwent a personality change, when he switched into his opposite persona. He was usually so quiet, shy, funny, and friendly, but, when drinking past that crucial point, he would become angry, jealous, unreasonable. And, now I definitely knew, also violent and physically abusive.

My friend Sheila, my maid of honour at my wedding, listened to my tale of woe during the days after my wedding. One evening, Mikiseetee was again drinking a lot, perhaps as a way of trying to cheer himself up after being so contrite about abusing me. I had a feeling that things would again get dangerously out of hand for me. I called Sheila by telephone without Mikiseetee knowing. She was to be on standby to pick me up in her car to take me to her place if I needed a safe refuge. The signal would be that I dial her telephone number and hang up when she answered without saying a word. That way, Mikiseetee would not know who I was calling.

I kept a clear head and noticed that, yes, Mikiseetee had again flipped over, personality-wise. I dialed Sheila's telephone number. She picked up and I disconnected.

Mikiseetee and I were in the bedroom when he began to push me around. A sudden feeling of white-hot rage overtook me. I balled up my fist, pulled back my elbow and pushed against his face with all my strength. It may just be that my push became a punch in the heat of the moment. He fell down beside the bed and seemed to pass out. I did not wait around to find out. After all, I had just hit him. If he were not passed out, only dazed, I was surely in greater danger. I ran outside to Sheila's waiting car, jumped in on the passenger side, slammed the car door and we were off. I spent the night at her house, relieved that I had a safe place to stay.

The next day toward suppertime, when I thought Mikiseetee would be sobered up, Sheila drove me back to the apartment. All was quiet. I went into the bedroom. Mikiseetee got up from the bed and embraced me. I tried to hug him back and but it was awkward for me.

He spoke, "I don't remember anything. Did I hurt you again?"

"Not this time. But I did go to spend the night at Sheila's house."

"My head really hurts," he groaned.

"Oh," I said and felt the sore knuckles on my right hand.

He asked, "Did anyone come here last night?"

"I don't think so, but then again, I was away. Maybe you fell and hit your head?"

Perhaps it was the way I asked this question.

Suddenly, Mikiseetee's face broke into a broad grin. "I know. It was you. You hit me."

"Yes," I said, "I did." I wondered what would come next.

He grabbed my hands and kissed them saying, "Thank you, thank you. I felt so bad for having hit you on our wedding night. Now we are even."

I was definitely relieved. Sheila, who had waited in the living room ready to whisk me away should things go bad, left to go home, satisfied that I would be all right alone with Mikiseetee.

My retaliation ploy did not prevent Mikiseetee from future overdrinking. But the next time he had that personality switch when he was drunk, he reacted defensively, not abusively.

"Oh, yeah. You're that dangerous woman who fights back," he would mumble. And he would not bother me.

From this I learned several things. Mikiseetee's identity, his sense of self, was as shaky as my own. When overdrinking, Mikiseetee tended to turn into an abusive person afraid of strong women. I could not stop Mikiseetee from overdrinking. It was imperative to get Mikiseetee home to Pond Inlet very soon.

Ten

Near the end of November 1974 after Mikiseetee and I were married, Papa called me and asked me to come see him at his house in St. Catharines, that he needed my help. He must have gotten my telephone number from Mama. He said he had to made a quick trip home because a certain well-known businessman was to make an evening visit in two days to complete buying the patent of the oil-boom Papa had invented. The oil-boom was a device used in retrieving oil on the water surface after oil spills from tankers. He said he needed the proceeds from this sale of his patent in order to continue his Pond Inlet projects as he had lost some of his government support, implying that this was partly my fault.

Still, he spoke to me in friendly terms and, I guess I hoped to mend broken fences so he would have the ban on my return to Pond Inlet lifted. I agreed to act as his hostess for the evening, dress well, prepare hors d'oeuvres, serve drinks and be as charming as I could be. The gentleman came and all went well. They discussed the sale of the patent, transfer of funds and other details. Then Papa showed the man some photographic slides projected on a screen of his Pond Inlet activities. It was a successful evening.

After the businessman left, Papa told me that certain government people had accused him of arranging the liaison between me and Mikiseetee, "the son of a prominent Pond Inlet elder", to further his business aims. I said I was sorry to hear this. Even though untrue, no one can fight a rumour, I knew.

Papa said, "You did owe me for setting me up for this rumour that put my training project at risk."

I apologized.

He said, "Well, you've made up for it now by helping me as hostess to clinch the sale."

I knew then that he was no longer quite so angry with me. He returned to Pond Inlet the next day. He said he did not like to leave Mama on her own there for too long. I hoped that all this would help to get my troubled husband and me back to Pond Inlet soon.

A few weeks later, a day in mid-December, Mikiseetee told me he had news from his mother after he spoke to her on the telephone.

"My mother said she sent my brother Josepee to visit your father and get him to take back the RCMP order that is keeping us from going home. Your father agreed and talked to the RCMP. We can go home at last." Mikiseetee could not have been happier and I was so relieved.

My new mother-in-law told Mikiseetee that Papa had relented because, after all, we were now all related by marriage. I suspect that Papa thought I was pregnant and had married Mikiseetee for that reason. That may be what he thought but, no, at least, not yet.

I stopped taking my birth control pills when Mikiseetee and I married. Both of us desired a child and I wondered how long it would take for me to conceive. I had read that conception usually takes about a year after stopping "the pill". Only a month had passed and so I must be patient. It was good to know that when I conceived, the child would be wanted by its father also, not just by me.

In the last year of my marriage to my first husband, Michael, I began to have nagging thoughts of wanting a baby. Before then, I'd had my doubts about launching a new life into this unfriendly world. When we married in 1968, Michael and I had both agreed that we would not have children. He warned me then that he would certainly leave me if I did become pregnant. Perhaps it was my perverse hormones nudging me as I was then fast approaching thirty, after which my optimum time for having babies would be over. I had been using birth control pills, once they were available, since I'd left my parental home.

A few months prior to our break-up, Mama told me about Michael worrying to her about my suddenly wanting children. He told her he was counting my birth control pills every day to make sure I was not going to claim that I had "forgotten" to take them.

Mama pointed out to him, "If my daughter really wanted to trick you into fatherhood, she would simply replace them." But she tried to reassure him that I would never be that underhanded and disloyal to him. Michael's reaction had been to replace me with someone else a few months later. This is how little he trusted me.

In the meantime, my pregnancy was yet to come.

I was suddenly very busy making arrangements for our departure. First, I made our flight bookings. Luckily, I had been frugal enough to have the airfare for our one-way air tickets home to Pond Inlet on hand. Then, I gave notice at my waitressing job and paid for the lease termination of my apartment. What little furniture I owned, my old upright piano, and household goods I parcelled out as giveaways to my local relatives and friends, but I had my custom-built bed put away into storage for future shipping north. That bed was a special consolation gift Mama had built for me when Michael and I parted. It divided in two sections that connected together, and could easily be moved. Sometime in the future, I thought, it could be sent up to Pond Inlet by ship as sea-lift cargo.

Mikiseetee's older sister, Mary, my new sister-in-law, had sent down the parka she made for me, a light-blue, embroidered, wool duffel undercoat covered with a tightly woven wind-proof cotton shell in forest green. The hood and cuffs were trimmed with white arctic fox fur with little white fox forepaws hanging down in front from the hood on each side. I was delighted with this parka. It replaced the ratty navy-blue expedition parka I had worn on my arrival in Pond Inlet the previous

My new parka 1974

July. I knew my new "saki", mother-in-law in Inuktitut, had arranged this for me, her new "ukuaq", daughter-in-law.

After that, I packed some clothing, a small selection of books, and little things I thought I might need, into several boxes and bags. We said goodbye to my friends and family and my uncle drove us to the Toronto airport. In Toronto, Mikiseetee and I boarded the airplane to Montreal and Resolute Bay and then flew by Twin Otter to Pond Inlet. To me, it felt like Mikiseetee and I were on our delayed honeymoon, going home. Mikiseetee was so happy, he did not overdrink on this trip, but he did bring along a large bottle of rum in his bag.

I had no conception of what winter would be like in Pond Inlet. But I now got a taste of it when we changed planes in Resolute Bay from the big Nordair plane to the little Twin Otter on winter skis that now replaced the summer's wheeled pontoons. The airplanes and buildings, hydro poles and wires, fences and trucks were all thickly frosted with ice rime. Our breath was visible as thick fog as we exhaled. They said it was only minus 22 degrees Fahrenheit (minus 30 degrees Centigrade), mildly cold, relatively speaking, I was told. We did not linger long outside but it felt to me as cold as it was on the airport runway in Montreal at 14 degrees Fahrenheit (minus 10 degrees Centigrade). At that time, Canada was still using Fahrenheit for temperature measurement and would not switch to Centigrade until the next year. I really could not tell the difference between Montreal and Resolute Bay coldness. And, it was already quite dark in the early afternoon, the complete opposite of what I had experienced that past July.

The flight on the unheated Twin Otter was noisy, dark and cold. It seemed to take much longer than the same flight in the summer for the same length of time in the air. Not being able to see anything out of the porthole windows of the small plane and its being far too noisy for conversation, left me with nothing to distract me from my discomfort. The plane was packed with mostly Inuit, all of us sitting shoulder to shoulder in the narrow fold-down seats. The remaining space was filled with luggage, parcels, mail bags and boxes secured by webbing. It looked like everyone was going home for Christmas.

Finally, the pilot indicated that we were approaching Pond Inlet. He did not have to tell us to buckle our seatbelts. No one had unbuckled them as it had been such a bumpy ride. The descent was like being on a carnival ride swinging back and forth inducing nausea. The landing was anything but soft, with a loud jarring thump. We taxied on packed snow, strangely smooth compared to that dusty ride in on loose gravel on this same runway the previous July. We stopped at the side of that strangely shaped orange airport hut.

The plane was met by the RCMP officer and settlement officials as well as a few Inuit meeting relatives disembarking the plane. At least it was warm in that misshapen hut, the air terminal, while we waited for the baggage to be unloaded and organized. Mikiseetee's brother Josepee drove us down from the airstrip in his truck. I noticed that when we reached the beach road, we turned right to go up the hill toward Takijualuk School. I knew that to get to my parents' house and laboratory, one needed to turn left. I tried not to think about Mama and Papa. I was just so happy that we had finally arrived.

Mikiseetee and I entered House Number 69, which was to be our home.

Since my father-in-law and my mother-in-law were both in Inuktitut referred to by the word saki, that is, parent-in-law with no differentiation, I decided to call my mother-in-law Sakikuluk, little parent-in-law and my father-in-law Sakialuk, big parent-in-law.

My Sakikuluk and Apphia, my new sister-in-law, hugged me in welcome while my Sakialuk just hung back and smiled his welcome. The open living-room/kitchen was packed with relatives to say hello to Mikiseetee and to greet me. I could see how relieved and happy Mikiseetee was to finally be home again, able to speak his own language among his people. He just kept laughing and smiling, such a switch from the moroseness and despondency that he seemed to have left behind in southern Canada.

Soon, when most of the relatives had gone after about an hour, I moved my things into Mikiseetee's bedroom. Somebody had decorated the wall with small, coloured, Christmas lights that glowed softly. Mikiseetee's single bed was wide enough to accommodate both of us. It was a small room, but it would do for us for now, I thought.

Finally, the visitors had gone, leaving only James, Mikiseetee's brother-in-law, and those who usually lived in the house. These were, aside from my parents-in-law, Apphia whom I knew from the summer, young Peea, James's younger sister adopted by my Sakikuluk, and young Natanai who was James's son but also lived here.

The first rule I learned from Mikiseetee and Apphia was that I was never to speak directly to my Sakialuk, my father-in-law. The second rule was to never speak the names of my parents-in-law. These were Inuit taboos, rules that must not be broken. If a taboo was broken, the family would be cursed with great misfortune. I wondered if there were many of these kinds of rules that I must keep. There was so much that I did not know, so much to learn, not just the language, but also how to live as part of my new family.

Soon, Mikiseetee brought out that large bottle of rum he had brought to share with my Sakialuk and James. This man was married to Mikiseetee's sister Joanna, was some years older than Mikiseetee, and was his good friend. Drinks were poured into mugs and glasses. Mikiseetee seemed to be telling funny stories about what he saw in the south. The men laughed a lot.

I could not understand, of course, so I went to sit with my Sakikuluk, and Apphia, who had acted earlier as my translator but by now was tired of translating for me. And, I was tired from the long trip and finally announced that I wanted to go and get some rest. Mikiseetee was not happy to hear that. His face went from smile to menacing grimace as he grabbed my arm and pulled me down to sit beside him on the couch.

In English, he snarled, "You're tired? It doesn't matter! I'm your husband and you must sit with me!" He gripped my arm holding me against him.

This Apphia translated for my parents-in-law and James. They all stared at Mikiseetee in silence. My Sakialuk took his pipe out of his mouth, looked sadly at his son and shook his head. Slowly he got up from his chair, stepped closer to Mikiseetee and lightly slapped his face. He said something quietly to Mikiseetee in Inuktitut. No one translated this for me.

I could see that Mikiseetee was not actually hurt, that he was more embarrassed and humiliated. Real tears ran down both cheeks and everyone in the room knew that he was sorry. Later, in our room, Mikiseetee told me that his father had never ever punished or admonished him before, had never raised his voice at him in anger. He said in bitter terms what his father had spoken to him in Inuktitut, "You must not mistreat my ukuaq."

My Sakialuk had defended me.

This incident recalled to me one of my early childhood memories when I was about four years old when my maternal grandfather defended me. My grandfather, too, had struck my father in the face and told him he must never mistreat me like that again. My father did not break down in tears. Instead, he absorbed the humiliation and shame as well as his helplessness and resentment. This was when the first seeds of escape from his father-in-law and my mother's family took root, I believe. My parents had been planning to build a house in Erlangen close to my grandfather's house at this time, but these plans were quickly abandoned. Suddenly, we were emigrating to Canada. We were leaving my beloved grandfather's house, Germany, and it was my fault.

On this particular day, Mama had left me in Papa's care while she and her father went into Nuremberg on an errand. All the others who lived with us in my grandfather's house after the war, my great-grandmother, my Great-uncle Lobel and Great-aunt Batty with her many children, my step-grandmother, aunts, and uncles, were all away. I only knew Papa a little from the occasional weekends he spent with us. His work had him away from home most of the time. I knew him as that tall handsome man whom Mama loved and missed so much when he was away. That he was jealous of Mama's attention to me, I also knew, and that he could not see why she cared for me at all. I was thin and small, slow to learn and when I did actually speak, spoke with, to his mind, a horrid lisp. I did not show much character, only cowered in fear behind my mother with my fingers in my mouth when he criticized me. Still, I loved him. He was my handsome father whom everyone adored, the war hero who had returned from the Eastern Front, one of those rare ones who had survived the war. He was the one who could fix anything and built my beautiful bed that he painted blue.

I am not clear on how it all escalated into a nightmare for me. A while after Mama and my grandfather left, Papa must have caught me dreaming with my fingers in my mouth, which he abhorred. When he shouted at me, I must have shrunk from him in fear.

"I will teach you what to be afraid of!" he shouted.

He picked me up and ran down all four flights of stairs, mumbling about hairy spiders and rats with long teeth, into the cellar of the house, a dark place where root vegetables and coal were stored and which had only two small grimy half-moon windows that did not let in much light. He opened the cellar door, thrust me to the top of the cellar steps, and flung the door shut, bolting it on the outside. It was dark with only the two distant glimmers of light across the cellar. Papa's spider and rat mumblings had me screaming in frantic gusts that hurt my throat. I have no idea how long I kept that up, but suddenly the cellar door flew open and Mama hugged me to her body.

"Why did you lock her in the cellar?" demanded my grandfather.

"She did not obey me," Papa replied.

My grandfather struck my Papa's face and said, "You must not mistreat my granddaughter!"

My Sakialuk had said almost the identical words to his beloved youngest son, my husband, when he intervened and prevented him from mistreating me. These words affected me on a fundamental level. My Sakialuk, too, was an older man willing to protect me, like my grandfather had. I knew then that I was safe from violence from both my husband and my father as long as my Sakialuk was alive.

Eleven

During the first days after my arrival in Pond Inlet as Mikiseetee's wife, my Sakikuluk worried about what I, her new ukuaq, should eat. Apphia showed me the ten Hungry Man frozen dinners stored in the refrigerator freezer compartment. She said her grandmother, my Sakikuluk, had asked her to buy them from the HBC store. I knew that these dinners were quite expensive. I did not let on that I did not actually like these types of dinners, with their paper-thin sliced beef or turkey in mystery brown gravy, lump of reconstituted mashed potatoes, a sprinkle of vegetables, and a little wad of baked apple dessert. I ate them dutifully for ten days for dinner. Finally, they were all gone.

When Apphia said, "My grandmother said to buy more of those dinners so you'll have something to eat," I said, "I want to eat what everyone else is eating, cooked caribou or seal meat or fish, or whatever is available for family meals."

Days after our arriving home 1974.

She translated this for her grandmother. I saw my Sakikuluk's face fold a little, eyebrows raised in disbelief.

I did not want to become a financial burden to my new in-laws. I knew that money was scarce for the family. My parents-in-law received old age pension from the government and Apphia earned wages as translator at the nursing station. This combined income paid for the electricity, telephone service, some grocery staples, and the token rent on their house as well as the monthly payments for the snowmobile they had bought for Mikiseetee. Then there was the gasoline, ammunition and whatever was needed for hunting. When they were very short of cash, I knew that Joseph Koonoo, Mikiseetee's brother, employed as school custodian, contributed money to help his parents. I was quite willing to learn how to live as they lived and eat the food they ate.

Bethuel Ootoovak, Mikiseetee's oldest brother, James Pewatualuk, husband to Mikiseetee's sister Joanna, and Phillip Issigaituk, husband to Mikiseetee's oldest sister Mary, all supplied the house with meat and fish according to their hunting successes. Mikiseetee and Apphia told me about how the hunters of the community shared food and how our closest relatives always brought a portion of their catch to us, as my parents-in-law were their respected elders.

My Sakialuk, my father-in-law, no longer went out hunting regularly, but he still kept a dog team, just in case they were needed. Occasionally he went to hunt on foot when his arthritis did not bother him too much. Now Mikiseetee went out seal hunting regularly, often returning thoroughly chilled and disheartened after standing motionless for hours over an aglu, a seal breathing hole, on the sea ice and, more often than not, coming home empty-handed. He had better luck in shooting ptarmigans and arctic hare. Still, with time, and much patience, he did bring home seals for us and his parents were able to invite others to come and take a share.

It took me a while to become accustomed to eating seal meat, our staple meat, although I had to force myself to eat it after the frozen dinners ran out. Seal meat is a dense dark meat laden with blood, very different from meat I was used to. I ate it cooked, not raw as Mikiseetee and the others did when it was very fresh and laid out cut open after skinning. The seal lay, innards removed, on the cardboard-lined metal meat tray on the floor beside the stove while those eating crouched around it. I enjoyed the seal's liver fried and found it just as good, maybe even better, than any liver I had ever eaten, beef or pork.

For cooking, cut-up seal meat was placed in salted water in a pot on the stove to boil. Seal meat broth tended to form dark pink froth when

As newlyweds 1974.

it boiled, leaving clumps of congealed froth on the meat. I quickly found that I could ignore that and just scrape it off as I ate. Any meat, seal, caribou, hare, ptarmigan or fish, was prepared like this, simply boiled in a pot on the stove, admittedly rather boring to my taste. Only rarely was meat fried or roasted. Seal ribs were very tasty fried in bacon fat, but that was done so seldom, it was a special treat. Bacon available to us came in a can and, whenever we got one, I always saved the rendered bacon fat and stored it in the freezer just for this purpose. Caribou and arctic char I enjoyed eating frozen like the others did, but it left me wanting warm, cooked food after getting my mouth so cold.

I learned to enjoy cooked inaluaq, seal intestines. As the hunter removes the inaluaq from the seal carcass, he squeezes out the contents and then braids them. I watched in fascination as my Sakikuluk cut up the braided inaluaq into four-inch lengths and put them into the cooking pot with water and salt. Although the intestines came from the seal, the broth formed did not foam up. Of course, I thought, the intestines had no blood, unlike the seal meat which was quite blood laden. When they were done cooking, my Sakikuluk put a few inaluaq pieces on a plate for me. I did not know what to expect. They smelled good, so I went ahead and tried them. I really liked the taste and texture of the cooked seal inaluaq, almost like a bland sausage. They became a treat for me.

Tea and biscuits or home baked palaugaq, that is, bannock, were what we ate after our dinner of meat or fish, as well as for breakfast and at other times of the day, or when there were visitors. There were three kinds of dry pilot biscuits for sale at the HBC store at that time: the square, very hard kind that came in a long white and green paper box, the round, flaky kind which was much easier to chew and came in a shorter white and blue paper box with a cellophane panel, and the sweet, very hard, tiny, three-inch loaf kind that came in a red paper bag. These biscuits had been used since the whaling days on sailing vessels and were called siva in Inuktitut. In Pond Inlet, the word for Saturday was called Sivataarvik, biscuit-day, because that was the day the whaling ship captains distributed biscuits to Inuit, the day before Sunday. I discovered later that Pond Inlet's name for Saturday was not used in other Inuit communities on Baffin Island.

The most available and therefore most popular hard biscuit had to be broken up and softened before anyone could chew them, often in the hot tea served up in an enamel tin mug along with lots of sugar. To my mind, they were make-work projects rather than food because of the effort it took to eat them. I preferred the round, softer, flaky ones when I had a choice, which was not often. When visiting in Inuit homes, it was polite to accept whatever was on offer as there often was nothing else. It took me a while to comprehend that pilot biscuits of any kind, as well as sugar, are actually luxuries for traditional Inuit, not the staples they had already become by the time I arrived.

The preferred hot drink in Pond Inlet was tea. This was usually Red Rose Orange Pekoe tea bags bought at the HBC store that stocked no other kind of tea. I was used to steeped tea, but the way I saw tea prepared and kept by the people of Mittimatalik was foreign to my tastes. Out travelling on the ice, when we stopped for tea, fresh snow was melted in the metal tea kettle and boiled over the propane camp stove. When the water boiled, a few teabags were added to the water in the kettle. I learned to try to be first to pour out tea into my mug so that mine was not quite so strong. At home in the mornings, I usually dumped out the old tea from the day before and boiled fresh water for new tea, adding only three bags to the large metal tea kettle on the stove. The kettle stayed warm on the stove and by the afternoon, others had added more water and tea bags as people poured tea for themselves and our visitors. By evening, the tea kettle might have about nine or so tea bags and the brew would be quite dark and bitter. I began to understand why everyone in my extended family used so much sugar in their tea. My Sakikuluk even added a measure of canned condensed milk to her tea mug. I was the only one at our house who ever drank coffee and I was fortunate to have a small jar of instant coffee that no one else used. I only used a half teaspoon of instant coffee in my cup in order to make it last as long as possible. But instant coffee was a luxury and when it was gone, I had to switch to the bitter strong tea, diluting it with condensed milk, like my Sakikuluk did, so I could drink it.

When I arrived, my sister-in-law Rhoda, Josepee's wife, had sent a few loaves of her baked yeast bread. I knew that she used to bake for my mother's table and for the Qallunaat who stayed at the transient centre for whom she often prepared meals. At that time, there was no hotel in Mittimatalik. These loaves did not last long. Pilot biscuits are fine occasionally, but not on a day-to-day basis, at least not for me. I soon began to miss the baked yeast bread to which I was accustomed.

One day Apphia said, "My grandmother will bake bread today."

I was interested to see how she did that. My Sakikuluk called for her agvik, a support for flensing, that is, scraping the fat off sealskin. It was a wooden platform topped with a smooth layer of Arborite, about the size of a large square tea tray, raised on an attached support. It was like a short-legged sloping little table. On this she placed large lumps of seal fat. The agvik was slanted over a large metal bowl to catch the oil that ran down when my Sakikuluk struck the seal fat with a smooth rock, rendering out the oil. I noticed flecks of red flesh and other bits land in the oil. When she had enough seal oil in the bowl, she added flour, baking powder, salt and water. Kneeling in front of the metal bowl, she stirred the mixture with a fork until it began to clump, then kneaded the dough with her hands, divided and formed the dough into oblong loaves and placed them into bread baking pans.

I wondered about the baking temperature because the dial thermostat, on the front of the oven door on the converted diesel stove we used for heating and cooking, was broken.

Apphia said, "Watch and learn."

My Sakikuluk placed an enamel pie plate with some white flour on it into the oven and left it for a few minutes. When the flour turned light brown, she had Apphia place the loaf pans in the oven to bake for a little less than an hour. Apphia watched the clock. She took the pans out of the oven and tipped the loaves onto some clean cardboard on the floor to cool.

My Sakikuluk gave me some of her baked seal oil bread to try. The slice had little brown flecks in the very dense white bread. I have to admit that I did not like it much, but kept my distaste to myself. This seal oil bread was actually baked bannock, I thought. I later discovered that I liked the taste of bannock fried in seal oil on top of the stove, but found bannock using seal oil bannock baked in the oven not at all to my liking.

After this, I made it a point to learn how to make my own yeast bread. I found a basic yeast bread recipe in the cookbook I had brought north with me. I had to wait until the monthly payments arrived to go grocery shopping for not only flour, sugar, and salt, but also dry yeast and milk powder, as well as a large new plastic mixing bowl. Following my Sakikuluk's example, I devised a way that I could mix and knead the bread in one bowl. Kneading the dough was easier on my back when done in the bowl on the floor. This method confined the mess and I really liked that I did not have such a large clean-up afterwards. Setting the bowl on the kitchen counter, I let the dough rise one time covered with a clean plastic garbage bag. Then I put the bowl on the floor, punched the dough down and kneaded it again. After that, I formed the loaves into their pans, placed them onto the counter, and covered them with the plastic bag to rise again. I used my Sakikuluk's method for judging the oven temperature, and baked the loaves for about the same length of time. I also dumped the loaves onto a clean piece of cardboard to cool on the floor. I knew the bread was done because there was a hollow sound when I knocked on its bottom.

I had baked six loaves that morning and by evening it was all gone. Everyone, the family and visitors, loved my bread and I did, too. My Sakikuluk saw my disappointment when the bread was gone. She spoke to Apphia.

Apphia said, "My grandmother says you should keep your yeast bread under your bed so it is not eaten up so fast. That is what she does with her bread to protect it from those who would just eat and eat until it is all gone."

I saw the sense in that. I found a clean cardboard box that became my bread storage for under my own bed. I did not hoard my bread, but only brought out measured quantities at meal times and when there were visitors.

Suddenly it was Christmas. I did not yet understand much Inuktitut, but I was aware of the excitement building. The school children of the family who could speak English talked to me about presents they would like to get from Santa Claus. The little St. Timothy's Anglican Church near my parents' house that we attended on Sundays was decorated with a gaudy little fake Christmas tree and bright decorations. Mikiseetee went to hunt caribou with the other men to supply the community feast that was to be held in the Takijualuk School gymnasium on Christmas Day. He said there would be games every day and a big dance on New Year's Eve as was their custom. Everyone was very excited. The Pan Arctic Oils company sent a great number of turkeys and other foodstuffs for the feast so their Inuit workers would enjoy their Christmas with their families.

On Christmas Eve, there was a special ecumenical service held in the school gym, featuring the Anglican Church minister, Reverend Laurie Dexter, and the Catholic missionary, Ataata Mari, whom I had met in the summer. Chairs had been set up and a raised platform with a microphone stand at the front for the speakers. The settlement manager spoke a few words before the service, telling us to bring our eating utensils to the next day's feast.

On Christmas Day in the late afternoon, we all went to the school gym. As instructed, we had brought our mugs, spoons, forks, knives and plates in our bags. My Sakikuluk brought her ulu, her woman's half-moon-shaped knife. Chairs had been set up all around the walls of the gym. The various family groups sat and stayed together. Women carried their babies and toddlers in amautik, parkas that had a pouch for the child on the back under the hood. A mother would lay her sleeping child on the floor on the child's amautik, so she could be free to eat. There was always someone near to watch if the child woke and would alert the

Christmas feast with traditional food 1974.

mother. Mikiseetee and I sat with my parents-in-law, Apphia and the children of our household. My sisters-in-law with their husbands and families sat to either side of our group.

There were portions of frozen char and caribou arranged at intervals along three long butcher paper carpets laid out in the open space of the floor. Along the far end of the gym, folding tables were set up laden with large pots and baking pans of cooked food. The local women had been cooking and roasting turkeys since yesterday evening. After the Anglican minister, Laurie, said a prayer of thanksgiving, the people hurried to the frozen food, crouching and kneeling on the floor as they

Lining up for cooked food, Christmas 1974.

ate with their knives and ulus. I did not participate in this but waited for them to finish. Then the call came to line up for the food arrayed on the tables. There were many turkeys, but also various versions of caribou stew, some with vegetables, some without. There was one interesting combination stew of caribou meat, rice and raisins. I tried a bit of that, but preferred the other versions. Tea urns had been set up, and for dessert, there was fruitcake. Almost everyone in Pond Inlet was there and enjoyed the food. Only my parents and those who could not come were absent.

Finally my turn, Christmas 1974.

After the meal, the leftovers from the floor were gathered up and the butcher paper underlay put in the garbage bins. The tables were cleared and removed. The excess food, I was told, would be distributed to various needy homes around town. We all went home ready for bed.

The next day was Boxing Day, so that meant relatives visited our house all afternoon bringing presents and it was often very crowded and noisy.

That evening, we all returned to the school and the games began. It was a bit confusing for me because I did not really know what was going on. There was one game where people sat around in a large circle on the floor, passing a dice that they would throw. When the desired number turned up on the dice, the person who threw it would run into the middle of the circle, put on a pair of padded oven mitts, with them on their hands grab the dinner knife and fork and try to undo the wrapped parcel with them. The attempts made everyone laugh. Everyone took turns until the parcel was finally unwrapped by the winner. It was quite fun. We played musical chairs to recorded music which had lots of people laughing, too. There were also many other games. Mikiseetee urged me to join in. He seemed to be showing me off, I thought, proud of his new Qallunaq wife.

The games continued each evening until New Year's Eve. Sometimes there were games just for women, just for children, and just for men. The men's games were eagerly attended. These were the Inuit high-kick, finger wrestling, mouth pulling, and more, often very painful-looking tests of strength and endurance. Of course, they were cheered on by their families. It was amazing how the men were so polite to their opponents, even after they lost. The men kept their emotions well under control, I thought, even when they were utterly humiliated.

On New Year's Eve, the platform was dragged out again at one end of the school gym and musicians appeared with their instruments, a button accordion, a guitar, a drum set and a fiddle. The microphone was plugged in and the music began. The musicians played what sounded to me like square dance music, a Scottish reel, perhaps. It was quite lively and couples joined into a large circle and began to dance. Everyone seemed to know the moves to this dance and automatically broke into their dance figures, glad-handing or twirling the next person, or whatever, all around the circle until they arrived back at their partner. I was not very adept at this dancing at first but I soon learned the steps and movements. Almost all the adults danced, even the old people who danced until they tired. It was energetic and all of us sweated copiously. During the dance breaks, people would go outside into the freezing air to cool off. Then, when the musicians started up again, the dance would begin again. Children ran about playing tag, up all night. The older people and exhausted mothers with babies gradually left for home, while the younger ones continued. The dance went on all night. By early morning, the exhausted musicians had to quit and everyone went home.

One late afternoon nearing suppertime that first January, I returned home from visiting my sister-in-law, Joanna. At the door, my nose detected a lanolin-like smell, like hand cream, not unpleasant. That changed as soon as I neared the circle of older people crouched around over the meat tray on the floor from which rose, it seemed to me, a foul odour. Being closer now, my eyes began to water from this stench that made it hard for me to breathe. Obviously, the people loved what they were eating. Curiosity overcame my revulsion and I took a closer look. I saw what looked like meat that had been rolled in layers of decaying fat and skin. The meat itself shimmered in rainbow colours like those seen in pools of gasoline in the summer sun. I asked Mikiseetee what this food was, he and the others were eating with such relish.

"This is igunaq." he said.

He told me how in the late summer they would process walrus meat, roll it up and store it in a cache under a pile of large rocks near their camp at Igarjuaq, at the foot of Mount Herodier, until after freeze-up in late November. Then the igunaq would be good, ready to eat. I began to understand. This is fermented meat, what was sometimes referred to as "rotten meat", fermented much like the German Limburger cheese that I was familiar with that was also definitely smelly but vastly enjoyed by many German people. That was not my favourite cheese. Mikiseetee gave me a piece of igunaq to try. I was able to get it past my nose to swallow it but, unfortunately, it came right back up again. My stomach rejected it in no uncertain terms.

Mikiseetee smiled. "The old people do not encourage young children, except for their special loved ones, to eat igunaq. That way there is more of it for themselves."

I have always enjoyed any kind of fish or seafood, so I found arctic char quite tasty. It is like a more-delicate kind of salmon, very fatty, but, to me, delicious any way it was presented: frozen, raw, cooked or dried. During the winter months, Mikiseetee and other hunters fished using fishnets through holes augured through the thick ice of the local freshwater lake. I learned to repair our family's fishnet with a bone shuttle made by my Sakialuk that had the net filament wound on its inner spike. I learned to pass the shuttle through a loop, unwind a length of filament, and knot it in places around the torn portion of the net so that the openings were like the rest of the net.

"My father made this net last year. We bought rolls of fishnet filament at the HBC store after that summer sea-lift," Mikiseetee said.

I was amazed because the net looked like it had originally been made commercially, like the ones I had seen used by the professional fishermen on Lake Ontario where I had spent my childhood. Usually, Mikiseetee told me, the hunter's wife repaired any rips in the net, so I was happy to learn how to do this.

During the summer months, I knew, arctic char swam and fed in the salt water of Eclipse Sound but before it froze for the winter they migrated, like salmon do, up the rivers to spawn and spend the winter at the bottom of freshwater lakes. I noticed there were two kinds of arctic char caught in the nets from the under the lake ice. There were the usual orange-fleshed ones but also those that had white flesh. Mikiseetee said the white-fleshed char were the ones that never migrated from the lakes to the sea in summer.

"I don't eat the white-fleshed char," said my husband.

I always ate those and left the orange-fleshed ones for him. The only way I could tell what colour the inside flesh was, would be after I cut into the char. I could not know if it was ordinary or white-fleshed char just from looking at the outside of the fish, but Mikiseetee could. Mikiseetee said he usually gave the white-fleshed fish to his father for his dogs. I noticed that the older folk all ate the white-fleshed char when there were none of the preferred kind left.

There were long periods when char was not available, especially in winter. The hunters usually concentrated on hunting seal and caribou. Lake ice fishing was an occasional pastime or resorted to when other game was scarce. Fish and caribou meat, along with arctic hare and ptarmigan, were enjoyed but it was seal meat that kept us warm, healthy and strong because of its fat and nutritious blood throughout the meat. I noticed that after eating char or caribou, I would become sleepier than usual. If I were feeling cold or chilled, seal meat would warm me up right away.

About a month after my first Pond Inlet Christmas, I became sick. I had diarrhea and spent much miserable time on the honey bucket in our tiny washroom. My Sakikuluk cooked a special soup for me of seal meat pieces and potato chunks and then added a dash of bottled ketchup to my bowl before encouraging me to eat it. It was absolutely delicious and soon I began to feel much better. I later learned that she had bought the potatoes from the supply flown in for the new Co-operative store at great expense.

Apphia said, "My grandmother learned how to cook for Qallunaq police officers so she knows how to make the food tasty for them and knows what to feed a sick Qallunaq."

Twelve

Of course, since I was home most of the time during those early days, housekeeping was my lot. Every day I washed and dried the dishes; sometimes all the many mugs and cups were used when the old people had many visitors. I swept the house, the bedrooms, the L-shaped kitchen/living-room area, the tiny washroom, and the short hallway. Once a week, I washed the floors with a string mop and bucket of hot soapy water. If Mikiseetee was at home, he would help me with that chore.

One of my household duties was to ensure that visitors left the house when my Sakikuluk and Sakialuk retired to their bedroom, usually at the time when the short-wave radio program from Greenland went off air for the night.

Mikiseetee said, "It's your job to make everyone leave at night when the old people go to bed." I felt uncomfortable bossing people about, being so new to the family.

"What makes you think they will listen to me?" I asked.

"You're a Qallunaq and everyone is afraid of Qallunaq anger."

I often heard visiting mothers warn their children, "Behave or the big Qallunaq woman over there will get you!" And the children would hide behind their mothers and stay quiet throughout the visit. I loved the beautiful children and it saddened me that I was seen as a threat. But now I saw that it did become useful to keep the house quiet so we all could sleep at night.

One of my least enjoyable jobs was to tie up the honey bucket securely when it was full and carry it outside to place in a half metal barrel provided for sewage truck pick up. I always lined our honey bucket with an extra bag because sometimes the bag would spring a leak and the liner bag then caught whatever leaked out. It took only that one time of my having to wash out our dirtied honey bucket with disinfectant to learn about this. Rubber gloves dedicated for honey bucket use became my friend. It was a smelly job, certainly, and I wanted to avoid having to do this again. It was enough just to have to tie up the bag and carry it out.

We usually kept a can of Pine-Sol disinfectant beside the honey bucket. Everyone was to pour a dash of that disinfectant onto whatever they did in the honey bucket. We usually kept the washroom door closed to contain the strong smell of the disinfectant and what it masked. After a while, I got so used to the smell and it no longer drew my attention, not like when I first wondered what that smell was on my first visit to my future home that past summer.

Bathing or showering was not done at home as we lacked the facilities, no bathtub, no shower stall, no hot and cold running water either. The drains we had from the kitchen and washroom sinks emptied onto the ground outside the house and often froze during the winter. These pipes were heavy-gauge black plastic that often got blocked by frozen water.

We had to remove and thaw them standing in a bucket near the stove in the kitchen. I discovered that when we pour wastewater down the sink drain, it must be done all at once, not little by little in a trickle. It was the trickles that froze quickly and new trickles got frozen onto the former until the drain was blocked. I kept a plastic basin over the drains in the washroom and kitchen sinks to prevent such trickles as much as possible.

Every morning, I poured water into the washroom basin from the kettle on the stove and the water tank in the kitchen so the water was warm in order to wash my face and strategic parts in our bathroom. I also brought in a glass of water and I brushed my teeth over the basin and rinsed my mouth.

"Where do I go for a shower?" I asked Apphia. She said I had to go to the school and use the facilities there.

I did that a few times, but soon made friends with some Qallunaq school teachers and town officials who had running hot and cold water and full bathroom facilities in their government-provided, insulated homes. Luckily, I could live a week without showering without too much trouble provided I did my morning ablutions. It was the dream of every adult living in Inuit public housing at that time to have, some day, complete plumbing and bathroom facilities along with a washer and dryer for clothes, not to mention insulated floors and walls like those teachers and government officials. It became my dream, too. Meanwhile, I rotated my weekly showers among my Qallunaq friends.

Doing the laundry without running water was a make-work challenge and we did this once a month. My Sakikuluk owned an old-style wringer washer, a tub with an electric motor to run the agitator and the electric mangle through which the clothes were fed to squeeze out most of the wash water. We filled the tub with heated water from the stove and buckets of cold water from our indoor water tank and added laundry detergent. The white laundry load was washed first followed by the lighter-coloured load, and then by the mid-colours, and finally by dark. The same water was used for the entire laundry and the wash water was muddy dark grey by the time I finished washing my jeans. Then I pumped out the washing machine and refilled it with clear water for rinsing, following the same pattern, from light to dark clothes. When I was a child in our early years in Canada, my mother had a machine like this, so I knew the routine. I knew to use a wooden spoon to fish out the clothes from the tub and guide them through the mangle. I knew how easy it would be to get my hand caught in the tight rubber rollers. Doing laundry this way felt like a throwback. As an adult, I was used to automatic washing machines where every load got its own clean water and was automatically rinsed and spun and required only loading in the laundry tub and removing it for drying in the automatic dryer.

I ventured to ask, "So where do I hang the washed clothes to dry?"

Apphia pointed to the rows of those mysterious suspended copper pipes I had noticed on the first visit to the house that past summer, the ones that looked like they were for piping running water. My Sakialuk had scrounged them from the garbage dump, possibly left over from when they built the teachers' houses. They functioned much better than an indoor wash line because the pipes were rigid and did not sag, but we had to climb onto a chair to hang up the clothes to keep them up over our heads. I welcomed the warmer days of March when I could take the laundry to hang outside on the wash line strung between the house and the storage shack. The temperatures then hovered around minus 20 degrees Celsius (minus 4 degrees Fahrenheit). I had to wear gloves inside my rubber gloves to keep my hands from freezing and I had to be quick. There was no need for clothes pins because the laundry froze onto the line in moments. Taking in the clothes after a day or so was a challenge as they were all frozen stiff. I put them on the overhead pipes for an hour to thaw and then they were dry, ready to fold and put away.

Doing the laundry was a group effort when I was lucky. When I was not lucky, I had to do it all myself and it was exhausting. It did alter how I thought of changing my clothes, now done on a weekly basis, while I washed out my underwear and socks each evening and hung them to dry

Laundry drying was easier in summer 1975.

behind our bedroom door. How I envied those who lived in fully equipped houses with their automatic washers and dryers and, of course, running water from their huge water tanks.

When I asked how laundry had been done before they got the wringer washer, my sister-in-law said, "We used to have a community wash house that was equipped with a few automatic washers, but one sea-lift supply ship brought in a lot of used wringer washers so that all the families got one and the wash house is now the community freezer."

She continued, knowing that I would ask, "And before that, out in the camps, we did our laundry only in the summer months when the streams flowed to the sea."

One time, when I was filling the washing machine, I did not notice that the bottom drain spigot had not been tightly closed, and the water flowed across the kitchen floor. I shut the spigot right away and tried to soak up the water with the dirty laundry I had sorted into separate piles on the floor. But there was too much water.

My Sakikuluk calmly took the homemade metal dustpan her husband had made out of aluminum sheeting and wood, and opened the front door. She hauled in a great lump of frozen snow and dumped it onto the spilled water. Right away, I saw, the water froze into the snow. My Sakikuluk picked up the frozen lump with the dustpan and threw it out the door. I got the picture and took the dustpan from her to complete the job of clearing away the spilled water, letting the freezing snow soak it up. I had thought about other occasions in the south when there was a spill on the floor, a calamity that demanded mopping up with towels and cloths. Using frozen snow was so much faster and cleaner. I was impressed by my Sakikuluk's cleverness.

Living in a heated, uninsulated house frosted up the windows and outside doors, front and back. I noticed the strips of caribou fur tacked around the inside of the doorframes as well as all around the door itself, hair facing outward. It was during the times of doing laundry, when the inside of the house was more humid than usual, that I found the reason for the caribou fur on the doors. It functioned better than weather stripping. It kept out the cold while at the same time prevented the doors from freezing shut. Caribou hair is hollow and brittle so that if the hairs freeze together, as they did, and pressure was put on them, like when pulling a door open, they would break, releasing the door. It was a way to keep the family safe, to be able to escape in case of fire. Another instance of Inuit ingenuity, I thought.

Mikiseetee helps with laundry 1975.

Although I learned to enjoy seal meat, I did make a rude discovery that February. The sun was just beginning to show over the horizon, a pink haze over the mountains of Bylot Island to the north across Eclipse Sound. Mikiseetee came home after spending hours over a seal's aglu on the ice at temperatures of about minus 40 degrees Celsius which was pretty extreme. In fact, minus 40 Celsius is almost equal to minus 40 Fahrenheit, I discovered. Luckily, maybe, when it is that cold there is usually not much wind. We were all joyful that my husband had such success that day and were looking forward to fresh seal meat. While Mikiseetee thawed himself out, I helped cut up the meat. I got some seal blood on my hands and my Sakikuluk noticed.

"Ukuaq, you have blood on your hands," she said.

She sounded so upset, that this was not right. I did not understand, until Mikiseetee told me in English what she said.

I replied, "Please don't worry about that. I can always wash my hands." Mikiseetee translated.

She looked at me strangely when they told her what I had said, but then seemed pleased with my response.

I put the cut-up seal meat on to boil in a pot and added salt. As expected, the broth foamed up while boiling and I moved it to the back of the stovetop to finish cooking over lower heat. This seal meat had a somewhat different smell to it while cooking, I noticed. The others had gathered to eat the seal meat raw and I ladled out some seal broth in enamel mugs and laid out some boiled seal meat on plates to cool for those who wanted it, as I had learned to do. I took some on my plate as well. I cut a piece and put it in my mouth. I had to spit it out right away. It tasted like some kind of chemical had been poured over it, like lighter fluid or diesel fuel.

I asked Mikiseetee, "Is there something wrong with this seal meat?"

"No."

"Okay," I said, "it tastes so very different than the seal meat we usually eat. Why could that be?"

"February is the month for seals to mate. This was a male seal in rut. This is known as tiigak," he said.

"That explains it. I don't like the taste."

He seemed disappointed about my saying this. "You can see that everyone eats the seal meat anyway, no matter how it tastes," he said. "None of us are complaining about it except you. You can at least not complain. We are all just grateful for the meat and so should you be, too."

I felt humbled and ashamed.

Later, I asked Apphia if the female seals also tasted like this in February and she said, "No, they don't."

I learned to be careful about seal meat in the month of February from then on and to ask if the seal meat was tiigak. One time, I even tried to boil the tiigak seal intestines to see if they were also affected. Usually, I enjoyed eating cooked seal inaluaq, but I found, to my great disappointment that, yes, intestines from a tiigak seal also tasted tainted to me. Oh, well, I did try, I thought.

I had always thought that I knew a bit about sewing and I said so. I had done embroidery, cross-stitch and chain-stitch and other stitches for my mother as a child. I had learned how to do basic crocheting and knitting, but never really got into knitting. I had been given an electric sewing machine when I was twelve and had sewn my own clothes for school. Unfortunately, during that time, home-made clothes were ridiculed by those students whose parents could afford to buy store-bought clothes. Home-sewn clothes were to me a reminder of that humiliation. In my new life with Mikiseetee, I began to see that I knew nothing and had to learn a new way of sewing.

My Sakikuluk bought some heavy, cream-coloured duffel material at the HBC store. Duffel is closely woven woollen material suitable for blankets and coats. My Sakikuluk had my sister-in-law take the measure of my foot which she could do by just looking at it and then cut out the foot and leg parts of a pair of duffel socks for me. I was to sew them together, the V-shaped upper foot part to the elongated oval sole and

Learning to sew duffel socks 1975.

then the one-piece legging with the seam at the back, to the top of the completed foot at the ankle.

Sakikuluk removed her glasses, licked the end of a long piece of heavy-duty white cotton thread, squinted as she threaded the needle pinched between the forefinger and thumb of her left hand. She put her glasses back on, twisted a knot at the end of the thread, and handed the threaded needle to me. I set to work. She watched me closely through her glasses and frowned. She sighed and indicated to me that I should give her what I was sewing. I did and she pulled out all the thread from the seam I had sewn. I had clamped both pieces of cloth layered one over the other in my left hand and had sewn them together pushing the needle underhand from the bottom. I watched closely and noticed that she used her needle overhand, over the top, as she put a stitch at the toe holding the foot top to the sole, and began about ten stitches of a seam she was making, holding the edges to be sewn together abutted against each other with no overlap. I got the idea but it took many doings and undoing before I realized that I was to take slight gathers of the sole while stitching so that the sole curved into the upper part of the foot portion. I even cried in despair at one point because I could not seem to get it right. I had to be extremely careful when I undid stitches so the material did not get frayed.

My sisters-in-law all came to watch me sew and made no comment, but I could tell by their smiles that they were satisfied that I, a Qallunaq, could not sew and had to learn like a young girl. At long last I finished the duffel socks for myself and also a pair for Mikiseetee. Then there was the task of embroidering the turn-down portion of the duffel socks without using an embroidery pattern. I thought this was the fun part where I could design a pattern for myself. This was allowed for my own duffel socks now adorned with alternating upside down V's and sideways C's in blue and green embroidery floss. Nobody would care what I wore anyway, I guessed. But for Mikiseetee's duffel socks, my Sakikuluk urged me to copy her simple cross and dot motif in red and blue. After I got the hang of sewing duffel socks, I was shown how to make a duffel sock pattern. I practised making duffel socks for the boys who lived with us. It was good to finally be useful to the family.

Thirteen

Our family's old age pension and translator's income was augmented by selling prepared sealskins to the new local Co-operative Store that we called the Co-op. I had seen a little of how preparing sealskins for sale was done when I visited my sister-in-law's houses but did not yet know the entire process.

One day, my Sakikuluk placed a large piece of packing cardboard on the kitchen floor and on it put her agvik, her flensing board, the one she used to pound out her seal oil for making bread. It had a laminated top that reminded me of a kitchen counter surface. She brought out her long, sword-like, sharpening steel and her large ulu, women's knife, and sharpened the ulu's cutting edge all around its half-moon edge. She took a sealskin thawed out in a large enamel pan near the stove, grasped it by its nose end, with the inside fat facing up and positioned the skin on the surface of the agvik. She began to flense the fat from the sealskin starting from the nose. I watched carefully as she made pushing motions of her ulu to cut away the fat. I saw that she only partly removed the firm, white layer next to the hair membrane under the fat. She sat before her agvik on a cushion, one foot under her like she usually sat on a chair, with her other leg stretched out before her on the floor beside the agvik. She looked comfortable and used such smooth fluid motions that soon the small sealskin was half flensed. She indicated for me to try.

How hard could it be? Selling clean dry sealskins was how the family got extra income. I could help with that. Mikiseetee and I had discussed my doing sealskins and I had arranged for my hunting license so I could sell my husband's processed skins to the local Co-op or HBC store.

I sat down on my Sakikuluk's cushion in front of her agvik, holding the partly flensed sealskin with my left hand. I did not sit on my foot. I bent my knee with my foot hard against my inner thigh instead and stretched out my other leg in imitation of my Sakikuluk. She, meanwhile, had sharpened the ulu again and put it into my hand. She had to correct the way I held it, placing the handle in my palm-up right hand. She turned my hand over and spread my index and middle finger on the blade to get a firm grip. She then guided my hand over the place I was to start and gently pushed my hand down holding the ulu until the blade came in contact with the fat. I knew I should push forward, away from me, slicing the fat with the ulu. I was aware that the ulu had just been sharpened and I had pushed hard. Suddenly the ulu seemed stuck and would not move forward. My Sakikuluk took the ulu and resharpened it. This time it worked better and I was surprised at how much force I had to use. I felt pleased that I was beginning to get the hang of this. I continued removing the fat.

My Sakikuluk indicated the part that she had flensed that had a slight bluish tinge and I understood that I had to copy that, remove enough fat and thicker white layer until I achieved this bluish colour. At first it went fine, with lots of stops to resharpen the ulu blade. Then, oh, I nicked it, cut through the skin. I had made a curved slit, a hole. My Sakikuluk frowned. I knew that a skin that brought top dollar had no holes other than at the head and the slits along the edges for stretching it on the drying frame. I was ashamed but my Sakikuluk said nothing. I finished the skin after a long hard effort. I then learned how to sew up my cut with waxed nylon thread, repairing the damage I had done.

My Sakialuk, my father-in-law, showed me how to sharpen my ulu for myself. That made the flensing easier for me and I now know that each woman doing skins must be able to sharpen her ulu for herself. Someone else doing it for her would not quite do. Only the top curved edge should be sharpened all the way around the curve. The other side is only smoothed to remove any roughness. I learned that I could shift my hand slightly as I pushed the ulu forward as soon as the cutting edge began to drag, and keep shifting like that until I had used the entire ulu's curve. Of course, these fine points I had to learn over the years. My Sakialuk honoured me by making a large flensing ulu for me.

Mikiseetee made a smaller all-purpose ulu for me. He also made an agvik for me out of a sink portion cut from the laminated kitchen counter at Mama's house. I was able to buy a good sharpening steel at the store. My Sakikuluk gave me both a flat scraper and a curved scraper. I was grateful because now I had all the tools I needed for seal flensing and cleaning sealskins to help make money for our household.

The flensing, cutting away the fat, of the sealskin was just the beginning. After it had been flensed, any holes repaired, and stretching slits cut along the edges, it must be washed in soapy water and hung outside to drip. The wet skin is then placed hair side up on the agvik, and the flat-edge scraper is used to squeeze out the excess water from the fur.

The damp skin was now ready to be stretched. We used wooden rectangular-shaped stretcher frames that had the corners stabilized with cross pieces of wood. A long length of thin rope or twine was looped over the top of the frame so that there was a line to the left and one to the right. We started with the head and worked both sides of the sealskin, threading the line through the edge slits of the skin then around the frame and back until all the slits had been threaded to the tail on one side. This is then repeated from nose to tail on the other side. The cross pieces helped the skin stretch properly.

The tension of the stretch was now adjusted. I was told to stretch sealskins as tight as I could when they were for sale. At the tail end of the skin, both ends of the lines were tied in a slip loop for fast release. The stretched skin in its stretcher was then placed in the shade. Care must be taken to keep it in the shade throughout the day when the sunlight circled the house to avoid burning the skin. Burned sealskin becomes rigid and unworkable, I was warned.

Once the skin was dry, it was taken out of the stretching frame and the lines were wound up and fastened to the stretcher. The flensed side of the dry skin was now quite dark and sticky with dried seal oil in spite of the soapy washing it had undergone and often insects and air-born dirt clung to the black tarry surface. The next step, then, was to wash this surface with soap and water and work the soapy solution into the oily surface with a scraper or, as I did, with a steel-bristled brush. The skin was then again hung to dry on the clothesline. After that, the skin was taken inside the house. The flensed side of the sealskin was thoroughly worked with a curved scraper to remove all the black stuff until the inside of the skin was all white and clean. It sounded easy, but it was hard, backbreaking work. Mikiseetee often helped me with the final scraping during the time I was learning. Finally, when the skin had been processed, my Sakikuluk would decide which finished sealskin to keep for sewing and which to sell.

The first sealskins I worked were mostly of young Ringed Seals called Silver Jars because of the bright, silver-coloured hair with black circular markings. They were about half the size of full adult Ringed Seals. The adult Ringed Seals were often yellowed and covered with seal lice. Sounds crazy, but sea mammals are often afflicted with sea lice. The Ringed Seal baby seal is born in April and is covered with yellowish fur that looks a bit like sheep wool. This woolly baby fur is moulted after about a month or two, revealing the distinctive silver and black fur it had covered. The shin portions of kamiks, sealskin boots, were usually sewn from Silver Jar sealskin.

My sisters-in-law prepared the skins of the large Hooded Seal or Square Flipper Seals that were used to make kamik, that is, boot, soles. These seals were double and triple the size of the Ringed Seals that formed the basis of our regular diet and they did not sell as well at the stores as the popular Silver Jar.

Occasionally, a local hunter would catch a Harp Seal, which brought a good price because of its silver hair and black harp shape on its back, but they were not normally in our waters, I was told. Walrus was not hunted for its skin like it once was for making an umiaq, a women's boat, or a traditional kayak, but now rather for its tusks, making fermented igunaq, and used as dog food. We did not often eat walrus meat.

I was so proud that day when I received top dollar for a sealskin I had worked, thirty Canadian dollars. When I think of the many hours I had spent flensing, washing and scraping, I had to realize that I was only being paid pennies for each hour of heavy work. It was not surprising to me that many young local girls did not seek to do sealskins as their life work when one is better paid at an easier job, provided one had the required education. Still, most adult Inuit women I knew took great pride in their abilities cleaning and bleaching sealskins. It was ranked next to sewing skills.

I noticed that the older Inuit women, especially those more closely related to our family, watched me carefully. I sensed that they were interested in how I adjusted to life with my Sakikuluk. I was not the first Qallunaq woman to live among them. Although there was much that displeased me, like the lack of insulation and plumbing, at House 69, I had signed on to this simple, hard-working life and had vowed to myself to make the best of things, and learn as much as I could to the best of my ability.

I felt I was doing well in everything new put to me except learning to speak Inuktitut. I began to learn the old-style syllabic symbols from the Anglican syllabic prayer book and hymnal and would make out some parts of words. Reading Inuktitut was made difficult by the language's being set up differently than English and following its own distinct syntax and grammar. Instead of separate words strung into sentences like in English, Inuktitut had word parts all connected into what looks like one long word with the end of it showing the action and who or what did it, reminiscent a little of German sentence structure with the verb at the end. I had some sort of mental block, I thought, in making out the sounds of Inuktitut words and retaining them in my memory. It did not help that whenever I tried to speak Inuktitut and made mistakes, Mikiseetee and everyone else, except my parents-in-law, would burst out laughing as if it were the funniest thing they ever heard. That really discouraged me.

At times, after long periods of not speaking, only smiling and nodding, I felt as if I were fading away, that I might soon cease to exist as the person I thought myself to be. From what Mikiseetee told me, it seems he had problems with his identity as well. This uncertainty of not really knowing who we were and what each of our roles in life should be, may have drawn us together that first summer when we met.

One day, Mikiseetee drove me and my Sakikuluk to the store for grocery shopping after the old age pension cheque had arrived, leaving my Sakialuk at home alone. When we returned after about an hour, I saw him talking to his wife and how she laughed and slapped his head. Mikiseetee said that his father had answered the telephone while I was out. The person calling, a Qallunaq woman, had asked in Inuktitut to speak to someone by the name of Tuasi (how my name is pronounced in Inuktitut) and he said he did not know such a person and hung up.

I knew right away that it was my mother who had called. My Sakikuluk told him that the name asked for was me, his ukuaq, his daughter-in-law. He was surprised and I could see right away that he was sorry.

Of course, I was never called by my name in my new home. I was always called ukuaq. Of course, Sakialuk would not have known my name. In our family, baptismal or Qallunaq names were discouraged except for children. Instead of Mikiseetee, I was to call my husband Aiguu, and my brother-in-law Ait, I discovered. I knew my mother would try to call again and, when she did, I explained. My Sakialuk thereafter also avoided answering the telephone.

Another time when Mikiseetee and I were at the check-out counter with our purchases at the HBC store, a short elderly Inuit woman dressed in a very intricately made caribou amautik smiled at me and asked me something in Inuktitut.

Mikiseetee translated, "She wants to know if you would like to have her amautik."

"Thank her and tell her it's a very beautiful amautik. But I could not take it," I said. After all, I had been raised by Mama to be polite and not take what was not mine.

After we returned home, Mikiseetee told his mother about this. My Sakikuluk was amazed and slightly upset with me. She told me that I should have taken it, that no one will ever sew such a beautiful caribou amautik for me. Mikiseetee told me I had missed the opportunity for owning such a fine piece of clothing, my loss for being such a Qallunaq. Oh, well.

Later that day, that little old lady came to our house wearing a parka, not the fancy caribou amautik. Perhaps she had given it to someone else? My Sakikuluk had me take down the two decorated fine porcelain cups with matching saucers she had stored away at the top of the kitchen cabinet to keep out of harm's way. I had to think this little woman was an important visitor to rate drinking her tea from these special teacups.

My Sakikuluk smiled a lot at her and they seemed to exchange gossip. After a time, the little woman pulled a colourful blouse out of her parka pocket and gave it to my Sakikuluk. She examined it and made sounds of praise and thanks. My Sakikuluk then went into her room and brought out a blouse of her own to give in exchange, equally colourful. After that came words of farewell.

The little woman stopped to shake my hand before leaving, smiled at me and said, "Ukuaga", my ukuaq.

I did not know what to think. Mikiseetee told me that this woman had come to Mittimatalik from Igloolik just to see me when she heard that my Sakikuluk had a new Qallunaq ukuaq. She had been my Sakialuk's wife before he chose my Sakikuluk as his second wife. The two women were rivals, I could see now, and my Sakikuluk wanted to show off for her. She was proud that her son married a Qallunaq who was now her ukuaq, wife of her youngest son. I found that a little amazing because I had never been valued like this before, almost like a commodity.

Fourteen

The weather was extremely cold that first February in 1975 as the sun finally broke over the peaks of the Bylot Island mountains during the last part of the month, marking the return of daylight. The sunlight did not stay long at first, but it did lift my spirits. In January, it seemed as if the long winter dark would last forever. On Sunday mornings I rode, clasping Mikiseetee on his snowmobile, to St. Timothy's Anglican church near my parents' house. I knew I was lucky not to have to walk the distance in the extreme cold like many other people without transportation. We went back again for Sunday evening service. I learned early that we were not to go hunting on Sundays or work in the house except for cooking food. We were not allowed to play either, so no card-playing, or doing jigsaw puzzles, either. Bible reading was encouraged, so I did that. There was not much to read except the few books I had brought with me that I had read and reread many times. Otherwise, Sundays were reserved for visiting relatives and friends, and attending the two church services.

In the early days, I was shy and reserved and did not enjoy being shown off as the family's very own Qallunaq ukuaq. I went along to visit with my husband, but since I did not at the time speak or understand Inuktitut, I was often bored and somewhat annoyed at not being able to communicate except by body language which was a bit limiting, I felt. Those friends and relatives we visited who spoke English were more interested in how I was able to cope in our rather more traditional Inuit household. I was offered Qallunaq store-bought food by some who thought I missed that. Often, even though they spoke English, I could not really make out what they were trying to say. Mikiseetee was himself somewhat shy, so I found visiting the houses of his second-oldest sister, Johanna, of his older brother, Joseph Koonoo, and of his oldest brother, Bethuel Ootoova, the best. In each of these houses, Mikiseetee was at ease and there were his nieces and nephews, a few who were older than Mikiseetee, who could speak English with me. This did not help me learn Inuktitut, but it did dispel some of my feeling of isolation.

On one Sunday afternoon after the sun came back, I remember how bored I was after our return from morning church service and visiting. I was sitting with Mikiseetee on our bed when I had an inspiration about how to relieve my boredom. My idea was to draw a portrait of my husband. I took out a pad of letter paper and began to draw with a pencil sharpened with a knife. I asked him to pose for me.

I said, "Hold still. Turn a little. Now, look up."

My voice must have carried and my strange words were probably overheard. There was little privacy in our house, I had discovered. My sister-in-law looked into our room on her way to the kitchen. Her jaw dropped in horror and ran in, grabbed the paper on which I drew and tore it up. She was very angry.

"Don't you know that you should not make a graven image on Sunday? Do you want someone here to die or that we have sickness or bad luck in hunting?"

I was dumbfounded by this reaction. I was doing something harmless, I thought.

I said, "I've heard about graven, that is carved, images being prohibited by Moses only in connection with the Israelites worshipping statues of animal gods on their flight from Egypt, but not about drawing pictures." It sounded a bit feeble in the face of the accusation.

Mikiseetee told me later that he also did not know that drawing pictures on Sunday was a Christian or Anglican taboo. Clearly, the way our family practised their Christianity was different from what I was used to.

My Sakikuluk was Anglican, as was the rest of the family, but Sakialuk, her husband, was Catholic. He had been born and raised in the Naujaat, in the Repulse Bay area, south of Igloolik. Most of the Inuit in that area were converted by Catholic missionaries during the time of the whaling ships, the late 1800s and early 1900s. The Inuit of Pond Inlet were mainly Anglican and there was only one extended Catholic family during the time I lived here. There was definitely a rivalry between these denominations of Christianity, I found.

The local Catholic missionary, Ataata Mari spoke Inuktitut as well as any local elder, healed people, and, according to my Sakialuk, hunted to feed others, cared for the sick, and had proven himself as a superior human being by never showing anger. He was often away from Pond Inlet ministering to his other congregations in Arctic Bay, or on archaeological digs, or away at meetings. He edited the *Catholic Diocesan Eskimo Magazine* in which he recorded what he saw and heard of Inuit culture and traditions, graced with his superb drawings, cartoons, and photos, as well as personal histories and writings by other Catholic missionaries. He came to visit my Sakialuk whenever he returned to town after a long absence. Occasionally, Attaata Mari would ask my Sakialuk to carve something for a museum, such as a replica of an Inuit artifact, or perhaps inscribe scrimshaw on walrus tusk or make a walking cane made out of narwhal tusk. By the proceeds from these efforts Sakialuk was able to augment the family income.

My Inuit family thought it strange that I had a Catholic father and a Lutheran mother. Lutheranism is Protestant in Germany. I had been raised as a Lutheran with the permission of the Catholic Pope because my father served Germany as a soldier in World War II on the Eastern

Front. Most German soldiers at that front never returned. My mother, a Lutheran, was allowed to raise me in her Lutheran beliefs and traditions. When Mikiseetee and I met, I was neither Anglican nor Catholic, but I had been baptized and confirmed as Lutheran. Because Lutheran is close to Anglican in basic beliefs, the local Anglican Church minister, Reverend Laurie Dexter, accepted me at Pond Inlet's St. Timothy's Anglican Church. That Greenlandic Inughuit were Lutheran and that Labrador Inuit were Moravian (a German Protestant missionary sect introduced there in mid 1700s), most local Inuit had heard, but that did not mean they accepted these different Christian denominations.

When gathering at the new community hall built up on the hill, I often heard children chant, "My Father is better than your Father!" sung in the taunting, mocking style of "nya-na-na-nya-nya."

I asked Mikiseetee about this and I laughed as he explained. The children were referring to the Lord's Prayer that begins, "Our Father …" used in both the Catholic and Anglican religions. The Anglican children liked to pick on the few Catholic children whenever they could.

Even Christian children can be cruel, I thought to myself.

There were a few Inuit elders who visited our house regularly, the men to swap stories, and the women to gossip — that is, to exchange local information — and all smoked and drank tea. There was usually much laughter but at this point, I did not understand what was being said, but I knew that my parents-in-law lived to enjoy these visits in their old age. They themselves did not often visit other houses, possibly because they had trouble getting about and were the oldest local elders at that time. That meant there were visitors almost every day.

I noted that most of the other older women had grey or white hair while my Sakikuluk still had black hair. Often on quiet Sunday afternoons, a grandchild was called to sit on the couch while my Sakikuluk lay with her head in his or her lap. The child's task was to find and pull out my Sakikuluk's grey hairs. After a time, my Sakikuluk complained that her hair was getting thin from having her grey hairs plucked out. A granddaughter was then recruited to buy black hair dye at the HBC store and to regularly dye her grandmother's hair.

When I asked why my Sakikuluk was so concerned about showing her grey hair, her reply was translated to me this way, "I dye my hair black because I care about our elders' feelings. When they see my hair grey and see me as old, then they will also feel old. I help them to feel younger when they see me with my hair as black as it was when I was young."

I could follow the reasoning but it still struck me as odd.

One day after the sun had returned. Mikiseetee's nephew, Jayko, son of his oldest brother Bethuel, who was a few years older than Mikiseetee, came by the house to bring a freshly caught seal. He sat to drink tea and removed one kamik and sock. By his facial expression and the sound of his voice as he talked to my Sakikuluk, he was in pain and I could see that his big toe was very swollen and infected. Mikiseetee told me that a sliver was embedded in Jayko's toe.

"Can you help him?" asked Mikiseetee.

I said I could and got some warm soapy water in an enamel bowl, some clean cloths, a new roll of toilet paper, a rolled gauze bandage and a tiny bottle of iodine from my first aid kit, a pair of nail scissors, a needle, and my tweezers from my wash kit.

Meanwhile, Jayko took a seat at the table under the window where the sunlight streamed in. I placed Jayko's foot to soak in the warm water in the bowl on the floor. Then I moved up a chair and sat to hold his foot in my lap. I carefully dried his foot with a clean cloth. I disinfected the point of a needle in a match flame. Then I slowly scratched away a bit of softened skin with the needle from around where the sliver was embedded so I could grasp it with my tweezers. It took two tries and I got the tiny thing out. I squeezed out the pus from the infected toe until bright blood began to flow. I caught the pus in a wad of toilet paper. I

Jayko Ootovak, my nephew by marriage 1975.

applied iodine to disinfect the wound and Jayko winced. I cut a piece from the gauze bandage to make a hood for his toe and then made a bandage around it with ties. I told Mikiseetee to tell Jayko to keep his foot elevated for a day, it would hurt less. Jayko stayed a while, then put his sock and kamik back on and left after thanking me in Inuktitut. Everyone had watched what I was doing with great interest and I saw that they were pleased.

A few days later, I was alone in the house, when Jayko entered the house with a cardboard box. He put it on the table and I opened it. It was full of books. I was amazed. I was even more amazed when Jayko spoke to me in English. I thought he spoke only Inuktitut.

"This is a thank you for helping me out with my foot the other day."

"I didn't know you spoke English," I said.

"Well, yes. Nobody told you yet, but I am the town heavy-equipment mechanic and spent some time away in Alberta getting my mechanic's license. I read these books when I was homesick during my training. I thought you might enjoy them, too."

I was overwhelmed with gratitude. I had so few books to read and really missed reading. I had expected to have access to books through the town lending library project. But because Mikiseetee had left town with me the year before, the town did not pursue funding for the local lending library he was to have managed. Even though he had wanted to take on library duties as wage employment, I found I had to be careful not to get too deeply into reading around him. He told me that it was anti-social for me to stay in our room and read when there were people out in the front room. I also think he may have been envious of how I could escape into a book.

Over time, I became friends with Myna, Mikiseetee's niece, and her boyfriend, Leo, who was a member of the one local Catholic family. They were obviously in love. Although Mikiseetee was Myna's uncle, he saw her as a sister. She was the oldest daughter of Mary, Mikiseetee's oldest sister. In 1957, when Mikiseetee was six years old, my Sakikuluk suffered from tuberculosis and was taken away from Mittimatalik by ship leaving him in Mary's care. To him, still so young, Mary was his mother and her children he saw as his siblings. When his mother, my Sakikuluk, returned after a few years, Mikiseetee did not know her at all.

I have since learned that when a relative is away from the community, or at a distant hospital, no mention is ever made of that person so as to avoid causing painful feelings in the people left behind, especially the children. This was to curb worry, as in, one should not worry, I was told. For this reason, it was not unusual that Mikiseetee should have forgotten his mother. He related how, when she returned, he called her ningiu, paternal grandmother, just like the other children his age, his uncles, aunts and cousins did.

"My mother scolded me, frightened me," Mikiseetee said. "She warned me that I was always to call her anaana."

He was so used to listening to and obeying his oldest sister as if she were his mother, he said, that it was difficult to change, to listen and obey this old woman whom he hardly knew. Mikiseetee was my Sakikuluk's last born child and so he had to move back into his father's house from his sister's place when his mother returned from the sanatorium. By custom, he, the last-born son, was responsible for supporting his parents, providing them with food and necessities. And, my role, as his wife, was also to care for them, I gradually discovered.

During my early days in Pond Inlet, Mama made several secret visits with me that she did not want Papa to know about. I would meet her at the school. She told Papa that she was practising piano in the school gym where there was an upright piano. Mama had been training to become a piano teacher in Germany during the 1940s and played superbly. Papa valued her piano skills and bought the story. She would call me by telephone to let me know when she was going up to the school. I was grateful to be able to see her and talk with her. I was often lonely so was relieved that I had Mama as a friend while I adjusted to my new life. She helped me to understand a few things that I found puzzling but came clear as we discussed them. She told me Papa could not keep her away from me. I felt her love for me and that helped me through some difficult times.

In late March, Mikiseetee told me he was going to take me out to the family's home camp at Igarjuaq at the foot of Mount Herodier, east of the town. We would travel over the ice by snowmobile.

His sister Mary gave me a new pair of sealskin kamiks that she had just finished making for me. They were beautiful but the fit was on the snug side, quite tight.

I dressed warmly in my parka and wind pants, borrowed gauntlet caribou skin mitts, and put on a knit hat and scarf for under my parka hood. I was ready and excited to go. Mikiseetee took along a thermos flask of sweet tea.

Mikiseetee pulled hard on the starter cable and the snowmobile's engine sprung to life in a cloud of gasoline fumes. I straddled the seat behind Mikiseetee and held on to him. We took off in a blast of noise along the snow-packed street to the east end of the town where Igarjuaq could be seen from top of the cliff. Mikiseetee pointed us down the steep trail to the sea ice while I hung on to him tightly, afraid of slipping off the snowmobile. This was definitely not like going along the west road toward the HBC store or the church — an easy ride. The ice looked smooth and level from a distance, but the way was very rough and I had to brace my legs to absorb the shock of the bumps along the trail that we followed. Igarjuaq looked to be fairly close when viewed from town, but I was soon to learn that what I perceived to be close was a deception. It took quite a while to get there.

I was thoroughly chilled by the time we arrived at Igarjuaq. Mikiseetee poured out tea, still warm, into the lid of the flask that served as a cup. Drinking the sweet tea helped warm me. Mikiseetee took me up into the little house where he and his parents had lived before the coming of the school and prefabricated houses that formed the settlement of Pond Inlet in the late 1960s. The little house had been built by my Sakialuk of found lumber and had a sheet-metal roof made up of pieces joined together. The low doorframe was lined with caribou fur and I had to stoop down to enter the single room. I was fascinated by the newspaper and magazine pages pasted on the walls in layers for insulation. It looked like interesting reading to me. There were two sleeping platforms, one larger and one smaller and were, essentially, big boxes built of wood filled with gravel on which Mikiseetee told me bear and caribou skins were laid as mattresses. Almost against the wall opposite the doorway stood a battered little coal stove with a chimney that led through the roof. In one wall was a window with glass panes that his father had been given, he said. It was frosted over but let in light. Mikiseetee pointed out the little wooden fold-down ledge attached to the smaller sleeping platform closest to the window.

"My father attached this so that my brother Josepee would be able to put his book and a small qulliq, seal oil lamp, on it when he was reading," Mikiseetee said.

Much was expected of Josepee, he told me, because he was part Qallunaq and his parents wanted him to be able to read. They wanted all their children to read the syllabic Anglican prayer book, but they hoped that Josepee would read English as well.

After looking inside this little one-room house, Mikiseetee took me out to look at his older sister Mary's former house close by where he had spent much of his early childhood. This house was already falling apart and Mikiseetee said that parts of the house had been taken to town to build storage shacks for their houses there. He said no one used these houses anymore, that everyone preferred to stay in tents when they came here in summer.

The next stop on our walk was to view an area of snow-covered boulders across a frozen stream to the west of the two little houses that Mikiseetee said was the old Inuit cemetery, where some of his ancestors were buried. He showed me arctic hare tracks and I actually saw one, white with black-tipped ears, for a second before it flashed away. He also showed me tiny lemming footprints in the snow, and arctic fox tracks. Mikiseetee said that as soon as the sun returned, these animals would come out of hibernation to run about on the snow. A pair of black ravens, each the size of a house cat, flew around following us. I had seen big ravens in town and wondered if they were the same ones.

Soon, I was succumbing to the cold again and Mikiseetee decided to head home. When we arrived and were inside where it was warm, I removed my kamiks. My toes were numb and looked much whiter than they usually were. My Sakikuluk lifted the front of her blouse and pressed my feet against her warm tummy to thaw them out. I had never experienced such cold feet before. When the numbness subsided and I began to feel them again, it was pain I felt and a kind of uncomfortable hotness in them, too. It took a few hours before I could walk again. My Sakikuluk examined my kamiks and said that they were too tight and had her husband manipulate them over a scraper attached to a wooden stand used to stretch or soften kamik soles. It was not long before I received a pair of kamiks that had split cow-hide foot portions and white fabric leg coverings, what the women in our family wore on a daily basis. The white material was taken from Canada Post mail bags that were coated inside with a rubber coating to keep the mail dry. I preferred these kamiks to the ones made of sealskin and I think this may have offended my sister-in-law Mary who had made my sealskin kamiks. I think my feet did better with the rawhide because it let my perpetually sweaty feet breathe. The only drawback was that the rawhide was not waterproof like the sealskin kamiks.

Fifteen

The first long hunting trip I took with Mikiseetee was in May 1975 to the floe edge off Bylot Island's Button Point to the east of Pond Inlet on Baffin Bay.

"What should I bring along? Food? Biscuits?" I asked.

"Bring nothing," said my husband, "I will hunt along the way."

I had spoken to my mother on the telephone earlier and she had urged me to, at least, put some dry biscuits in my parka pockets just in case. I did that, thinking, maybe she was right.

I saw a large metal barrel of fuel, our down-filled sleeping bags on a layer of caribou skins and the grub box holding the Coleman stove, teabags, sugar, metal tea kettle and enamel cups were already tied onto the qamutik, the sled. That in turn was attached to the back of Mikiseetee's snowmobile by a toggle and two ropes connected to each side of the qamutik runners. I was to sit on the top of the bedding holding onto the binding line looped and pulled around the slats that held everything together on the qamutik.

I was excited about this trip. The weather was clear, the sunlight brilliant and warm, and there was no wind. Just perfect. I even became anxious to leave because I was soon getting too warm dressed in full travel gear, with my heavy expedition parka over my normal parka, wind pants, kamiks and caribou gauntlet mitts. And suddenly, the qamutik jerked and we were off. We left by the east shore of town and bumped along over the ice.

Holding onto the line across the sleeping bag on which I sat became a problem as I could not get a good grip on it with my thick caribou fur mitts. The caribou hairs made them slippery and I had to keep changing my grip to stay on top of the qamutik while we bounced along over the hummocky ice that looked so deceptively smooth from a distance. It was my first experience riding on a qamutik and now I saw that this, too, was something I had to learn how to do. It looked effortless but I soon knew that it was actually hard work to keep from falling off. Mikiseetee was way ahead on the snowmobile, intent on following the trail, and enveloped by the noise of the snowmobile engine. There was no way I could communicate with him. He occasionally looked back to see how I was doing and I forced myself to smile at him thankfully for thinking of me while I bounced around. The qamutik seemed like a bucking bronco to me and soon my arms and back began to tire from the strain of trying to hold on with the constant jarring.

Finally, after a few hours, Mikiseetee stopped for a tea break. He set up the Coleman stove, gathered up some new snow into the tea kettle and placed it on the stove after pumping it up and lighting the flame.

It was so intensely quiet that, to me, it was almost deafening, like an implosion, when the snowmobile engine was shut off. The scenery was superb with the high snow-covered mountains on each side of Eclipse Sound, the sunlight glinting off the new snow on the ice, the different blues and blue-greens of the bergy bits of ice frozen into the sea ice. It was so still, reminding me of a great cathedral I had visited as a young child before leaving Germany, so silent, so grand, so awe-inspiring.

Mikiseetee said, "I feel so close to God out here, so small." I felt this too.

We drank our sweet tea and ate a biscuit from our grub box. I felt renewed and warm again. Mikiseetee dumped out the tea kettle and repacked the grub box. I climbed back onto the qamutik as Mikiseetee pulled the snowmobile's starter cable a few times until the engine roared back to life. We were off again, me hanging on for dear life. I noticed that we now crossed quite a few narrow leads in the ice, long cracks that seemed to stretch from shore to shore. These were filled with dark midnight blue water. Mikiseetee stopped to hunt seal a few times, and tried to approach basking seals beside their aglu, their breathing hole in the ice, but the luck of the hunt was not with him. I admit that, at times, I became somewhat impatient waiting in the cold but tried very hard not to show it.

I was thoroughly chilled and weary long before we arrived at the little shack at Button Point where we were to spend the night. We dragged the sleeping bags, caribou skins for a sleeping pad, and the grub box into the shack and set up for the night. With the Coleman stove providing heat and Mikiseetee and I sharing the zipped-together sleeping bags, it was warm and comfortable enough that we even made love. Perhaps it was all the effort and excitement of the days, the sweetness of Mikiseetee's skin, warm against mine, but I felt at the moment such love for this man who was my husband. I felt then that life had nothing but good things to bring us.

We had eaten the last biscuits from the grub box for our supper. Mikiseetee worried about having only tea for breakfast. Surprise, I was able to provide breakfast biscuits from my parka pockets. I was glad I had heeded my mother's advice.

The next morning, we repacked the qamutik and headed off toward the floe edge. Soon I saw Baffin Bay where the sea ice ended. The bay water was the same dark, midnight-blue colour of the water I had seen in the leads on our way here. I could see icebergs floating like majestic sailing ships on the water.

We followed along to the south along the floe edge. Mikiseetee had told me that we were to join his niece Myna and her boyfriend, Leo. I looked forward to seeing them. I was becoming weary of travelling over the ice. Finally, I saw a yellow nylon tent set up off the ice on two qamutiit. We had arrived.

Travelling May 1975.

Myna and Leo in May 1975.

Mikiseetee had told me that we would have seal meat to eat once we had joined up with Myna and Leo. I looked forward to that because I knew eating seal meat was a sure way of warming up. Then Leo told us that he and the others had hunted for seal for days but could find none. He seemed a little disappointed that Mikiseetee had not brought one for them. Instead, for food they shot akpa, murres, duck-like white-breasted black seabirds, that Mikiseetee called arctic penguins. These were plentiful, I saw. Mikiseetee and Leo ate their akpa raw, while Myna boiled some for me in a pot over her Coleman stove. After a few days of eating only akpa, which tasted unpleasantly fishy to me, we were all overjoyed when Leo caught a small seal.

One afternoon, Leo and Myna, along with the others, went on an excursion farther down the floe edge, leaving us alone. I thought Mikiseetee would like to take advantage of our solitude to be able to make love like we had at Button Point. When I touched his arm and tried to kiss him, he pushed me away.

He said, "We don't make love when out camping, ever."

I guessed our overnight at Button Point did not count to him as camping. This was a surprising new rule. It was the first time he had ever rejected me or passed up the opportunity to have sex with me. I knew enough not to react and kept my disappointment to myself. It was certain that I knew nothing of camping protocol and still had much to learn.

The weather remained gorgeous and now my problem was to find shade from the unrelenting sun. I spent as much time as possible in the tent, but I could not stay there all the time. I had on my sunglasses but still the glare of the sun glancing off the ice, snow and water blinded me at times. I could see that Mikiseetee's skin was getting darker than its usual bronze colour, now deeper, more like copper.

Mikiseetee was upset that he had not yet caught a seal while Leo, younger than he, had done so. This hunting trip was proving to be difficult for my husband, I began to understand. After a few days, he told Myna and Leo that we would be leaving the next day. Leo asked him to take back a large empty fuel drum and he agreed. We left the one we'd brought out with us.

We packed our gear and the fuel drum onto the qamutik and restrung the line over the ends of its cross slats to hold it all. I climbed aboard. Mikiseetee started up the snowmobile. Then with a mighty jerk we were off with me again holding on for dear life. This time, I had found a piece of rope to make a loop through which my mitts fit to hold onto the qamutik cargo line making it easier to hold on. Mikiseetee often stopped to hunt along the way. The leads or ice cracks that only a few days before had been so narrow, were much wider now. At one lead, Mikiseetee finally shot his seal and pulled it out of the lead with his gaff hook. He tied the seal to the back of the qamutik behind the grub box.

He was happy that he was not returning home empty handed. I was relieved and glad for him.

We travelled closer to the land on the north side of Eclipse Sound, near Bylot Island, and the mountains threw their huge shadow over the ice. I felt much colder in this shadow than I did in bright sunlight, so tried to settle into a doze and just brave it out. We passed over a lead that was a few feet wide. Then I felt the qamutik jerk and swerve in an arc. This snapped me out of my doze. I caught a glimpse of a lead ahead that was wide enough to swallow a truck, menacing with black water. At the last moment, Mikiseetee had stood up on his legs riding the snowmobile, saw how wide it was and immediately turned his snowmobile to try to avoid it. But the momentum of this sudden change in direction swung the qamutik into a curve. It flew, with me on it, over the open lead and then back again. It overturned on top of me. Mikiseetee instantly shut off the snowmobile and ran up to tip the heavy-laden qamutik off me. I was in a state of shock, but all my bones were intact, nothing broken, nothing damaged in my body except the skin on my cheek where the sharp ice crystals had grazed me. I was just lucky that the fuel drum on the qamutik was empty.

I knew Mikiseetee was profoundly sorry and worried about me. He saw me shivering and broke out a sleeping bag to wrap me in and secured me in my bundle onto the qamutik.

"Try to sleep. It will be better for you," he told me.

I stayed awake until he found a place to cross that lead, way on the south side of Eclipse Sound, but then soon dozed off. We did not stop for tea on the way back but pushed through except for pee breaks. It seemed to take forever and I felt so frozen but eventually we did arrive at Pond Inlet's east side. Somehow, I was able to walk up the hill to our house.

My Sakikuluk was overjoyed that I had survived the ordeal and roundly scolded Mikiseetee for not taking better care of me. I was just relieved that we were back home where it was warm and where there was food to eat other that the eternal fishy akpa of the floe edge. I even appreciated the honey bucket. Not having to pull down my pants to pee while being buffeted by the cold wind was such a blessing.

One of the things that had occupied all our minds that winter and spring was my fertility, or my apparent lack thereof. Everyone wondered why I was not yet pregnant. After all, it had been many months since I had stopped my birth control. I wondered, too, about what I had read, that sometimes there was a year or so delay after stopping the pill before one could expect to become pregnant.

My Sakikuluk watched me carefully and grumbled about Mikiseetee's plan to take me out to camp closer to home to the west at Anaviapik's home camp before the ice on Eclipse Sound broke up. On this trip, I remember having an unusually frequent urge to pee, much more than usual. This was a problem for me because I had to catch Mikiseetee's attention way ahead of the qamutik on the noisy snowmobile. He looked back to check on me more often since our last trip, so it was manageable. He was annoyed by the frequent stops, I could tell, although he did not say anything. I knew that the stops made the relatively short trip that much longer. But I could not ignore the dictates of my body. This time, we were travelling out with Mikiseetee's oldest brother, Bethuel, and his family. This was, to me, embarrassing. On the ice, there is no privacy and I had to expose my nether parts to the open air to do my thing. I was used to having privacy for tending to my body functions.

When I spoke about this, Mikiseetee said, "You must announce to everyone that you need to pee and everyone will look away."

He told me how to say this in Inuktitut. All this was distressing but necessary. The adults did look away but the curious children did not, much to my chagrin.

Bright sunny weather had blessed our trip to the floe edge that May, but now it was late June. It looked like the mists from the evaporating snow had massed into great clouds and it rained for the entire week we were out.

Mikiseetee hunted in the rain and left me in the tent.

I was massively bored spending time in the tent to keep dry and this forced me out to visit the other tents in spite of my shyness. I noted that the other women had brought along all kinds of things I had not thought to bring, for instance, shampoo, scissors, needles and thread as well as unfinished sewing work, magazines and books. All I had brought along were my little pocket bible and a ball of wool with a crochet hook as these easily fitted into my parka pockets. My visits to the other tents were brief, just the time it took to drink a cup of tea, after which I always had to go pee. That was really beginning to annoy me. By the time we broke camp I had re-read much of the Old Testament and had rediscovered how to crochet.

On the way back home to Pond Inlet, it rained in earnest for the entire trip. I was soaked, a sodden lump of misery clinging to the qamutik. Mikiseetee took pity on me and had me sit behind him on the snowmobile with him to keep me warmer. By now, instead of narrow leads, there were now broad rivers where the sea ice parted from the shore and the ice was covered by deep pools and puddles of snow and ice melt. We passed close to the mouth of a thawed-out river flowing down from the land on the south side of Eclipse Sound where I saw a kind of whirlpool.

I said to Mikiseetee, "I'm afraid of that."

He grinned and teased, "Want something to be afraid of?" and confidently turned the nose of his snowmobile toward the whirlpool for a closer look.

Suddenly, the snowmobile slipped into the pool and sat on the ledge of ice surrounding the big black hole down into which the river water swirled. We were both up to our waists in breathtakingly freezing water. We immediately climbed up onto the surface ice. Mikiseetee stepped down onto the ice ledge and tried to lift the snowmobile up off the ledge onto the surface ice without its slipping into the black vortex. I could see that he could not do it alone. I knew that we were stuck without this snowmobile. I slid into to the icy water onto the ledge beside him and helped him hoist out the machine. Somehow, desperation had lent us the strength to succeed.

Mikiseetee said, "Now, let's see if it will start." He pulled the starter cable many times while I shivered and prayed to myself.

Finally, with a cough and sputter, the snowmobile's engine sprang to life. We were so relieved, both of us shivering with cold. Mikiseetee unhitched the qamutik and we raced on the snowmobile to Pond Inlet, landing after about a half hour later at the HBC beach near my parents' house. We squelched up the road in our soggy kamiks to my Sakikuluk's house.

I entered the house with supreme gratitude. This flawed substandard humble residence took on a new significance. I felt blessed to be home, warm, and where I could urinate in private and relative comfort as often as I needed. We changed out of our wet clothes and hung them up to dry. My Sakikuluk stuffed our kamiks with old newspaper so they would dry slowly and not get hard and tough. Soon my feet began to painfully overheat, just like they had after my March visit to Igarjuaq and after the May floe edge trip. A few hours passed before the pains subsided. I was not in a hurry to go camping anytime soon.

It did not take long before it became clear to me that I was, indeed, pregnant. That explained my frequent need to urinate on this last camping trip. My parents-in-law were overjoyed as was Mikiseetee. I tried not to think about anything except that I was finally going to have a baby. I hoped it was a girl, a daughter who would become my friend like I was to my own Mama. News travels fast in a small community and soon Mama heard. Papa still forbade her to make contact with me, but one day she called me by telephone and asked me to meet her at the school as we had done before. I could see that she was not as overjoyed about my pregnancy as I was.

Sixteen

In July 1975, just before the annual arrival of the sea-lift supply ships, Mikiseetee had the opportunity to work away at the Pan Arctic Oils exploratory field camp with the local work crew. The winter before, Pan Arctic Oils had signed an agreement with the government to hire local Inuit to provide them with wage employment. I saw Mikiseetee off on the plane, knowing he would be away for three weeks. He was happy to go because the pay was good. We had been trying to get by on my parents'-in-law Old Age Pension payments and the proceeds of my sister-in-law's medical translation job. There were seven of us living in our house at that time. The telephone bill and the modest rent was due for the house, and the snowmobile payments also had to be made to the Hudson's Bay store.

I spent a lonely three weeks with Mikiseetee away. I read books and played solitaire. I helped my Sakikuluk with her massive jigsaw puzzles. I did the daily housekeeping and visited. It was summer, so most of my extended family had gone to their summer camps. No one wanted to stay in town in the summer except those with local jobs, the sick, and the elderly, who no longer travelled.

Occasionally there were films or dances held at the new community centre. I went to one dance just to break the monotony. I accepted a lift home from Mikiseetee's best friend, Samuel, on his motorcycle. He worked regularly for Pan Arctic and this was his three-weeks-off-work period to spend at home with his family and hunt for their meat supply. He told me he had just come back from a successful hunt and was looking forward to going out to the work camp when Mikiseetee returned. My Sakikuluk watched from the window as I got off the motorcycle at the house and it drove off. She had withdrawn into her room by the time I entered the house. It was late so I undressed, pulled the blackout curtain over the window, and went straight to sleep.

When Mikiseetee finally returned home, we were very glad to see each other. It took a few days before someone told Mikiseetee about how I had been seen riding with his friend on his motorcycle. I was surprised at how Mikiseetee was overcome by anger on hearing this. After all, it was just a ride. I had not spent time with Samuel otherwise. I noted, too, how his friendship with Samuel suddenly went cold. Mikiseetee did not have many close friends his own age and I felt the loss for him. I had not been aware that accepting a lift home would be such an issue. Had I perhaps breached a taboo?

Now Mikiseetee had money of his own to order alcohol which arrived a few weeks later. Many people got drunk when the monthly liquor orders arrived, and it was party time until all the alcohol was gone. While drunk he scolded me fiercely for getting too close to his friend. I promised to not take a ride from anyone again. My Sakikuluk wanted me to go with my husband whenever he went to other houses to drink and I did so. I tried, at first, to be a good sport and have fun. But the fun soon evaporated.

Mikiseetee's drinking companions at the beginning of his drinking sessions were usually his older brother and brother-in-law. My sisters-in-law watched me carefully and I noted that they did not usually drink. But soon, Mikiseetee would get bored and want to leave them.

My husband also had a few drinking companions who were not so closely related and with those, there was often trouble when things got out of hand. Mikiseetee showed himself intensely jealous of me while his less-related drinking companions seemed to all want to have a piece of me. I know that I was considered attractive, but I did not welcome all this physical attention. I quickly learned not to drink at all so as to avoid family trouble as well as unwelcome attention from lusty drunken men.

I learned to fear the arrival of the monthly liquor orders. The orders were submitted to a local committee that approved or prohibited a local person's liquor order. Sometimes locals were prohibited and these men then went to visit those who had been approved for their share when the orders arrived. They had, after all, provided those men with alcohol when they had been deprived. It was a reciprocal arrangement. Often, there was much community uproar and panic when drunken men staggered about the town, wives and girlfriends were threatened and beaten, and children and old people frightened. The whole community seemed to sigh with relief when, finally, all the liquor was consumed.

In late July, during the time Mikiseetee was away at the Pan Arctic worksite, my Sakikuluk once again worried about what I, her pregnant ukuaq, should eat. It had been some time since we'd had fresh meat or fish as was often the case in summer months. The HBC store had also run out of food items and the expected sea-lift resupply ships had not yet arrived. Some relatives finally arrived from the floe edge where they had caught a beluga whale and a narwhal. We received some maktaaq, narwhal and beluga whale skin, and we survived on that. I found raw maktaaq difficult to eat. The black, grey or white outer skin layer was chewy, rubbery like raw squid, and tasted like raw coconut. That outer layer, about an inch thick, was attached to a thinner, very firm gristle

We loved each other, summer 1975.

layer that my Sakikuluk scored crosshatch-wise with her ulu, having first removed most of the thick, pink layer of fat that was the layer beneath that. It was this gristle layer that was so hard for me to chew. It did not seem to break down as I worked it with my teeth and I usually just swallowed it when my jaws got tired of chewing. My stomach did not appreciate this and I suffered tummy pains from the semi-masticated food.

When my Sakikuluk noticed that I was not eating as much as she thought I should in view of my pregnancy, she urged me to eat the maktaaq she had boiled to fork tenderness for herself. She had a set of false teeth, but always took them out to eat and therefore lacked the ability to chew with them. She said that the false teeth hurt when she tried to chew with them and only used them to improve her looks for visitors. She said she lost her teeth by chewing sealskin for sewing kamik soles, like so many of the Inuit women I knew. I looked in the pot of boiled maktaaq and saw curled chunks covered with grey thick foam that had boiled out. I speared a playing-card sized piece, and put it on my plate. It smelled pungent, food-like, and that gave me appetite. I was hungry and ate the boiled maktaaq. I found it tasteless after having tasted it raw. Everyone in our home loved to eat fresh raw maktaaq and I felt left out of the enjoyment by having to eat it cooked in order for me to get enough to eat. Occasionally, I ate small pieces of the raw outer maktaaq because I could chew that and actually enjoyed that. Still, maktaaq was not my idea of an actual satisfying meal.

That summer, we had several visitors from outside Pond Inlet. One was

Hugh Brody, a British anthropologist who had visited my parents-in-law several years earlier. By this time, he was involved in making a film about the impact of non-Inuit activities and resources, like shipping and air traffic, on the Inuit and their hunting lifestyle. Both my parents-in-law spoke about the disturbance of waterfowl on their summer nesting sites on Bylot Island across the water from Pond Inlet and also the lack of sea mammals, caribou and other animals in the area surrounding the town, requiring hunters to travel far in order to hunt. Mr. Brody was less than thrilled by my presence in the household and looked away from me when we were introduced. I think he gave the old people a sum of money for their participation and the promise of being able to see themselves speak on film before the public airing, which he kept. I recall that my parents-in-law were not overly pleased that much of what they said had been edited out of that video.

The other summer visitor was the Prime Minister of Canada, Pierre Elliot Trudeau, and his two young sons. My Papa had finally waived the no-contact prohibition between myself and Mama when he heard from his trainees that I was pregnant. That meant that Mama could now telephone me openly and tell me that the Prime Minister was coming to their house from the air strip. The Prime Minister left his sons in Mama's care surrounded by armed security officers while Papa took him out on a snowmobile trip across to Bylot Island. Mama was very much honoured to have been able to babysit the Prime Minister's children. Papa was very pleased to be able to act as the Prime Minister's tour guide and to tell him

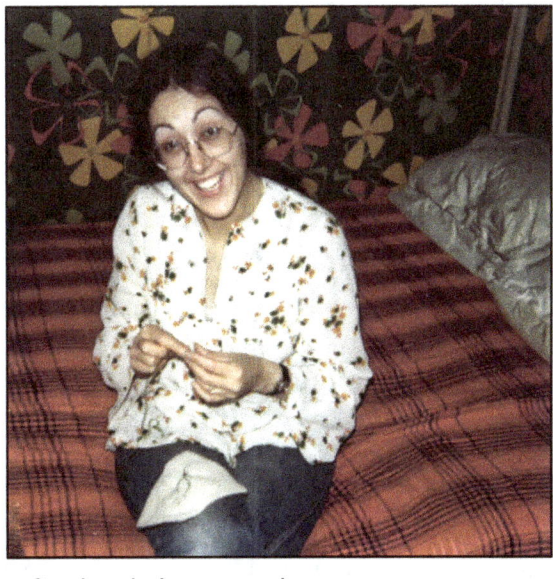

Sewing during my early pregnancy, summer 1975.

of his work projects training Inuit in Pond Inlet. After their return, the Prime Minister and his security officers did a walk-about in the town with a great crowd of children and young people following him. He made a stop to shake hands with my parents-in-law, which delighted them. I was surprised at how short our Prime Minister was, a little shorter than I am. From newspaper and magazine pictures, as well as his appearances on southern television that I had seen, I always assumed he was taller. Had I been in southern Canada, I would never have seen the Prime Minister close up like this. Only in Pond Inlet.

In late August, about four months into my pregnancy, my sister-in-law said that the school had received some funding for holding a pre-school program at the black-roofed, pink and grey building closest to the school. She said that I was to run the program and that I would have an assistant, a local Inuit young woman, a member of our extended family, who had trained as a kindergarten teacher in Greenland. We would both be paid by the school from the annual school program funds. The school provided a barrel of milk powder, a barrel of flour, and a supply of oats, sugar, lard, and cocoa powder. They also donated a large roll of brown butcher's paper, a few blunt children's scissors and a large box of broken crayons. Our building was furnished with a few low modular tables and little chairs left over from an old portable school as well as an old worn couch and easy chair. For our activities, we would have a large airy space with windows looking over Eclipse Sound.

Our pre-school space had a small kitchen that featured a converted diesel fuelled cook stove like we had at home. It needed priming before it could be lit as it had stood idle for some months. I had trouble with that and succeeded in flooding it. My brother-in-law, Josepee, the school custodian, came to show me the proper way to light the stove. I had planned to make simple oatmeal cookies and hot chocolate for the children's afternoon snack. After a few experiments, I worked out the temperature and timing for baking these cookies. The hot chocolate was much easier to make using the milk powder, cocoa and sugar. I showed my assistant how to bake cookies and make hot chocolate so she could do them on her own, if need be. The kitchen came with a large number of thick Melmac institution-style plastic mugs and plates, as well as metal mixing bowls, cookie sheets and other equipment that made our life easier. And, most welcome of all, it had running water from its large water tank, a flush toilet and even a shower. I took happy advantage of the shower after hours during my pregnancy.

Our pre-school hours were from one to four o'clock in the afternoon. That meant that older children could bring their toddler sisters and brothers on their way to school for the afternoon. We limited participation in our pre-school program to those children who were toilet trained. We felt that such young ones not yet toilet trained should be with their mothers, and besides, we could not deal with diapers and diaper changes in our program. We were not a daycare centre, after all. Some mothers brought their children just to look at first and, when the children began to relax into our activities and snacks, they would quietly leave without their child noticing. Usually that went well, but occasionally a child would make a fuss, screaming for its mother, and we had

a tough time trying to quieten the child. My assistant was a gentle young woman who told stories and sang songs in Inuktitut with our children. I supervised drawing and paper crafts. And, we both played and danced with the whole group. Of course, the children loved our snack time with our hot chocolate and oatmeal cookies, things they did not normally get at home.

Myna and me, later that fall 1975.

I was slow learning to

speak Inuktitut at home because of my shyness and reluctance to have any Inuktitut words I tried out loud laughed at with such glee by most of the adults. My Sakikuluk and her husband did not laugh at me, though. They appreciated any effort I made to learn Inuktitut. The others who could speak English preferred to practise their English with me which did not help me learn to speak Inuktitut. But at the pre-school, the children who were themselves learning to speak Inuktitut helped me learn. They never laughed at me. They enjoyed being able to teach me, the ilisaiji, the teacher, and were very patient with me. My Sakikuluk had a tough time in correcting my Inuktitut speech that I learned at pre-school. To my dismay, I discovered that there was a distinct difference between Inuktitut children's talk and Inuktitut adult speech. Still, my pre-schoolers opened me to the language. I knew that I needed to learn for my coming baby.

My husband's alcohol consumption remained a problem for me. On one occasion, after supper in November when it was already dark outside, Mikiseetee called me to join him at his drinking buddy's place. By then, my belly protruded quite noticeably. I remember that I was tired and had chosen to stay home that evening, but I put on my parka now stretched over my baby bump and began to walk down the road lit by electric streetlights. New snow covered the ground and my kamiks left oval footprints behind me on the road. Suddenly, I found myself down on my side lying in the snow. I had slipped on a piece of cardboard hidden under the snow. I took a few deep breaths and got up. I was somewhat shaken by the fall and hoped I had not hurt my baby. I should have gone back home, but I didn't want Mikiseetee to be angry with me. He was very strict about me obeying him when he was drinking.

I got to the house he had directed me to and pushed the door open. It was dark and behind me a person, stinking of alcohol and body-sweat, grabbed me around the middle and began kissing me. I jumped, yelled and batted this person away just when a door across the room opened giving some light. I saw it was Mikiseetee's drinking buddy who had grabbed me.

My husband stood in the lit doorway, and I saw a naked woman sitting on an unmade bed behind him. I did not know what to think.

"What is the matter with you? Go ahead, make love to him. I just finished with his wife. I owe him," Mikiseetee said to me.

I could not believe my ears. This was my husband, the man I loved, the father of my coming child. I slammed the house door as I ran out. I had reached halfway up the hill toward home when Mikiseetee caught up with me, puffing with loss of breath.

"Why did you run away? Did he hurt you? What did he do to you? I'll kill him." He was pretending that he had not set me up for his drinking buddy.

I clung to his arm so he could not get away and make good his threat.

"He just tried to kiss me," I told him.

Mikiseetee was quite drunk, but I convinced him to come home with me, and fell down a few times as I supported him home. There, he passed out and left me in peace.

Finally, it dawned on me that all that unwanted attention given me by Mikiseetee's drinking companions was because he had used their wives before he and I married. He'd had sex with them, and now I was expected to repay my husband's sexual debts. I had read about how Inuit used to swap wives in some of the older writings by northern explorers. Could this be what they meant?

Since the summer, Mama came to visit at our house whenever she had time. I was fortunate, I thought, to be able to talk to Mama face to face. Of course, I did not share with her the problems I saw developing in my marriage. I kept that to myself. My main purpose in life at that time was to get through this pregnancy and deliver a healthy child.

Mama told us that Papa was providing support for the upcoming

Inuit moratorium meetings to halt arctic oil exploration, providing information about sea ice and its importance to Inuit hunters. Otherwise, Papa continued to provide sea ice data to the Polar Continental Shelf Project that protected Canada's offshore natural resources, provided support for arctic researchers and extended Canada's arctic sovereignty. I was happy that he could see the Inuit point of view on these issues and was no longer supporting the oil companies and their goals.

That winter, Inuit from across the arctic from as far away as Inuvik and Nain, Labrador, came for this meeting. Inuit meeting delegates were boarded in Pond Inlet homes, and Francis Ruben of Paulatuk, a community near Inuvik, stayed with us. Mikiseetee became instant friends with Francis throughout the meeting week. After the delegates left, Mikiseetee announced that he would like us to name our child Ruben to remember his friend, if it was a boy.

I said, "And if we have a girl, we could call her Ruby." I was hoping for a girl throughout my pregnancy. Mikiseetee said he liked that, but he was sure it would be a boy.

Part 2
1976–79

Seventeen

As the sun crept back over the icy mountain tops on Bylot Island in February 1976, the weather was again extremely cold. It was a year and two months since I had returned to Pond Inlet as Mikiseetee's wife. By now I was nearly poised to give birth. The public health nurse, a young woman who had not experienced childbirth herself, nor had much midwife experience, tried to argue with me about when my due date would be. She claimed it would be sometime in the latter part of March.

"That could not be," I said. "Mikiseetee was away for a few weeks that past June and I was sure I had conceived in May at Button Point during our first trip to the floe edge."

About two months before at Christmas, I had stopped working at the pre-school program when unaccustomed heaviness and fatigue forced me to stay home. My Inuit assistant carried on without me, hiring someone to help her, until the funding ran out the following May. I applied for unemployment benefits due to maternity. With the few unemployment benefit payments I received, I was able to buy an apartment-sized washer and dryer before I was informed that I would not receive more payments because I had not worked long enough. I contented myself with the fact that these new appliances replaced the old labour-intensive ringer washing machine and the need to hang up wet clothes to dry. These appliances would certainly make my life easier with a newborn.

In the final trimester of my pregnancy, I suffered with aching back and swollen feet. I had gained an enormous amount of weight and my belly pressed hard into my diaphragm so I often found it difficult to breathe when seated. My Sakikuluk kept saying that I would surely have a boy because my baby bump was so high. I actually wished for a daughter, but by this time I did not care. I was so weary of carrying this bulky, kicking child.

During the annual Christmas/New Year games and dances at the community hall, Mikiseetee demanded that I go with him whenever he went and even to dance the energetic square dance. I usually liked dancing but not now and I refused. My Sakikuluk warned Mikiseetee that dancing would now be dangerous to my coming baby. I was grateful she intervened. I was always tired and sleepy these days and did not welcome my bulk being shown off at the dances.

Mikiseetee liked to play card games late into the night after his parents were asleep and could not comprehend why I would not want to sit up with my hard belly pressing painfully into my lungs. I thought it was because he was used to seeing pregnant women being able to do anything and everything up to the very moment that they gave birth. I had to remind him that this was my first pregnancy and I was not like the women he knew, not like the historically hardy Inuit women in his family who gave birth out on the land without any help at all. It could have been that he was worried about my constant tiredness, how big I had gotten in pregnancy and so was constantly testing my stamina. Making love, too, was difficult at times with my now ungainly shape. I am almost certain that this also upset my husband although he never said so.

Perhaps as a result of my uncomfortable pregnancy, I became more and more aware of the many dissatisfactions about my new life, those I had until now ignored. It was not the impoverished lifestyle we were living nor the lack of the comforts I had always taken for granted before coming to Pond Inlet. I would have been content had Mikiseetee been more considerate of me and the tremendous adjustments I had to make in getting used to this new life. He seemed to me to be fully absorbed with showing everyone that he was able to catch a Qallunaq wife and make her pregnant, thereby fulfilling his family duty. It turns out that he was not the good hunter he had put himself out to be when we first met. In fact, he had been quite inexperienced. His mother often criticized him, mentioning how his nephews hunted better than he, to his great chagrin and embarrassment. The happy Inuk I had been captivated by at the beginning was now a sour, defensive, and short-tempered man.

When I met him, he enjoyed getting inebriated with drink and smoking up dope, but in the early days before our wedding, he did not lose control of himself. Now I did not like my husband's almost monthly binge drinking and smoking hashish and weed, all to the point of passing out. At the start of our relationship, Mikiseetee's drinking alcohol and smoking up struck me as only what other modern young people did. I mean, even I drank to excess when my first marriage broke up, but I did not continue to crave alcohol all the time. I found during my adolescence that I could not tolerate smoking up, so that never became a thing for me. I found it increasingly difficult to accompany him when he was drunk going from one house to the next in search of alcohol, weed, and hashish. What I was beginning to see with my husband, was something that looked quite unhealthy. Still, I had to remind myself that I had married him in church, making vows "in sickness and in health" and now I was about to have our baby. I decided to get a grip on myself and try to make the best of things as they came.

I sorely missed modern plumbing and other household amenities in my unhappy pregnant state. I was not the only non-Inuit woman married into the community. I had made friends with the other one and I was able to use her bathtub every now and then during the early months of my pregnancy. She had demanded that her Inuit husband provide her with a proper house and she got what she wanted as soon as her son was born the year before. Her husband was well-educated, government employed, and for these reasons, it was not impossible for him to improve her living conditions. I did not have that hope, my husband being relatively uneducated and sporadically employed with no permanent employment prospects in sight. Of course, I had not considered these details before I'd committed myself to Mikiseetee and my future in Pond Inlet. I had gone into this union blindly, in a fog of romanticism as well as in the heat of defiance of my Papa's trying to control my life.

My Sakikuluk must have sensed how unhappy I was, that I was not just tired of being pregnant. Before I told her that I was pregnant, she had often said that I would soon leave them. At that time, it was still early days and I was still enamoured of my new romantic life as the wife of an Inuit hunter. I denied that I would ever leave her and my husband. I knew that my Sakikuluk was quite religious and paid attention to teachings of the Anglican Church. She had an Anglican Inuktitut prayer book and hymnal as well as several books of the Old Testament, and the New Testament Bible translated into Inuktitut syllabics, issued in pamphlets, that she often read. She showed me her old leather-bound King James version of the Holy Bible in English that she had been given in the late 1950s when she was taken away by ship as a tuberculosis patient and ending up at the Hamilton sanatorium, about forty miles (seventy kilometres) from where I was then growing up in St. Catharines, Ontario.

Earlier that summer, there had been a public panic spread by public radio by some religious fanatic claiming that the world would end on a certain date, which happened to be the next day. Mikiseetee's frightened niece came to tell her grandparents the dire news.

When I asked what was wrong, the granddaughter said with shaking voice, "The radio says the world will end tomorrow. My grandmother and I are so afraid."

"I am not at all worried" I said. "I have heard such stories before and the end of the world did not happen then," The granddaughter translated while my Sakikuluk listened with astonishment.

I told them my father's story. He, my father as a young man in

Germany, drove a truckload of plate glass after the war. He parked the loaded truck on the hill outside my grandfather's house one evening so he could visit with my mother. That was the same evening that the townspeople had gathered on the next hill, their naked bodies covered with blankets, expecting the end of the world that night. Our family chose to ignore the public panic. My father and mother heard a loud crash and looked out the window. They saw that my father's loaded truck had rolled down the hill and smashed into a stone wall breaking all the glass it contained. My father realized that the truck's brakes had failed. The next morning, the newspaper published a story about the anticipated end of the world and how the townspeople waited on the hill. They reported that on hearing a loud crash, thinking the moment was at hand, they threw off their blankets to reveal their nakedness. The delighted newspaper reporters photographed the scene and the photos accompanied the report. The newspaper, the day after, also reported how embarrassed the townspeople were when they discovered that the crash they had heard was only a runaway truck loaded with plate glass smashing into a wall, not the end of the world, after all.

"The Bible tells us that no one will know the time when the end of the world would come," I said and found the Bible passage for my Sakikuluk that said this, Mark 13:32, "But concerning that day or that hour, no one knows, not even the angels in heaven, nor the Son, but only the Father." She had it in Inuktitut and was impressed by these words.

Still, the next day, the end of the world day according to the radio, Sakikuluk sent her husband, the shaman, to go visit someone's house and he went, carrying his caribou skin drum and masks. She was convinced that he would probably not go into the afterlife where she thought she was going. She spent the day praying and reading her Bible, just in case. Nothing untoward happened all day. That night, she called her husband back to the house and, not saying anything, they went to bed. The next day she thanked me for keeping my faith.

She said, "I am no longer afraid of the end of the world because of you."

Little by little I was gaining the old woman's trust, it seemed to me.

When my Sakikuluk kept on saying each time she saw me unhappy, "You will leave us and go back south to your family," I had to take action. I reminded her of the story of Ruth in the Old Testament of the Bible which she knew well in Inuktitut translation.

I said, "Your people are my people," just like Ruth had told her mother-in-law, Naomi.

This seemed again to set my Sakikuluk's mind at rest. She stopped talking about my leaving.

Mikiseetee must have been worried that I would leave, too. He was so remorseful after each crisis-laden drinking bout, that I found I had to forgive him. I believed such incidents were just bad habits, that with settling into married life and fatherhood, he would leave off the drinking and riotous living.

Before I became pregnant, my Sakikuluk had often commented that I was taking so long to conceive. And, when he was drunk, Mikiseetee often criticized me, saying, "You're a barren woman," which was unacceptable.

At those times, I comforted myself with a passage in the Bible, Psalms 113:19, "He makes the barren woman abide in the house as a joyful mother of children. Praise the Lord." I did not show this passage to anyone. I did not want to admit that I, too, was worried about this.

After it became apparent that I was actually pregnant, things gradually began to change. My Sakikuluk became more caring and attentive to my comfort. Mikiseetee, on the other hand, became gradually less caring, as if that could be possible. It seemed as if he had done his duty by me for his family by getting me pregnant and was proud of that fact. He may not have been the hunter he had claimed to be when we had first gotten together, but here was proof that he could at least father a child.

The winter of my pregnancy I became very sick and I went to the nursing station, mercifully located near our house. The nurse told me I had amoebic dysentery. I had heard that this disease was going around in town, that a young pregnant Inuit woman had died of it recently.

The nurse said, that because I was pregnant, she would not give me the antibiotics necessary to recover. She said that antibiotics would compromise my expected child. Frustrated with the nurse, I called Mama by telephone for help and she came to the nursing station right away.

"I am not concerned about the loss of my unborn grandchild. I am concerned about losing my daughter. Alive, she could possibly have another child," she told the nurse.

Mama was so fierce that the nurse did give me the antibiotics after all. In a week I had recovered and was still pregnant. My Sakikuluk was relieved and happy about that, as were we all.

According to the nurse, since this was my first pregnancy, and because I was already over thirty years old, I was to make the long flight to Frobisher Bay to give birth. This was the location of the nearest hospital equipped to deal with all kinds of medical emergencies.

In spite of my knowing the exact date of conception, the nurse claimed I could not know this as I had not been pregnant before and so she booked me to leave mid-March. I felt certain I would give birth about the end of February. When I pressured the nurse about letting me depart by plane for the hospital a few weeks earlier than she would have liked, she possibly recalled how uncomfortable she had been with Mama when she defended me that time when I was sick with dysentery. The nurse relented and let me leave when I needed to go.

My departure for hospital was on February 16, 1976. It was a cold and supremely uncomfortable flight for me. I could not do up the front zipper of my parka over my huge baby bump and I was wedged into that narrow seat on the airplane. It was still fairly dark during the day in

Pond Inlet when we left as the sun had not yet risen above the mountains. We arrived in Frobisher Bay in brilliant sunlight. I was taken from the airport to the house of a young Inuit couple originally from Hall Beach where I was to board, in a room all to myself. I was pleased to note that their house had proper plumbing, but there was almost no food in the house except tea and hard biscuit. I made the best of that and went to bed early. I had an appointment to see a doctor the next morning at the hospital and a hospital car was to come to pick me up at eight in the morning.

The next day dawned in bright sunshine. I was up early as I had spent a near sleepless night and sat looking out the main window. The snow sparkled and dazzled my eyes. I knew that Pond Inlet would not have that kind of morning until the middle of the following month.

Looking out the window, I noticed a large dog on a chain in front of its doghouse across the way trying to defend the frozen meat someone had thrown him for a meal. He was jumping around and barking furiously. I went closer to the window and saw what was bothering him. There were three large ravens standing in a half-circle near the doghouse, just out of reach of the dog on its chain. These canny ravens worked as a team. One raven would step forward so the dog could almost reach it. The dog jumped toward the raven, trying to snatch it in its teeth, but it confidently flew up and settled back out of reach. While the dog was occupied with this distracting raven, the other two ravens dragged the meat away from the dog across the snow. Poor hungry dog. The ravens seemed to laugh at him as they broke the meat apart and flew away with it. It was child's play for the ravens with the dog chained up like that. But, I think, even if the dog were free, it would have had a hard time trying to outwit these canny ravens.

The car came to take me up to the hospital and the doctor examined me.

He looked at my file, at what our community nurse had written, and said I would probably deliver in about a week or so. I told him I felt it would be sooner. He told me, laughing, that he was going up island and would be away for a week.

"Just hang on until I get back," he said.

"I'll try," I said.

Eighteen

After my hospital morning appointment with my doctor, on February 17, 1976, the car from the hospital services drove me to my boarding home. I walked to the Frobisher Bay HBC store near the shore to buy food for myself and to share with my boarding hosts. I spent the evening getting to know the young Inuit couple who spoke English very well. They were both about a decade younger than my thirty and a half years and they marvelled that this was my first pregnancy "so late in my life." They were both homesick for their home and family in Hall Beach. After a light supper, I went to bed. I was exhausted after my long walk that day.

At about six the next morning something woke me. I got out of bed and went to the, thankfully, modern washroom. I felt a great gush flow from my body. I knew that this must be my water breaking. I telephoned the hospital and they said their car would pick me up at eight. My back was achy after I dressed so I walked around the house until the car came. I knew that my doctor, expecting me to give to give birth in a week or so, as he said, had left Frobisher Bay that morning. I wondered how that would play out.

At the hospital, then, a little after eight in the morning, I told the receptionist that my water had broken at six that morning. She told me to take a seat, that a doctor would see me as soon as one was free. I tried sitting and did manage this for about an hour, but after that, the pain in my back forced me to pace. More hours passed, and I went to the receptionist to remind her that my water had broken five hours earlier, and I was getting very uncomfortable. She said impatiently that I should sit down and wait. Then it was noon and a man in a white coat came out of the doorway beside my chair.

"Are you a doctor?" I asked.

He said, "I am." I launched into my story, six hours since my water broke and so on.

"Wait." He paused. "Six hours ago? Are you feeling any birth pains?"

"No, except for a huge pain in my back."

"Why hasn't anyone told me about you? This is trouble. And I was just off to have my lunch."

I was sorry for the doctor's lunch delay and said so.

Suddenly, I was surrounded by nurses and was whisked upstairs to the maternity ward, stripped, bathed in an antiseptic bath, dried, dressed in a hospital gown and prepped for birth delivery. Since it was lunch time, the nurse asked me if I would like to eat. I had not had anything to eat since the night before. The nurse brought the tray and I ate a kind of stew, I think. Then the labour pains started in earnest. I tried to be brave and not cry out, but after a while I could no longer control myself. A delivery nurse came to check me periodically all afternoon. Finally, toward evening, she said the baby was finally coming.

I was wheeled into the delivery room. The attending doctor, someone I had never met before, introduced himself. There were two nurses in attendance, one to watch and help me and one to assist the doctor. By now, the pains were unbearable and I screamed each time they tore through me. I vomited out the lunch I had been given into my long hair and the nurse said I should not have eaten anything. I said grimly that I would remember for next time. Between pains, I whimpered and called for Mama in German. Luckily, the nurse who was caring for me understood German and spoke comforting German words to me. Finally, the pains stopped altogether. I was utterly exhausted and welcomed the respite. The doctor said they would inject me with Pitocin to restart my labour which should take effect in about an hour, they said. They were all off to have their supper. I was feeling cold and sleepy when they turned the lights low and left. I slept.

About an hour later, the delivery team returned, switched on the bright overhead lights, waking me. Suddenly, a pain I had never felt before jolted through my belly. I had two more of them, with my attending nurse struggling to keep me from falling off the delivery table.

Then the doctor said, "Stop pushing. It's breach. I will have to cut."

Cut? I felt an injection but I could also feel every slice of the scalpel cutting my perineum. I heard the clank of some equipment and felt something being shoved into me. I felt a dragging pull from inside. Was that my child being pulled out of me?

"It's a boy," the doctor announced.

I did not have my glasses on so I only saw a dim shape as they whisked away the baby, a bundle wrapped in blue. Then the repair work began and I felt every stitch. After that I guess I passed out. This was the end of my son's birth day, February 18, 1976.

A few hours later, I awoke when a nurse shook my shoulder in the recovery room. Tears streamed from my eyes in grief.

I said, "I dreamed I had a baby boy and he had died."

"He didn't die," she said.

I asked to see my son, but she said that I had lost a lot of blood and should go back to sleep. I was still so exhausted that I fell back asleep right away.

The next morning, I was wheeled on a gurney into a semi-private room and transferred to the hospital bed. Then procedures were begun for drying the sutured cut the doctor had made during delivery. I was given light foods and drink that morning and at noon, but in the evening, they served a very decent caribou stew with bannock and later a cart came by with frozen char and maktaaq, all foods Inuit like to eat and me, too. I was pleasantly surprised that the hospital served such country foods.

A very pregnant Inuit woman who did not speak much English was moved to the empty bed beside me. I just had time to tell her who I was and where I was from when she indicated urgently for me to call the nurse. The delivery team came with their equipment cart and pulled the green privacy curtain around her bed.

I heard one nurse say, "It's too late. The delivery has to be here."

There were sounds of rustling sheets and movement behind the drawn privacy curtain. When it was pulled back a half hour later, the mother lay resting with her newborn nestled in her arms against her propped-up pillow. I was amazed that the woman had made no sound at all during her delivery because I had been much more than noisy during mine. She later told me that she had had a little practice as this was her fifth child.

"I had heard that Inuit women were admonished not to make unnecessary noise during childbirth," I told her.

"Yes, that is so, but it is not always possible," she said.

Her kind words comforted me.

That evening, I tried to reach Mikiseetee by telephone in Pond Inlet but was told he was out. That was disappointing, so I called my parents' telephone number. My Papa answered.

"You are now grandfather to my son," I said. "Can I please speak to Mama?"

"Not so fast," he said, "I want to know how many fingers and toes your son has. And does he have a Mongolian mark on his body?"

"He has ten toes, five on each foot, and ten fingers, five on each hand, and, no, he doesn't have a Mongolian mark," I said.

All except for the last part was true. A Mongolian mark is like a birthmark but blue in colour found on bodies of children of mixed blood, especially of Asian origin. I knew my Papa would never wipe my little son's bottom which is where his little blue mark was right between his tiny butt cheeks. It was a little white lie that seemed to relieve my Papa. He said he was happy that the baby and I were all right. I did not lie to Mama and she agreed it was better that Papa be spared this knowledge. In his early upbringing during the Nazi regime in Germany, I suppose he paid attention to the Nazi "purity of race" doctrines taught to children at that time. Mama was able to resist this kind of brainwashing probably because her genteel Christian family taught her to be kind to and accepting of everyone, no matter the racial origin. She had taught me the same, for which I was grateful.

Two days later, after supper and visiting hours were over, I had just put my tiny son to sleep in his little see-through plastic cot on a trolley beside my hospital bed, when, surprise, Mikiseetee staggered into the room, followed by a nurse and an orderly who were trying to make him leave.

"Where's my wife? Where's my son?" he shouted, shaking off the attempts to hold him and looking around frantically.

He finally focused his eyes and saw me. He staggered over to my bedside and planted a drool-laden kiss on my cheek. I was shocked and appalled. What was he doing here in Frobisher Bay? The plan was that he would wait in Pond Inlet for my return.

He said he had cried to his older brother, Josepee, and begged him to buy his flight ticket. I could not believe that Mikiseetee had such a hold over his brother. I suppose getting him away spared the family

Mikiseetee's frustrated temper. I was less than pleased to see him here at the hospital. I did not feel at all capable of dealing with him in his drunken state, especially as I was recovering from my childbirth ordeal. I urged him to come back tomorrow during visiting hours, now that he had seen us and satisfied himself that we were safe. I wrote out the address where I was boarding, told him to give the paper to the taxi driver, and to go there to sleep it off. After he finally left the room, I asked the nurse to call the couple where I boarded to warn them of his coming. When he returned the next day during visiting hours, he was his normal shy and quiet self, embarrassed when I told him about his drunken visit the night before. He had no recollection of it at all, of course.

I know that during the five days I spent at the hospital in Frobisher Bay, Mikiseetee went drinking at the local hotel bar at the Frobisher Inn after visiting me and our son every day. I did not look forward to the time I would have to leave the hospital knowing I would have to deal with him by myself. I hoped that our boarding with the young Inuit couple would somehow help. When the time came for me to leave the hospital, I found that Mikiseetee and the young husband and his wife had become drinking buddies. I did not know what to think of that.

It was good that Mikiseetee and I had a room to ourselves for privacy. There was only the single bed which made things crowded and a little uncomfortable for me as I had not yet healed completely. Mikiseetee didn't want to sleep on the floor, he said.

I actually looked forward to the hours he was away so I could get the rest I needed and get used to breastfeeding my child without critical witnesses. I yearned to return to Pond Inlet as soon as possible, but we were prevented from leaving immediately because there was a problem with my infant son that would need surgery to correct this problem, I was told. I was very eager to be at home again with my parents-in-law where Mikiseetee could not stagger around drunk at all hours. I was always so tired and dreaded the delay in leaving.

One afternoon a few days later, Mikiseetee had been drinking again, very drunk and unsteady on his feet. I lay on the bed in our room with my baby beside me, trying to nap, when he burst into the room, panting and swaying, wild-eyed and raving. I could not understand what he was shouting in Inuktitut. He bounced off the edge of the bed, losing his balance and bumped into the wall. The young couple ran into the room, to watch, I guess, because I knew they would not and could not control my raging husband.

He finally yelled at me in English when he saw I did not understand, "Give me my son. You're keeping him all to yourself." He snatched our son and stood swaying back and forth unsteadily, crooning to his son.

Perhaps it was because I was overwhelmed by all the noise, fear for my child and my utter exhaustion, not to mention physical pain, but some strength within me suddenly kicked in. I pulled myself up to my full height and glared at him. I calmly pulled our son out of his arms. He made to strike me, but something stopped him. Perhaps it was my intense stare.

I kept eye-contact with him and said, slowly and distinctly, "If you ever touch our child again when you are drunk, I will surely kill you."

The young couple gasped when they heard this and quickly left the room. Mikiseetee seemed to think over my words for a few seconds, perhaps deciding that I actually meant what I said, and then staggered out of the room. He and the young couple left the house. I was relieved to be alone with my baby.

The next day, Mikiseetee was relatively sober when we took our baby to the hospital for his daily check-up and were told by the doctor that our son's problem had resolved itself. Our baby did not require surgery after all. I spent the rest of the day trying to find the quickest way out of Frobisher Bay to fly home, while circumventing Resolute Bay which had a public bar where alcohol was served that I wanted to avoid. I booked our return flight via Hall Beach to Pond Inlet. We left the next day.

I did not have an amautik, a women's parka, in which to carry my baby. I had been told that first time Inuit mothers did not get an amautik until after the expected child was born so as not to bring bad luck to the birth. I had to make do with my baby bundled up inside the front of the parka I had worn on the trip down. My baby was small, so this was not too difficult.

On the flight, Mikiseetee, abjectly hungover, suffered motion sickness before we landed in Hall Beach. I could not help him much as I had my hands full with our child. I was happy to see my brother-in-law James, travelling with us and helping to distract Mikiseetee in his misery. James was the husband of Joanna, Mikiseetee's sister and also his good friend. He was the first of our family to see our son. On touchdown in Hall Beach for refuelling, we were told that we could not fly on to Pond Inlet that day because of a blizzard moving rapidly into the area.

From the air strip, we were led by the Inuit air agent from the air terminal through a covered walkway to the official crew's quarters that houses transient workers and pilots on layover. It was like a miniature hotel, with a small reception area with a coffee machine and a hallway with tiny rooms, each holding a narrow single bed, a compact chest of drawers, a chair, and a bedside table. James went off to sleep in a little room down the hall from us.

Mikiseetee did not want to sleep by himself, so I bundled my baby to sleep in the folds of my parka in a half-open dresser drawer and propped the chair under it so it would not accidentally drop. Since there was only one pillow on the bed, I took one from the next unoccupied room as well as the blanket. Mikiseetee and I slept on the narrow bed together. That is, he slept while I dozed, ever alert to my child's cry. He actually cries a lot, I thought, wearily.

The next day, we explored the quarters and found the coffee maker ready with hot coffee and a plate of cookies in the little reception area. I was grateful for even this meagre breakfast because we'd had no food since leaving Frobisher Bay the morning of the day before. We found our way through the walkway to the air terminal, the hangar that also served as the departure lounge. There, the Inuit flight agent told us we were weathered in for who knew how long by the blizzard howling around us.

We walked back to the crew's quarter to wait there. There were a few old *Reader's Digest* magazines and a checkers board game in the reception area. That gave James and Mikiseetee something to do for a time playing checkers, and me with something to read between baby feedings. We searched the place but could find nothing more to satisfy our hunger than coffee, sugar, fake creamer and bags of cookies. And drinking water, thankfully. Somehow, we got through the day and night. Mikiseetee complained about his hunger for "real" food while I was concerned about getting enough to drink so that I could breastfeed our baby.

On day two of our forced Hall Beach layover, we again walked to the airport departure area. There, the air agent told us the same thing, "The plane cannot take off. The blizzard is still raging."

He did tell us that we could buy frozen prepared airline breakfasts and heat them in the microwave oven on hand in his office. The cost was twenty-five dollars for each little breakfast tray. None of us had any cash on us. In those days, credit cards were not in as general use as they are today. I asked the air agent if he could bill us for the meals and I would mail him a bank cheque. He said he could do that. I had no idea how we were going to come up with the cost of these meals. Mikiseetee ate two breakfasts right off, while James and I only ate one each. The meals consisted of a rubbery lump of scrambled egg, two tiny sausages, a little wad of hash-brown potatoes, and a small bread roll. After we ate, we walked back to the crew's quarter to continue waiting.

On day three, we were told that we would be leaving the next morning according to the weather forecast. We bought four more breakfasts, and the agent gave me the bill, two hundred dollars for eight breakfasts. We returned to the crew's quarters. Mikiseetee kept complaining, acting as if the blizzard and our being stuck in Hall Beach like this was entirely my fault. And maybe it was, come to think of it. If we had flown via

Resolute Bay, Mikiseetee said, we would have been home already. James told him that was actually not so because the air agent had told him Resolute had also been weathered in by blizzard for these past few days. I was so grateful to have had James with us during this trial of uncomfortable waiting.

The next day dawned bright with clear blue skies and sunshine. The blizzard had blown itself away. We were having our coffee and cookie breakfast when the air agent came to alert us that we would be leaving in a few minutes. He reminded me to mail the payment of the airline breakfast bill.

Then, he kind of laughed and said, "You want to know something funny? I had just come back from hunting caribou and stashed my catch in the snow outside the hangar door when your plane arrived and we were all weathered in by this blizzard. I was going to take the caribou meat into town as soon as the blizzard was over. I should have shared the meat with you, but I forgot to tell you I had caribou meat. So sorry."

That left me stunned and even more than a little glad to be leaving when we boarded the airplane. I was so relieved, so happy to be on our way home again and looked forward to letting my Sakikuluk hold her new grandson.

Nineteen

The month of February 1976 passed by while James, Mikiseetee, my newborn and I were weathered in by that blizzard in Hall Beach. It was March already when we left there.

The flight home to Pond Inlet took place in glorious sunshine and light winds. The sun's rays sparkled off the brilliant snow of the blue-tinged snow-clad mountains of Bylot Island and everything looked clean, fresh and new. The little plane landed softly with its skis on the snow runway and taxied in to the flight shed where the fuel truck and other trucks were waiting. My brother-in-law, Josepee, was there to give us a ride to my Sakikuluk's house. There was no joy in Josepee's greeting to me and Mikiseetee did not speak at all. I was grateful for the ride in silence because I held my sleeping babe against my body under my parka, the empty sleeves tied in a knot in front to keep out the cold. In a few minutes we were home, inside House Number 69.

My Sakikuluk smiled from ear to ear making the creases in her face deeper as she took my tiny baby from me as I slipped him out of my

Proud parents of Ruben 1976.

parka. My Sakialuk stood behind her trying to catch a glimpse of his newest grandson. Suddenly, the house was full of my younger relatives-in-law and I saw Mikiseetee withdraw into our room. I was so weary and still so sore from my childbirth that I longed to join Mikiseetee just to lie down. But not yet.

Josepee asked, "What name did you and Mikiseetee choose for your son, the one to be used for his baptism?"

"Ruben," I said. "Mikiseetee wanted him named after our house guest, Francis Ruben, who stayed with us during those moratorium meetings last fall about the oil-drilling on Lancaster Sound."

My Sakikuluk said Ruben was one of the brothers mentioned in the story of Joseph's many-coloured coat in the Bible. It was this brother who prevented his other brothers from killing Joseph. The King James Bible had the name spelled as *Rueben*, but I preferred the simpler spelling of Francis Ruben's name. This baptismal name, Ruben, was passed around and approved by the family.

Very soon, everyone noticed that our baby Ruben was not at all happy. He fussed and cried, and refused to feed at my breast. He was not wet and his clothing was not binding. I could not figure out what was troubling him. My Sakikuluk sent for Josepee's wife who was still lactating. Her last child was about four years old by then and still on the breast. My sister-in-law was not too happy to be summoned, but came right away. Her mother-in-law's wish was her command, as it was mine.

One of my nieces whispered to me that my Sakikuluk said my breasts were too small, that I had not enough milk to satisfy her baby grandson. So, my babe was put to the new breast, large and overflowing with milk. He took one suck. He seemed to realize that this was not his mother's breast, pulled away, and howled. He was handed about and everyone tried to calm him and finally he was put to that strange breast again, but it became clear he really did not want it.

I calmly took my baby from my sister-in-law's arms and put him back to my breast. This time he accepted it, sucked his fill and soon fell asleep. My Sakikuluk told everyone to leave now, they could visit another time. Mikiseetee had fallen asleep on our bed, I saw, as I finally lay down beside him in our room while my Sakikuluk took baby Ruben to her room to let Sakialuk meet his newest grandson.

I thought over what had just happened about breastfeeding with my sister-in-law. It struck me that my Sakikuluk wanted a wet nurse for my baby to ensure that he was well-fed. She did not trust that my breasts could actually provide enough milk. They looked so small to her. I was so grateful that my little son preferred my breast. While breastfeeding remained painful for me, coping with overfull breasts was an agony I did not want to endure at this time. While my baby was being offered the strange breast, I had a sudden flash of insight that if he did prefer it, I would be redundant. It was my role to feed Ruben, necessary for keeping him alive and thriving.

I saw, too, that it was my Sakikuluk who had the final word on my son's care and keeping. I was to learn later that the first son of my Sakikuluk's eldest son, as well as the first son of her youngest son, by our Inuit family custom, belonged to her. She was ningiu, the paternal grandmother, to my son. He belonged to my mother-in-law and her word was law to me, her ukuaq, wife of her youngest son.

This reminded me of what I had read about ancient traditional Chinese family structure in the historical novels written by Pearl S. Buck, where she described the roles of the daughter-in-law subservient to her mother-in-law. Ataata Mari had told me that eons ago in prehistoric times, the ancestors of Inuit migrated from Asia. I also realized that the foot-gear of our modern Inuit, the dark bottom foot coverings with white insets over the top of the foot, were similar to those used by traditional Chinese. That Inuit were of ancient Asian descent made sense to me, especially since my baby also bore that Mongolian mark.

Ruben at my breast 1976.

After my nap, I emptied the middle drawer of our chest of drawers, propping it with a chair back, like I had in Hall Beach, to make a safe cot for my tiny son. I put the clothes in a cardboard box under our bed beside my bread storage box. There was not much room in our bed for the three of us and I was afraid that Mikiseetee or I would crush our newborn while we slept.

Later in the day, my Papa came by snowmobile bringing a cradle he made from plywood painted light blue. That was the same colour he had painted the bed he had made for me when I was four years old, still living in Germany. He knew I would remember.

"This is a gift to my new grandson from Mama and me."

He stayed only a few moments, held his grandson for a bit, congratulated us, and left.

I was surprised and quite touched by this gift and the thoughts behind it. Our clothes under our bed went back into the chest of drawers and I put the cradle on the metal trunk against the wall at the foot end of our bed. But my little Ruben did not sleep much in this cradle. He seemed to cry constantly. I spent many nights walking him about. Often, my Sakikuluk would take him from me so I could get some much-needed sleep. But, the mostly unused cradle acted as a symbol of Papa's change in attitude,

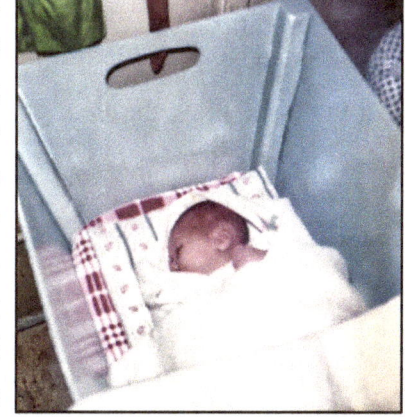
Baby Ruben in the crib Papa made for him 1976.

accepting me as the mother of his Inuit grandson. I was glad of that.

It took me more than two months to recover from childbirth. I had lost all the weight I had gained in pregnancy and now I was underweight, just bones encased by sallow skin. I had no energy, felt listless, had no appetite, although Mikiseetee and my Sakikuluk urged me constantly to eat and drink for the sake of my son's milk supply.

Mikiseetee began to lose patience with me, and continually pestered me from about two weeks after our return to let him have sex with me. I had to deny him because I had not fully healed. My Sakikuluk had good hearing and picked up on that. I thought at times that she understood a lot more English than she let on.

"My mother spoke sharply to me telling me to leave you alone," he told me bitterly.

Our marital relationship had not yet recovered from the Frobisher Bay and Hall Beach ordeals. He seemed to lose interest in his baby son, but he appeared content that his mother was happy with her new grandson. Mikiseetee's duty, as the youngest son, was to take care of his parents and by providing a son, a grandson for his parents, a future provider, he had fulfilled one part of this traditional duty.

My Sakikuluk heard from her granddaughters what a hard time I'd had giving birth as well as about our having been weathered in during the Hall Beach blizzard. I told no one about Mikiseetee's drunkenness, but I guessed that other local Inuit who had been in Frobisher Bay at the time had seen my husband there and had told her about that, as well. It was a lesson in the lack of privacy and the efficient gossip mill in this small settlement. One afternoon, when Mikiseetee was away from the house, Josepee apologized to me for having paid his brother's way to the hospital. I told him that I knew he had meant well, no hard feelings.

My Sakikuluk made a point of telling me and Mikiseetee that I should not have another child because the next one would most likely kill me. At this point, I had no intention of becoming pregnant and was using birth control again. Mama had warned me about having babies too close together, saying that it is better to space offspring by a few years. She spoke from experience. My younger sisters were born only a year apart. When the youngest was born, the sister ahead of her stopped walking because she wanted to be like the new baby that now had most of my mother's attention. I could try for another child in a few years, I thought, then, perhaps have the daughter I yearned for.

Now that I had a living infant, my Sakikuluk instructed Mary, Mikiseetee's oldest sister, to sew an amautik, a women's carrying parka, for me. No amautik had been made before my son was born to avoid bad luck, a stillbirth or worse. The outer cover of the amautik was of tightly woven, off-white, bone-coloured cotton with a wide blue border around the large hood with a distinctive peak. It had an A-line skirt trimmed with two lines of store-bought trim around the bottom hem to match the sleeve cuffs. The inner amautik was sewn of heavy wool duffel and had wolf-fur trim around the large, pointed hood. It fit well except that the sleeves were a bit too short. My wrists are unusually long when compared to Inuit body proportions. I crocheted myself some cuffs to protect my wrists to solve this problem and that worked well. I also learned to tuck my hands into the alternate sleeves like Inuit women do. I was proud to own an amautik as a mark of my new status as mother.

    I learned to finger-weave a long woollen tie belt that was to go around the back of my new amautik. My Sakialuk presented me with a large, oblong, eight-sided button he had carved from narwhal ivory, decorated with black narrow baleen inlays forming a cross with a red plastic circular inset at its heart. My Sakikuluk had fashioned a finger woven harness for me which she instructed me to sew to the front in three places of my amautik from the shoulders forming a "W" shape with two loops. One downward loop was to hook the new decorative button that was sewn about a foot and a half from the end of my waist belt, and the other downward loop was for knotting the other end of that

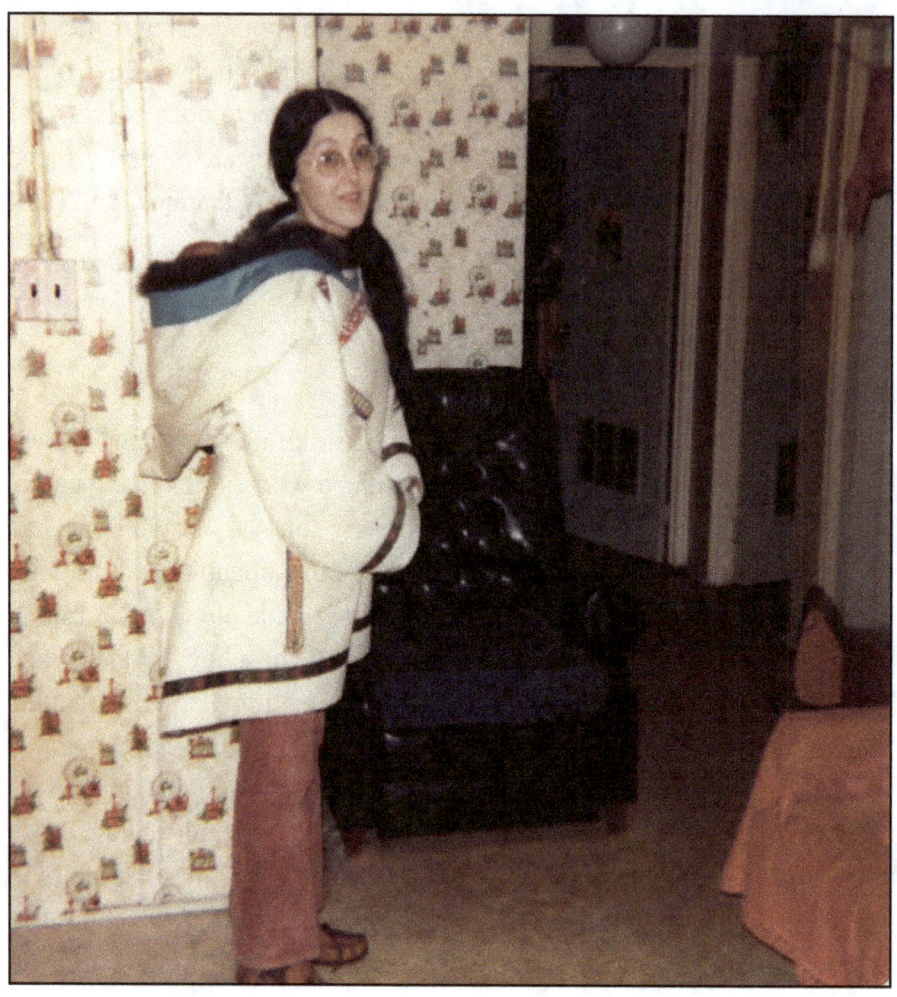

My new amautik 1976.

belt with a slip-knot. The knotted end was adjusted so that the belt sat snuggly under the back pouch that held my baby so that he would not slip out of the bottom of it. I had not yet seen this style of amautik harness on any other amautik in Pond Inlet. The usual style was as a "V" from the shoulders, or simply a loop from the middle of the neckline, through which the amautik belt is passed and then tied tightly all around the waist, not using a button at all. My Sakikuluk told me that the "W" harness shape with the button was what she wore on her amautik for her children. I found this harness convenient because I did not have to untie my belt when I wanted to pull off my amautik nor did I have to retie the belt when I put it on. After I had the amautik on, I just slipped the button into its loop. Different, but very handy.

When in the amautik, my baby lay upright directly against my back with the wide hood covering my baby's back. When it was cold and windy, I pulled the hood up over my baby's head as well as my own and secured the hood with a finger-woven band attached to the side of the hood passed in a slip knot through one loop of the amautik harness.

"Care must be taken so the newborn's face is turned sideways to avoid him smothering to death," my Sakikuluk instructed.

She made sure I understood this by having stories told to me of ignorant young mothers who had accidentally suffocated their babies by not being careful. As long as the baby was still so small, I had to rely on others to help me place my baby into my amautik and to turn his head sideways. I did not dare to do this myself in fear of accidentally dropping him or smothering him. Taking him out of amautik, I learned almost immediately. I just had to lean far forward and catch him as he slid out over my shoulder.

After baby Ruben had grown a few months, I was impatient to learn how to put my baby in and out of the amautik without help. I did not always want to be so dependent on others, disturbing them to help me put him into the amautik each time I wanted to go out. I practised over my bed until I was sure about how to pull up the back of the amautik with one hand forming a space into which my son could slide, all while holding him balanced with my other hand on the back of my neck with his feet poised to go down my back into the amautik's back pouch. He thought it great fun, but I soon tired. I had to keep trying until I got it right and became adept at this procedure. I did the practising only over a bed or well-padded couch in case I missed, but I was so careful that I never dropped him. This learning took about a year to master completely.

A few weeks after I got my new amautik, Mikiseetee took me to see the

Igluvigaq exterior 1976.

inside of an igluvigaq, a snow house, that had been built entirely of hard snow blocks by one of the elders to demonstrate how it was done. I already knew that the Inuktitut word iglu means house or building. We crawled through the igluvigaq entrance tunnel on our hands and knees. I was afraid I would bump my baby's back, but we got through without mishap. I was able to stand up inside.

I saw that it was a bit dark towards the back of the igluvigaq. There was a sort of tent of sewn-together army blankets had been stretched over the sleeping platform that was held to the roof and sides by toggles made of bone passed through holes in the snow blocks. The area around the entrance was quite light in contrast. When we went out again, I noted the toggles on the outside of the igluvigaq that held the inside tent. Mikiseetee told me that when the igluvigaq was used for longer than just an overnight, this kind of inside tent arrangement was used. The snow walls of the igluvigaq were always wet, and dripped when there was any source of heat, even just people breathing.

"It is dangerous," he said, "to have water dripping onto the bedding because of the risk of freezing the sleepers."

It made me glad that I did not have to live in an igluvigaq. I had the feeling there was much I did not know about how to live in one safely. Mikiseetee told me that Inuit usually no longer lived in igluvigaq for extended periods, but it was used for emergency shelter when the weather went bad while travelling over the ice.

In this igluvigaq there was a qulliq as well as a

Inside the igluvigaq 1976.

propane camp stove. Caribou skins, hair side up over a layer of skins hair side down, formed an insulating mattress under the bedding on the snow block sleeping platform. The igluvigaq was circular with the raised sleeping platform taking up a little more than half the space and was about four feet higher than the floor of the entranceway tunnel. The floor space was narrowed by the snow block storage platforms to both the right and left of the entrance. Whatever warmth there was inside the igluvigaq was kept in by the entrance tunnel's being much lower than the sleeping platform and the sources of heat.

I was impressed by the ingenuity of igluvigaq construction, and knew that building one was a skill that needed intensive learning and much practice. I knew that Mikiseetee's family had lived in a qarmaq, sod house, at their home camp in Igarjuarq before my Sakialuk built the wooden family house I saw there. A qarmaq was laid out inside much like the igluvigaq but was made of rocks chinked with turf and roofed with sod over a frame made of driftwood or large whale ribs or even whale jaw bones.

I heard that the family was always so glad when spring came to be able to leave their qarmaq to live in igluvigaq because the qarmaq was so dark and damp inside and over the winter would become quite dirty and smelly. But they said they were the happiest in the summer when they lived in their sealskin tents, with the translucent hairless skins covering the front half and the back half covered by sealskin fur turned to the outside to darken the sleeping area. In modern times, those traditional sealskin tents were gradually being replaced by canvas prospector tents or nylon pop-up tents sold by the HBC store. Inuit life was changing rapidly.

Learning to tend the qulliq flame 1976.

Twenty

On that trip home from Hall Beach where we had been weathered-in, my brother-in-law, James, who had accompanied us home from Frobisher Bay, told of his trip to Ottawa. He was the member representing Pond Inlet at the meetings of Inuit Tapirisat, the national Inuit brotherhood, located in Ottawa. He told us the news that the Inuit Tapirisat had resolved to re-name the Inuit. Up until then they had been known as Eskimos.

"We are to be called 'Inuit' from now on, not Eskimos anymore."

My parents-in-law, Mikiseetee reported, found this a bit odd because in Inuktitut, the word "inuit" means people, as in humankind. There was, during this time, much political discussion about indigenous or native land and personal rights. It was during this time that I began to think of Pond Inlet as Mittimatalik like the rest of our family and other local Inuit.

My parents-in-law spoke about Project Surname just after they had moved to Mittimatalik from their home camp. A government person, an Inuit from the western arctic, came to give each male householder a last name so that Inuit would no longer have to use their disk numbers for identification. Their numbers were stamped onto a small maroon disk, made of the new plastic called Bakelite, or of pressed fibre or leather, suspended on a neck chain, like a military dog-tag.

The new names now consisted of the oldest male householder's main Inuit name as the last name and each member of the household using their Christian baptismal names as their first names. That had the confusing result in that Mikiseetee's brothers, the sons of my Sakialuk, Joshua Komangapik, each had different last names because they each had their own houses at that time. Mikiseetee's last name was the same as his father's for the simple reason that he still lived in his father's house. No one seemed to mind — or maybe they thought they had no choice way back then. The old people accepted the ethnic name change from Eskimo to Inuit without much surprise at the strange modern ways.

This was the last trip that my brother-in-law James made to southern Canada. Joanna, his wife, objected to his long absences from home and his overuse of alcohol when away. Soon after our return, he became a lay minister at our St. Timothy's Anglican Church. I knew that James had bouts of painful arthritis in his hands, especially when he went out hunting. Yet, in spite of that, he hunted regularly without complaint, to supply food for his family.

I saw Joanna, James, and their family regularly as she was my Sakialuk's favourite child and lived close by. She had been allowed to marry the man of her choice, while Mary, Mikiseetee's oldest sister, had been compelled to submit to an arranged marriage. Arranged marriages were another of the old ways that changed since Inuit moved from their home camps into settlements.

Joanna became my best friend in the family.

❄

Later that summer, the annual sea-lift brought my queen-sized bed that my Uncle Hermann managed to ship up from St. Catharines, Ontario. This was the ingenious custom-built bed that Mama had given me when my marriage to Michael had failed. It dismantled into two parts for easier transport and had two storage drawers. All it needed now was a queen-sized mattress. None was available in Mittimatalik, but we did find a used double bed mattress in good condition that was six inches too wide. Mikiseetee built a long bench for the support of the overlapping side of the mattress that worked very well.

Now we had a spacious family bed for ourselves and our baby, but now our bedroom was too small for this bed. So it happened that my Sakikuluk moved her adoptive daughters out of their larger bedroom into our small room and gave their former room to us. This room was right across from her bedroom and made it even handier for her to check on her grandson.

Mikiseetee was urged to go hunting regularly by his parents. His mother had bought him a snowmobile and his father had built him a qamutik. His father also gave him a gaff hook, harpoon and line for sealing and a kakivak, a trident-like leister for spearing fish. He had a .22 rifle for arctic hare and ptarmigan and used his father's higher calibre rifle for larger animals, like narwhal or caribou.

While there was still sea ice, he went out almost every day. Many times, he returned empty-handed but every now and then, his efforts were rewarded and he brought home a seal or two. At those times, he was proud and happy, especially when his mother was able to call everyone to share out the meat. She knew I liked seal liver, so she would always put some aside for me to cook later while everyone else would enjoy eating the rest of it raw. Happily, our household did not depend solely on Mikiseetee's hunting success. His two older brothers and three brothers-in-law also provided meat, seal, fish, and often caribou. In the summer months there was also maktaaq, narwhal skin, usually mottled black on grey, while the black kind was highly prized and considered a delicacy. When someone in our extended family got very lucky and was allowed by government tag lottery to hunt polar bear, we received some of that meat, too.

On one occasion in May, when Ruben was about four months old, Mikiseetee had gone seal hunting over the sea ice. He was gone longer than usual, staying out overnight, and my Sakikuluk began to openly worry about him, demanding from all who heard, why her youngest son had not yet returned. We all tried to reassure her and offered good reasons for his delayed return, but nothing would calm her. She was so upset that she did not even want to hold her favourite grandchild, my son Ruben, and he began to fuss at his beloved ningiu for being so upset. I put him into my amautik and took him for a walk to look over to the east of the settlement toward Igarjuaq, the direction that Mikiseetee had gone, to see if I could catch a glimpse of him returning.

It was already the afternoon and I chose to pace up and down the street beside the houses hoping to settle my son's agitation and my own worries. A little woman limped out of her house and asked me to come inside and visit for a bit. I had met her before and knew her as Martha Kautainuk, mother of Samuel and Aquila, widow of the reputedly black shaman, Kautainuk. Her son, Samuel, had been Mikiseetee's best friend until jealousy over me interfered. They had been the very best of friends in spite of the whisperings I had heard of some sort of feud between their fathers. I was ready for a distraction from my brooding thoughts and welcomed the visit.

Over tea, Martha told me briefly about how her foot caught between the slats of her father's qamutik, breaking her ankle which took a long time to heal and left her with a permanent limp.

"Because I had this disability, my limp, I knew that I would probably never be able to marry and have children," she said.

She explained that girls or women with some kind of physical deformity or other disability like blindness or deafness, were not seen as proper enough to be hunter's wives. They were condemned to becoming old maids in their parents' home, often being overworked and sometimes mistreated. This did not happen to her, she said, because her father loved her so much.

"So," she said, "I was completely surprised when my father told me that I was to go to Kautainuk's house and be his new wife."

She had heard, she said, all the stories about how Kautainuk was thought to be a black or evil shaman, how all of his wives had died, and how he had mistreated them while they still lived. She, like other local women, was frightened of him. But her father insisted that she go, and she knew she must obey her father. Her father was very much afraid that if she did not become Kautainuk's wife as he desired, he would curse both of them.

"I had no choice," she said, and agreed.

"When I entered Kautainuk's house, he greeted me kindly, had me sit down and gave me tea with a piece of bannock," she continued. "He saw that I was shaking with fear and he seemed to take pity on me."

She told how Kautainuk said to her that he did not care about her disability, her limp. He chose her, he said, as his next wife because she was a good woman and was praised for her sewing and other womanly skills. He assured her that he would not beat her or mistreat her. She reminded him that she was a practising Christian and that she had heard that he was a shaman. She said he laughed at that and told her he permitted her to continue her Christian religious practices. She then told him that she could not be with him if he did not agree to having the children they may have together baptized and raised as Christians. She thought he would refuse this, but he did not. Instead, he agreed. So, she became the shaman's wife and had two sons by him. She never saw him practising any form of shamanism, she said. He always treated her well and with respect and was a very good hunter. Now she was his widow for many years and had grown sons who support her.

Martha's story reminded me of the story Ataata Mari had told me of how he helped my Sakialuk overcome the curse of snow blindness put on him allegedly by his rival Kautainuk. He told me that my Sakialuk was what one can term a good shaman, a healer, and while Kautainuk was suspected of being a bad or evil shaman who had long had an animosity toward my father-in-law.

"Your father-in-law came originally from Naujaat, Repulse Bay area, south of Igloolik," Ataata Mari explained, "while Kautainuk grew up in the Mittimatalik area and probably felt, therefore, that your father-in-law was his rival. Your father-in-law was also Christian, a Catholic, as were many Inuit in the Repulse Bay and Igloolik areas. Since your father-in-law is Catholic, he sent for me when he suffered snow blindness.

"We went into a room and covered the window so that it was quite dark. I called for water and gave it to your afflicted father-in-law to drink, and closed the door. I had brought all I needed to do an official exorcism. I performed the rite. In the dark room, we fasted and prayed, drinking only water. After three days and two nights, your father-in-law regained his sight. Praise be to God," said Ataata Mari.

"Is not covering the eyes allowing them to heal from their burns, and feeding the afflicted a liquid diet, the modern medical way of dealing with snow blindness?" I asked.

"Oh, yes," said Ataata Mari, "what you say is right." He smiled a little. "But your father-in-law is a devout Catholic and a healing shaman. I knew that the exorcism ritual was a perfect solution for his ailment and would restore his sight, as well as satisfy his need to overcome the curse of his rival shaman. I wanted to put an end to that rivalry."

I thought on my Sakialuk's healing from the snow blindness curse while visiting with Martha Kauntainuk. She was aware that I, too, had heard bad things about her deceased husband, father of her sons. I began to understand how it was that Mikiseetee, with his father's blessing, could have become such good friends with Samuel, Kautainuk's son.

Before I left, Martha said, "Your mother-in-law is old and belittles her youngest son too much. He is safe and will come home soon, you will see."

I returned home. About an hour later Mikiseetee arrived and relieved his mother's worries.

"I became tired and visited at some tents at Igarjuaq," he said, "where I slept."

He was immediately forgiven for making the old woman worry because he brought home two seals.

In addition to seals, Mikiseetee often hunted ukaliq, arctic hare, and aqiggiq, ptarmigan, which his parents enjoyed eating raw as well as cooked. A ptarmigan is the size of a small chicken with almost completely white feathers with black on their wing tips. I watched in fascination whenever Mikiseetee stripped the skin with feathers attached off the little body all in one piece, like pulling a glove off a hand. The feathers were not plucked out as is done with chickens, turkeys, ducks, geese and wild fowl in southern Canada. The naked ptarmigan did not look at all like the skinned domestic chickens I was familiar with in southern Canadian supermarkets either. The flesh was deep red and there was little visible fat.

After he eviscerated the ptarmigan, Mikiseetee removed its croup, a membranous pouch almost like a balloon that held seeds and pebbles, stretched its opening end, blew into it to inflate it, and tied the opening with string. He put it up on the warming shelf of the stove to dry. When it was dry, the seeds inside rattled and this was then a favoured plaything for children. The feet were cut off and these also became children's toys while they were still pliable. Little Ruben loved playing with these toys.

When Mikiseetee brought in a winter hare, it was quickly checked for fleas. If it did have fleas, Mikiseetee would skin it outside the house, again stripping off the skin in one piece and turning it hair-side out again and would hang the skin up outside. When it was frozen, somebody, maybe even me, would hit the hare skin over and over with a stick to remove the frozen fleas. The frozen fleas just dropped off. I learned that hare fur, rabbit skin, was used like we would use paper towels to mop up spilled things. They were also used as diapers, when travelling, to soak up the baby's urine while in the mother's pouch on the back of the amautik. Later on, I would also learn that traditionally, Inuit women used such fur as sanitary napkins. This was no longer necessary because now such personal items were in stock at the HBC Store.

I used cloth diapers for baby Ruben. Disposable diapers had just come into use in southern Canada but were still very expensive. Since I had an apartment-sized set of electric automatic washer and dryer, my life was a bit easier doing Ruben's diapers without draping the entire kitchen in wet diapers. Since the washer was so small, I could go only about a day or so without washing and drying diapers. Instead of doing laundry once a month like we did with the old wringer washing machine before the birth of my child, I now did a weekly laundry for the household and diaper washes every day or so. The old wringer washer was now set aside outside for future sealskin washing.

The days grew longer and by the end of May, most families left over the ice to their spring camps. Not many were left in town. As soon as the ice broke up in mid-July Mikiseetee took me and our son by borrowed boat to camp in Igarjuaq, his parents' home camp. It was an opportunity for Mikiseetee and I to spend time with our son as a little family in a tent all to ourselves. We both welcomed our summer getaway.

Mikiseetee's nephew Natanai, Joanna's son who lived at our house, went camping with us to be our helper. That boy had been kept at hospital in Montreal after his birth when Joanna returned home alone. Baby Natanai had some sort of medical problem with his breathing. When he was finally shipped home, my Sakialuk took him in because Joanna had not bonded with him and she had also not yet recovered her health. He was a tiguarq, an adopted child, to his grandparents. I began to learn that adoption for Inuit was not always happy. Some, like Natanai, were not especially well-cared for. That changed a bit for Natanai after I arrived. I did not then know the reason why they treated him so badly. Perhaps they wanted to harden him up. To me, he was just an abject little boy. I made sure that he, at the very least, got enough to eat and had warm clothes to wear. I was learning a lot about my Inuit family's ways, and did not always agree with how things were done. But, as long as I was living in my Sakikuluk's house, I had to accept her will as my law.

Out in the freedom of our summer camp at Igarjuaq, Mikiseetee reverted to his playful, charming self that I had fallen in love with two years before. We spent much time together, laughing with each other. Mikiseetee showed me what he was like underneath the gloom he carried at home. He delighted in playing with Ruben and showing his love, something he rarely did at home where his mother took over our son's attention. I did not begrudge my Sakikuluk this, but I would have liked for Mikiseetee to be more part of our son's daily life. I began to dream about someday having a little house of our own to be a family just like out in our summer camp.

The freedom of summer can also bring tragedy, I learned. One August afternoon, someone came to the house to bring news from one of the camps. A boy had been shot dead. Apparently, the father had placed his rifle upon an upright fuel barrel believing that the children would not touch it there, while he surveyed the ice and leads for seals. The rifle was loaded and ready to shoot. The safety was off. The father hoped to catch a seal. He then slipped into the tent for a quick cup of tea. The young children ran about outside the tent, playing tag, having fun. A loud bang stopped everyone. The rifle had fired. The father, now out of the tent, saw his youngest son, still a toddler, dead before him, shot in the head. His older son stood frozen, terrified at what he had done. He had just playfully pulled the trigger. The mother ran out of the tent and fell grieving over her dead child. The father bundled his unfortunate older son into warm clothes and left with him by boat. We heard he was hiding out somewhere with his son.

"Why would he hide out with his son?" I asked. "Is he afraid of the police? It was clearly an accident."

"No," I was told, "he is not afraid of the police. He is afraid that the relatives of the deceased person his dead son is named after would seek revenge. They would try to kill the son who pulled the trigger that killed the little one. They would not see this as just an accident."

We heard that the father somehow sent word to the RCMP officer to come and get them from their hiding place so that he and his son would be safe from these vengeful namesake relatives. He knew he will be safe in jail with the RCMP here in town.

This was a revelation to me who had seen most of the population of Mittimatalik attending the local St. Timothy's Anglican Church. There were only a handful of people who were Roman Catholic, and even they attended the Anglican church when the Catholic missionary, Ataata Mari, was out of town. It seemed that Christianity was not quite as entrenched in Inuit daily life as the Christian missionaries had hoped. Some of the old Inuit ways were still being kept, it seemed, the old family feuds and vengeances still carried on, in spite of the mandate of both the Anglican and Catholic churches for Christian forgiveness. Later, I began to see that this forgiveness was, for some local people, from God for our personal sins only and not for one person to forgive another. Religion and daily life were kept quite apart, it seemed, except on Sundays. What concerned the spirit was kept at church while out in the community, Inuit traditional custom still operated within the restraints of Canadian rule of law as enforced by the local RCMP officer.

In this case, the unfortunate young boy and his father were protected by RCMP intervention. Nothing much happened to the boy who had accidentally shot his brother, but the RCMP did announce on local radio about taking the ammunition out of firearms when not in use to prevent such accidents in future. My parents-in-law and extended family followed this story closely to the end and discussed the accident and its outcome.

Around this time, Mikiseetee showed me an old article printed in *The Beaver*, the Hudson's Bay Company magazine that his parents had saved. It reported the alleged murder of Robert Janes by Inuit and the trial held in Mittimatalik in 1922 that sent two Inuit to jail in southern Canada while another was indentured locally to the HBC. This incident established the RCMP in Mittimatalik. The trial demonstrated to Inuit, without a doubt, that they were now governed by the foreign laws of southern Canada enforced by the RCMP officer.

Mikiseetee had shown me Robert Janes's grave on a low cliff overlooking Eclipse Sound when we walked out to Salmon River just after I had first met him in 1974. At that time, he had told me a little about the Janes case. Now I learned that local Inuit had been appalled by the trial and its harsh findings, especially since they had been so open about the incident, admitting what they had done collectively as well as their reasoning for doing so. The incident was locally considered a simple execution, according to Inuit custom and practice, of a stranger to their lands who had obviously lost his mind and posed a threat to others. I was fascinated by the old photographs that accompanied the article, and noted that it had not included the Inuit side of the story. I began to understand a little better of the love-hate relationship that Inuit developed over time with the RCMP, the Canadian and territorial governments, and non-Inuit in general.

Mikiseetee also told me of the connection between the RCMP and his parents. Both parents had been employed by the RCMP in the past.

During the 1950s, my Sakialuk along with other Inuit helpers in Mittimatalik assisted in settling the Inuit families who were relocated from southern Inuit lands to the northernmost uninhabited arctic islands, now Resolute Bay and Grise Fiord, north of Bylot Island. This took place during a time of a famine, a scarcity of game, in the areas from which they had been moved. Over several seasons, the Mittimatalik men taught the newcomers how to hunt in the new area and showed them the best places for camps. During periods of 1940s and 1950s, my Sakialuk also worked periodically as an assistant to the local RCMP officer in Mittimatalik. He hunted to supply food to the officer and his dogs and often accompanied him by dogsled when he made his rounds of the Inuit camps. At that time, my parents-in-law had their home camp in Igarjuaq while the RCMP had their headquarters in Mittimatalik beside the HBC store.

My Sakikuluk told of when she worked as housekeeper for the RCMP. She often walked with her small children from Igarjuaq to Mittimatalik over the ice in winter and spring and along the coast in the summer and autumn. She cooked the RCMP officer's food, his meat and bannock, washed his clothes, and kept his house clean. She also sewed his sealskin kamiks and heavy winter clothing, caribou qulittaq, hooded parka, and silapaak, wind pants.

Sakikuluk told me about how it came about that she became the mother of her son Josepee who was half Inuit and half Qallunaq. One winter, both she and her husband could see that the RCMP officer, a young man of whom they both had become quite fond, was suffering loneliness and homesickness for his southern Canadian family. My parents-in-law talked over between them how they could cheer up the young man for Christmas. They decided together that they would give him a small party with his favourite food, some alcoholic drink, and a romp in bed with my then still good-looking little Sakikuluk. She emphasized that her husband encouraged her to make the event as loving as possible for the lonely young RCMP officer. She told me that, when both the husband and wife agree, Inuit traditional custom allows the wife to be lent to another man, usually a good friend to both the husband and the wife. Their little party went very well and the young man did become much happier. And, she soon became pregnant with Josepee. I have seen a photo of my parents-in-law taken in that time period showing a smiling Inuit man with his tiny, pretty wife that helps me imagine that the young RCMP man was made very happy.

She asked me. "Ukuaq, do you think this was sinful? Especially since it was before I became Christian, me sleeping with a man other than my husband and bearing his child? Do you think I will go to hell for this sin?"

I was surprised that she should want to know what I thought of it all.

"Your husband agreed and is happy to be the child's father?" I asked.

"Oh, yes," she said. "Josepee is his favourite son."

"In that case," I said, "I don't believe you will go to hell for this. You did this out of love for another human being and according to your traditional custom. Love for another human is taught by the Christian churches, as you know."

She was very much relieved with what I said and thanked me. I had heard and read about the infamous wife-swapping of Inuit and now I understood better that marriage and extra-marital sex was traditionally bound with rules and taboos and was not a simple lack of morality. I was pleased that she had asked my opinion and that it mattered to her. We were becoming closer to each other, I felt.

Twenty-one

In July 1977, almost a year and a half after Ruben was born, I followed along as everyone gathered on the hill across the creek that bisects Mittimatalik, opposite the Co-Operative store. We had heard that workers would today dig up the graves in the old graveyard and move the corpses to the new cemetery much farther away up behind the airstrip overlooking Eclipse Sound. The old graveyard would become the new building site for about a dozen new fully equipped insulated houses that were to be erected for the local Inuit Housing Association that summer. Reverend Laurie Dexter, whom we all knew as simply Laurie, our Anglican missionary, was there to bless the cemetery move.

We all crowded around after the ceremony. Everyone wanted to see the bodies of their long-buried relatives. Some of the coffins were broken and I saw dried up skulls and bones covered in desiccated brown skin and partly rotted clothing. In one grave, I saw polished brass buttons on a well-preserved, almost undamaged, khaki uniform jacket even though it was said that this deceased person had lain buried there for twenty years or more.

After the ground was opened, the whole area was suddenly inundated with mosquitoes, drawn, no doubt, by the wet soil. Still, this did not drive the people away. I was struck by the way everyone reacted to seeing their dead relatives' remains. It was not at all with horror but with keen curious interest. I was told that the souls of these deceased were long gone after their Christian burial, so there nothing to be afraid of. As far as I could tell, the people of Mittimatalik had no superstitions about human remains.

After this event, everyone applied to the housing association for one of the new four-bedroom houses built that summer over the old cemetery. My Sakikuluk also applied for the eight of us since the birth of my son made living crowded in old House 69.

After the birth of my son, my relationships within our extended family seemed to improve. I thought they could now see that I was trying to fit myself into the family, contributing to the family welfare by learning new skills, gradually learning the language and customs, and respecting the elders of the family.

One sunny afternoon, Jayko, my nephew by marriage, who had given me all those books in thanks for removing the sliver from his big toe, came to visit for tea. The old people were back in their bedroom for their after-lunch nap with their little grandson. I had been resting, reading in my room. I gave Jayko some tea with fresh baked yeast bread, and we chatted a bit about the weather. Then, out of the blue, he said he'd like to ask me a question. I wondered why he'd hesitated so much.

"Okay," I said, to encourage him.

He twisted his hat in his hands.

"I really like our former nurse. Do you think I should ask her to be my partner at the community hall dance tonight?"

The woman he was asking about had been the community nurse

when I first came to Mittimatalik in July 1974. She quit nursing after my sister-in-law Joanna's baby daughter died unnecessarily due to the refusal of the remotely stationed head-nurse to authorize the MedEvac flight to take the child out to hospital. The head-nurse claimed that Mittimatalik had used up its quota of MedEvacs for that year. This had occurred during that time Mikiseetee and I waited to return to Mittimatalik in the fall about three years previously. This nurse had come to Mittimatalik years earlier from England and she had told me she did not want to return there. Since leaving nursing, she had tried living with a local Inuk, but that relationship had not worked out.

"Of course, you should ask her," I said.

"What if she says no?" he asked.

"Well, then, you will have your answer. But I am sure she will accept."

I did not attend the dance that night but stayed home with my son and the old people while the others went off.

A few days later, Jayko came by and let me know that the former nurse had accepted him at the dance and that they were now a couple. I was glad to hear this. Jayko had asked me, sometime after he had given me those books, why I had chosen Mikiseetee for a husband when there were any number of better local men available, like, for instance, him.

At the time, I think I said something like, "probably because at that time you did not let me know you were available." I knew he was the municipal heavy equipment mechanic, that he could support a Qallunaq wife.

I was happy to go to their wedding a few months later. Now she was my niece-in-law.

I was not the only non-Inuit woman married to local Inuit men. There were now three of us. Some kind of competition arose between the Inuit mothers-in-law of their sons' Qallunaat wives about who among these wives were most Inuit, that is, who had adapted the best.

Often Inuit women whom I barely knew would visit just to observe me and how I did things. I did not enjoy this sort of attention, but I tried hard to be polite, which impressed my Sakikuluk.

I also was closely observed by younger Inuit women who had been admonished by their grandmothers for being lazy at Inuit women's tasks and did not at all like me doing so well. I heard whispers that they thought I should be more Qallunaq, not so hard-working, care more about my appearance and hairstyle. I was even asked, "Are you trying to out-Inuit the Inuit?"

I ignored all this as much as I could. I was often unsure of what I was doing, but I knew I did not want to be a paragon of Qallunaq womanhood anywhere, and especially not in Mittimatalik.

My relationship with my father had also improved enough after the birth of my son so that Mikiseetee and I now regularly visited my parent's house. Papa's eyes lit up when he saw his little grandson, delighted to hold him, and I could see that little Ruben was equally enchanted by his Qallunaq grandfather. Mikiseetee and I, with Ruben in my amautik, went to church twice on Sundays, so it was no trouble to stop in after the church service to visit. Mama was as lovable and hospitable as always. I was so relieved that my parents and I could put aside our differences and enjoy each other's company. Mikiseetee was shy and did not speak much on these visits, but I thought he lost some of his fear of my Papa watching him play with our little son.

As the months passed, I was hired on to the Sanaugartaarvik skin sewing program funded by a government make-work project as their part-time

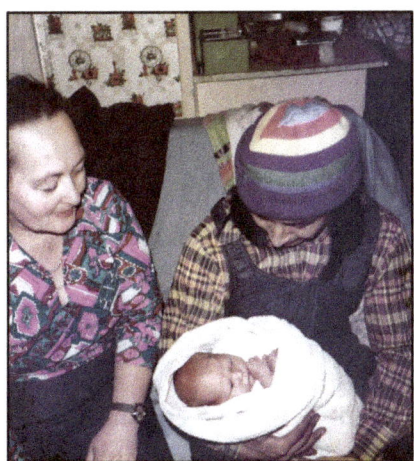

Mama with Mikiseetee holding Ruben 1976.

bookkeeper. This group was run by Mikiseetee's eldest brother's wife, my sister-in-law, Elisabeth Ootoova. I earned a small wage and I was happy to not always just keep the books or making out pay cheques. I learned quite a bit about sealskin processing beyond the initial stages, all the work that had to be done before the clean, dry sealskin could be sewn into clothing and foot-gear. They put me to some of this work softening a skin, for instance, by crushing, folding and refolding it and treading on it, dancing on it. It was fun and I got to know these women better while they were able to observe me close up, too, without my Sakikuluk observing or hearing their comments. I brought my baby son to work with me in my amautik just as the other women who worked there brought theirs. It was the perfect job for me while my son was small. It was a chance to spend time away from the house, to be useful aside from housework, and to earn money in a paying job. I found our hard-working Inuit women sewing group members were a joy to work with. I was beginning to understand more spoken Inuktitut, too. These women had a riotous sense of humour, especially when comparing their husband's body parts, that would often make me blush.

Soon we had news that the ANIK-B Satellite had been launched into space by Telesat Canada. This meant that the television set I saw first at my parents-in-law house in July 1974 was finally working. In fact, all the local telecommunications improved across the board. Long distance telephone was now reliable and somewhat more affordable, but still expensive. The old way of speaking on the telephone, like on a two-way radio, was no longer necessary. Commercial radio reception also improved and my parents-in-law began to enjoy regular programming from Greenland.

On television we enjoyed limited programming from the CBC, Canadian Broadcasting Corporation. I remember seeing Sesame Street and National Geographic shows, shows I had enjoyed in southern Canada. The children loved Sesame Street and I did it, too. My parents-in-law enjoyed the National Geographic program in spite of not being able to follow the narrator's English words, marvelling over the strange animals and people they saw in the documentary films. They were already keen on the National Geographic magazine that I subscribed to and shared with them and now they could see the photos come to life. It seemed to open up a whole new world for them.

Of course, many people were afraid that our hunters would now stay at home and become addicted to watching television instead of hunting for food animals. During the first few days of television service, some hunters did actually stay at home to witness the first programs, but soon lost interest. The television programming was not actually very compelling, especially daytime shows. Soon these hunters were back out there doing what hunters do best.

Along with the featured programs on television, there were the constant and relentless commercial messages that paid for them. Much of the programming was from the CBC but there was quite a bit of programming from the northern states of the USA. These commercial messages sold everything from soft drinks and laundry detergent to insurance products and more.

"Television lets us know that there is so much to want that we did not know about," said my Sakikuluk.

One evening, Mikiseetee was at home and we were all watching television when a commercial message interrupted our program. We saw a fluffy white dog jumping around in a back yard somewhere in the south on a sunny day. A family was about to

Papa playing his harmonica for his little grandson 1976.

barbecue hot dogs and they were set out on a plate. The white dog jumped up and snatched one hot dog and ran away with it between his jaws.

"It's a 'dog eat dog' world," the announcer intoned in a grave voice.

Mikiseetee, hearing this, burst out laughing and repeated in grave tones what he had heard, "It's a doggie-dog world." He said he loved the sound of it. He kept repeating it, "doggie-dog world" until it got us all laughing, too.

Perhaps it was the same insurance company that put out another commercial showing this same white fluffy dog knocking over a glass bottle of milk.

"It's no use crying over spilt milk," the announcer again intoned in a grave voice and went on how his insurance could prevent that. This also caught Mikiseetee's sense of humour.

Both the "it's a doggie-dog world" and "no use crying over spilt milk" became Mikiseetee's go-to expressions where he would usually have said "ajurnaqmat", meaning "it cannot be helped" or "there is nothing that can be done about it". This Inuktitut expression is like a shoulder shrug when things happen outside of human control, from disasters and accidents down to even slight annoyances.

Much of what Mikiseetee found amusing was in response to odd sounds and repetitions. I found some similarities between what was found funny in my native German and Inuktitut.

On one occasion, I removed a bit of white gunk out of the corner of Mikiseetee's eye with a paper tissue. He looked at it and told me that it had a name in Inuktitut. I found this strange because I did not know what to call it in English and told him so.

He said, "This is a 'siqpi'."

I repeated it, sirk-pee, and he burst into laughter, not because I pronounced it wrong, but because it sounded so funny. His parents overheard us and also laughed.

I found our family's sense of humour quite engaging. Everyone loved to laugh and tease, sometimes embarrassing the teased person. Making fun of others was encouraged and whoever was being teased was compelled to accept it all in good spirits and not take offence. I was often the butt of teasing and laughter because of my mispronunciation of Inuktitut I was trying to learn. It took a long while for me to be able to take such teasing in good spirits.

My Sakikuluk's application for one of those newly built houses near the former graveyard was approved by the local housing association. Soon it was moving time. We were all to move into this brand new, fully insulated, four-bedroom house with all the amenities. It had hot and cold running water, a full bathroom, and was equipped with all the modern kitchen appliances as well as a washer and dryer set. We were not alone in this. Mikiseetee's oldest brother Bethuel's family were also moving to a similar house nearby. Our four new bedrooms were divided among us and Apphia was able to move into her own room with her new Qallunaq partner, and soon gave birth to their daughter.

Because our new room was large, I was able to move in a proper crib for Ruben. He had long outgrown the blue cradle that Papa had made for him. I was attempting to train Ruben to sleep by himself in his own bed, but this caused some strife between Mikiseetee and me, not to mention also my Sakikuluk. I was still breast feeding and was hoping soon to be able to wean my son from the breast. He was already two years old. But, with Mikiseetee and my Sakikuluk both not liking such Qallunaq handling of my son, I knew it was an uphill battle as long as we lived in my parents-in-law's house.

One day, during the time I was working for the sewing group, Mikiseetee stopped by to tell me some news.

He told me, "Your father asked me to work for him and I said I would."

Now he will work for his father-in-law, my Papa. He was to train as a sea-ice technician and would work together with Koonark, his uncle.

Koonark had worked with Papa for several years already and functioned as a crew-boss for building and general equipment maintenance.

The most important part of Mikiseetee's duties was to carefully auger out sea-ice cores, long cylinder-shaped ice logs, taken from designated spots to transport back to the laboratory for examination, cutting, and testing. He was also to change temperature and wind-speed charts at certain locations.

Mikiseetee had already agreed, but I let him know that I was not completely happy with this arrangement. I felt it was a manoeuvre on Papa's part to control his grandson's life as well as ours. Papa probably meant well, but I was somewhat wary. I was happy about the steady wage and the ample time Mikiseetee was allowed for hunting while on

Mikiseetee preparing equipment for lab sampling 1978.

the job, but I felt uneasy about it, too. I decided to wait and see how things would develop.

Now that Mikiseetee could count on a decent monthly wage, we started talking over getting a small house for ourselves, to live away from his parents. One deciding reason was that Mikiseetee did not get along with the Qallunaq man with whom my sister-in-law shared her room. Mikiseetee was especially chagrined on those occasions when this man bragged and teased him about how he, the Qallunaq, was able to catch a seal while Mikiseetee, "the great Inuit hunter", as he mockingly called him, came home empty-handed. Of course, Mikiseetee did not answer him but I could see his face darkening and how his initial indifference to this man was hardening into intense dislike. Since my sister-in-law and her Qallunaq common-law husband were caring for our elders and the rest of the family at home, we thought it an opportune time to apply to the local housing association for our own house. And that is what we did. We knew that we would probably have to wait a long time before we got a decision on our application.

By this time, my Sakikuluk and her husband were noticeably aging. My Sakikuluk began to lose her ability to see enough to sew and began to move about more painfully. My Sakialuk no longer went hunting and had given up his sled dog team, although he did keep a few dogs, staking them out up hill in the fall and then down near the shore beside the mid-town creek after the snow had melted in the spring. His main worry in life these days seemed to be his supply of tobacco. I noticed when we moved away from House 69, that Sakialuk had many rusty old tobacco tins full of used cigarette ends he had saved over the years in case Mittimatalik ever ran out of tobacco altogether. During times shortly before the arrival of the annual sea-lift supply ship for the HBC, when tailor-made cigarettes and tobacco had long run out at the store, my Sakialuk stuffed his pipe with his hoarded bits of tobacco and smiled at those who suffered temporary tobacco withdrawal. We all still smoked cigarettes during these years and found it so difficult to quit. It was actually good for us to take a break from smoking like this each summer.

In 1978 my son Ruben turned two years old while we still lived with my Sakikuluk. That year we had a summer of visitors. My sister Ursula came first with her little son, Bjorn, who was then three years old. She stayed in the room I had used in Papa's house when I first came to Mittimatalik. Mama had sent her an amautik from Mittimatalik when her son Bjorn was born three years before and she used it here during her visit. She told me that, back off the east coast of Vancouver Island, having her son on her back in an amautik when he was still so small made it so much easier for her to row her boat from her island home to the town wharf in Tofino where she did her shopping.

I think I adopted my new lifestyle in Mittimatalik because I wanted a bit of that pioneering back-to-the-land that my youngest sister had found on that tiny island off the east coast of Vancouver Island a few years before. The idea of roughing it in the wilds was an ideal we had both fallen for, each in our own ways.

Ursula brought some of her silver and jewellery-making tools and tried to show Mikiseetee how to work silver wire into jewellery. It was not something that caught his fancy, but I was intrigued. She also sewed a little doll wearing a red duffel amautik as a gift for our Mama. It was a real piece of art, I thought. My extended Inuit family were enchanted with Ursula and she often visited at my Sakikuluk's house where Mikiseetee, Ruben and I still lived.

During Ursula's visit, Mikiseetee decided that we, that is, he and I with Ruben along with my niece Letia, were to camp for a week at Nallua. It was prime sealing time for catching silver jar and we were anxious to have as many sealskins for sale to augment our income as well as provide skins for clothing and food for the family. By this time, I had my own agvik that Mikiseetee had made for me from kitchen countertop material and I had my own large flensing ulu made by my Sakialuk. Mikiseetee had also made a regular-sized one for me. In camp, I did not use the big wooden stretcher frames for my sealskins. I brought along a bag of foot-long wooden pegs that I had prepared at home. I pegged out my flensed and washed sealskins on the ground, hammering in the wooden pegs all around the skins with a rock as I had seen done by my sisters-in-law. I enjoyed doing skins in camp because it gave me something useful to do when my son was napping.

Because we now had a child, Mikiseetee brought along a heater so we would be warm enough inside our tent. The weather was not always sunny and often we had cold rainy days, and sometimes even summer snow. After a few days, Mikiseetee announced that he had to return to Mittimatalik for more ammunition and gasoline for his snowmobile and

Papa playing with his grandsons, my nephew Bjorn on his back; Mikiseetee watching Ruben 1978.

Mikiseetee and Ruben on our hunting trip 1978.

would return the next day. Ruben and I were to stay behind. I knew how to operate the propane camp stove and the heater and felt confident we would be all right while Mikiseetee was gone. As soon as he left, the sunny weather turned. It began to rain, so I moved my flensing equipment into my tent and lit the heater. Ruben went to sleep and I continued working my sealskin. After a while, I began to feel sick, but I ignored that. I wanted get done flensing the skin.

The next thing I knew, my niece was shaking my shoulder. She had come in and saw that I had passed out and that the heater was smoking. She ran out and got my sister-in-law who helped to get Ruben and me out of the tent. By then I knew that the fumes from the heater had made me sick. I was afraid that Ruben had also been affected, but then saw that, thankfully, he was not. My guess is that my head was a few feet above his while he slept, so I had been affected more. I wondered about the fuel in my heater. Usually, we used naphtha, a clean-burning fuel, for the heater which was normally safe and did not affect me. But naphtha was very expensive. I did see Mikiseetee draw fuel from the tank that fed our furnace at our house. That was diesel fuel and I had wondered why, what was that for. Did Mikiseetee put diesel fuel into our camp heater? When he returned the next day, I asked him about it.

Rest stop, snowmobile overheating 1978.

Ruben and I inside our tent 1978.

"I did," he said. "I didn't think anything of it. I was just trying to save money."

Now he knew that using diesel fuel in a camp heater was dangerous, that we might asphyxiate, and was not a safe way to save money. I later learned that other families decanted diesel fuel for their camp heaters without suffering ill effects. I seemed to be the only one so sensitive. I began to yearn for a qulliq that I could use in camp for slow cooking and heating, reserving the propane stove for quick cooking and making tea. That way we could live without a camp heater altogether.

Returning to Mittimatalik. I was overjoyed to be able to see my

sister and my little nephew once again before they left for their tiny island home off Tofino on Vancouver Island.

Ruben at camp 1978.

Mikiseetee caught some geese 1978.

Ruben and his father's seal 1978.

Twenty-two

In the summer of 1978, after we had returned from camp, my Papa and Ataata Mari completed arrangements for the second exchange visit between the people of Mittimatalik and Qaanaq, Greenland. The first such exchange trip happened perhaps a year before my arrival in Mittimatalik in 1974. Qaanaq is situated across the bay from the Thule Airbase, of Second World War fame, a staging site in Greenland for the American air force.

Ataata Mari was at that time working on a genealogical table for his book about the Qillaq saga, mentioned in the writings of the explorer Hall about a hundred years before. Ataata Mari spelled the name as Qitdlaq in his book. Qillaq had been a shaman from south Baffin Island who led a large party of Inuit from the northeastern coast of Baffin Island on a legendary expedition over the ice to the north-western coast of Greenland in the area around present-day Qaanaq. The journey must have taken years.

These visitors stayed in Qaanaq area for several years. They made an attempt to return to Baffin Island but that was aborted when a murder interfered. Qumangaapik, Merqusaaq and three other relatives returned to Greenland where they remained. There had been some Inuit-style inter-marriage between the Canadian Inuit and Greenlandic Inughuit resulting in children that bound them all in kinship. My parents-in-law and their children are listed in Ataata Mari's genealogical charts as descendants of the Canadian Inuit who returned, and the Greenlandic Inughuit with whom they were affiliated.

Mikiseetee had participated in the first Qaanaq exchange trip and now looked forward to seeing his Greenlandic relatives come to

Games about to begin in Qaanaq 1978.

Mittimatalik on this second exchange trip while I was to go to Qaanaq with our two-year-old Ruben. Because Papa had assisted Ataata Mari with the flight and other arrangements for this charter, I was allowed a free seat on the plane. Papa also arranged for me and little Ruben to board as guests of a Danish scientist and his schoolteacher wife at their modern house in Qaanaq. I had heard that many Qaanaq people lived in impoverished houses like we did in Mittimatalik, but, instead of indoor honey buckets that we had, they used outhouses, even in winter. I was grateful and looked forward to staying in a house with indoor plumbing. I'd had enough of exposing my backside to the elements at camp for that year already.

Our Qaanaq visit went well. The local people planned daily events held in honour of their Mittimatalik visitors.

The day after our arrival, we visitors were taken as a group on a guided tour of the town. We viewed the medical clinic and dispensary. I was surprised to find not only a nurse, but also a doctor living in a building attached to the clinic. Only the patients who were too sick beyond their doctor's capabilities were sent away to hospital in Nuuk, we were told.

Attached to the doctor's house was a small operating theatre and a patient's ward that held ten beds.

Then we said hello to the elders who were housed in their group home that provided all the needs for those no longer able to live at home.

The power plant and administration buildings were next. There was an impressive modern school, too, that we looked into.

Finally, we were shown the exterior of a rowhouse separated into the special apartment units for young people who no longer lived with their parents. Mittimatalik did not have a special place for its elders nor for its young people, nor did it have the services of a real doctor. These were things we could aspire to in Mittimatalik.

In the section of Qaanaq known locally as the upper town, we saw newer houses equipped with plumbing and amenities. These had two-storeys with peaked roofs, not like the new single storey ranch-style

Dog sled race, Qaanaq 1978.

house we now lived in at home in Mittimatalik. There were many more older houses in the lower town that were very similar to our shacks, except that here, they each had their outhouses behind them. Many of these houses also had their dog teams staked close to the house and we had to be careful where we walked. A few hunters had a Danish version of a snowmobile, but most still used dog teams for hunting and transportation. There were many skin kayaks to be seen up off the ground on raised platforms, something we did not see in Mittimatalik anymore. I was told the Mittimatalik ancestors had actually taught the Qaanaq people how to build and use the kayak.

There were organized dances held every night at the Qaanaq community hall. Dog team races and games on the ice were held during the day for the length of our stay. When not attending these events, I walked around and looked about. I saw people carving outside and made some friends with what little Inuktitut I had learned in Mittimatalik. The older people who had been identified to me as relatives seemed to understand me when I spoke, but I did not understand them. This caused some embarrassment and a lot of laughter.

This trip was the first extended period of time that Ruben had ever spent alone with me. He fussed and cried much of the time so I thought he must sorely miss his grandparents. I tried to distract him in any way I could and found a solution when I visited the home of Orfik Duneq, a

Winner of the dog sled race wearing polar bear fur pants, Qaanaq 1978.

Qaanaq relative. The first time we met, Orfik had just come in from the hunt and was still wearing his furry polar bear pants. He asked to hold his little relative Ruben on his lap and I tipped him out of my amautik into his arms.

Ruben stopped crying right away. He was fascinated by Orfik's thick polar bear fur silapaak. There seemed to be an instant connection between my son and this middle-aged Inughuit hunter.

At Orfik's house, I noted that the tea cups and mugs were placed on the floor when the visitors were done drinking their tea. The schoolteacher I boarded with told me that in Qaanaq people did this to prevent the spread of tuberculosis. By putting the cups and mugs on the floor, everyone knows not to use them again until after they have been properly washed. Washing cups and mugs was also a bit different from what I was used to. Water was boiled in a great pot on the stove and detergent added. Then the cups and mugs were immersed and left to simmer for a few minutes. Then they were lifted out by their handles using a wooden spoon and set out on a rack placed over a tray to air dry. When dry, they were put away or put out for use.

I visited the Qaanaq community store and found grocery items with Danish and even German labels. I could read some of the Danish and, of course, all of the German, so I had no problem in knowing the contents of cans and boxes. I even found Earl Grey tea, a tea that I enjoy more than the orange pekoe available in Mittimatalik and bought a supply to take home with me. I also found plastic pants for babies, then the rage in Europe, that buttoned at the sides and held diaper pads. In Canada, plastic-plus-paper diapers like Pampers, were being used but they were too expensive for us, although I did have a small supply for use for when we travelled. I could adapt this new style I found in Qaanaq by folding cloth diapers to form pads and lining them with throw-away wiping cloths. The plastic pants I had been using had elastic binding at the leg and waist openings that chafed Ruben's tender skin. I bought three pairs of the new plastic pants to take home. I was looking forward to the ease of use of this new diapering system at home.

One evening at the house where I was boarding, the schoolteacher was preparing our supper. The scientist and his teacher wife had two children and two of my visiting Mittimatalik relatives had been invited, at the last minute, to share our dinner. I smelled delicious meat frying and went to the kitchen to ask what meat it was. Instead of giving me a straight answer, the teacher said she was a little worried about that.

"I heard that Mittimatalik people do not eat whale meat and it is whale meat that I am preparing," she said. "I bought it at the store just for us at home. What should I do?"

"They are your guests," I said. "You have gone to some trouble to cook for them. I think it will be all right."

The food was served and everyone thoroughly enjoyed it. My relatives asked for second helpings of the meat.

After they had finished it all, one of them said, "The beef tasted very good. Thank you."

"Oh, but it was not beef. That was whale meat," said the teacher.

Both relatives were suddenly angry with me because they had unknowingly eaten whale meat that was, they said, taboo for them, not permitted by tradition. I had not known about this suddenly revealed taboo. But I knew that all the people of Qaanaq ate whale meat of all kinds regularly and had assumed there would be no problem. Years later, I found that this Mittimatalik taboo was a local thing, not throughout Nunavut. Because they did not get sick and nothing bad happened to their families back home during our time away, these relatives forgave me for not giving them forewarning about the whale meat. Luckily, we had daily news from Mittimatalik because Papa had sent along a field radio for the scientist to keep in touch.

Finally, the last day of our visit arrived and we were about to leave. Those of us who could afford it, had bought souvenirs at their little gift shop, a little shack they opened only for tourists. As a memento, I bought a small white ceramic plaque with a blue Greenlandic logo showing a tusked narwhal and a star. Ruben's relatives whom I discovered in Qaanaq gave me gifts: a small colourful beaded mat, a miniature ivory-handled sewing ulu, a highly polished bear head pendant carved from walrus tooth, and a white dog skin for nuilak, among other things.

While waiting at the field radio at the scientist's house for word about the expected arrival of the airplane that was to take us home, I was told a Qallunaq man, who said his name was Kenn Harper, wanted to talk to me. I went to find out how I could help. Kenn Harper's request was to ask my father to let him board the plane back to Mittimatalik, that he would pay later. I went on the radio and asked Papa. He said no, the flight was only for charter members returning to Mittimatalik. No others were allowed because of international visa regulations between Canada and Greenland for this special charter exchange. I had to turn Kenn Harper down and I could see that he was very disappointed when he left the house. At the time, I thought, "Poor man, stuck in Qaanaq."

Today Kenn Harper is a respected writer and historian of Inuit, author of *Minik, the New York Eskimo* (1986 & 2000), *Thou Shalt Do No Murder* (2017) and the 5-volume series *In Those Days: Inuit and Explorers* (2022).

When we returned to Mittimatalik after a week away, I watched how my Sakikuluk and Ruben hugged each other with such joy, it left me feeling envious.

I had spoken with Mama about how I felt shunted aside from my son's affections by my Sakikuluk directing all details of Ruben's care. I had hoped that by spending more time alone with me, my son and I could form a closer relationship. This did not happen and Ruben was never happier than when we visited his ningiu. I could not deprive my son, so we visited every day as much as possible, even after Mikiseetee and I moved away from the old people.

Mama had tried to console me. "Every child has the right to know their grandparents. Your mother-in-law is getting older and will pass away. Then it will be your turn. In the meantime, do the best you can and don't give up."

I appreciated her words because I had been allowed to get to know my grandfather and great-grandmother when we were still living in Germany before we came to Canada. I knew how much it meant to have fond memories to carry me though a tough childhood.

On the Saturday of the Easter holiday weekend, Mikiseetee announced that we were going out baby-seal hunting because this was the time the mother seals begin to leave their newborns behind in a snow den connected to the seal's aglu while they hunted fish. I had seen baby seals in past years when they were brought to my Sakikuluk. Old people liked eating baby seal because their flesh was very tender and easy to chew. The baby ringed seal has thick tawny yellowish fur that looks a bit like sheep's fleece. This moults away as their fur grows in underneath. After moulting, the baby seal is called a "silver jar" because its fur shines like patches of bright polished silver.

Since it was Easter, I had a little joke going in my mind. In the rest of Canada, the Canadian Cancer Society had its annual Easter Seal fund-raising promotion where they provided sheets of perforated postage-stamp-like images of daffodil flowers. These stamps were known as seals and were used to solicit donations for the Canadian Lung Association. People used to stick them on their mailing envelopes after they donated. It was called the Easter Seal Campaign and was promoted by all Canadian media including television.

"Our Easter seal is not paper, it's the real thing," I told Mikiseetee. I was pleased that he got the joke and laughed.

A few days before we were to leave on this trip, someone had given our little son a dog, not quite a puppy, but still not yet fully grown. By this time, Ruben was three years old and could walk but he was still a little unsure around his new dog. Mikiseetee said we would take the dog along and tied a rope to its collar. He tied the other end to the last cross slat of the qamutik. We had loaded on a tent and bedding even though we were only planning to be out for the day. I wanted a place where I could breastfeed our little son in a protected shelter since he was not yet weaned. The sun was bright and the sky cloudless, but I knew that weather can change very quickly.

Holding Ruben in my lap, I sat on the qamutik facing back so I could watch the dog. Ruben was excited that his dog was coming with us. Mikiseetee revved up his snowmobile and the qamutik jerked forward. Mikiseetee thought to look back to how the dog was keeping up and saw that the dog was having trouble, being dragged a bit. We stopped and Mikiseetee picked up the dog and placed it on the qamutik with me and Ruben. I was to hold on to my son as well as this exhausted young dog. Mikiseetee, confident that he had solved the dog problem, jumped on his snowmobile and began to speed, pulling us along on the qamutik. The ice became rough and we bounced up and down, me holding on to the qamutik binding as well as my boy and his dog. Suddenly, the qamutik tipped a little to one side. I had only two arms, of course, and my main concern was that my son and I stay on the qamutik. The dog slipped out of my grasp. He fell off and, because the rope still connected him to the qamutik, he was dragged while we sped along. There was no way I could alert Mikiseetee so far

Ruben's dog skin 1978.

On our Easter Seal hunting trip 1978.

ahead on his noisy snowmobile. Before long I saw that the dog had given up trying to run. When we arrived where we were to camp on the ice beside an ice-locked iceberg, Mikiseetee was shocked to see the dog was dead.

"Why didn't you hold on to the dog better?' he demanded. "It's your fault our son's dog is dead."

"I have only two arms," I pointed out. "One arm I used to hold on to the qamutik binding to not fall off and the other I tried holding on to both our son and his dog. When we almost tipped over, it was either the dog or our son."

Poor Ruben cried about his dog, now dead.

After setting up our tent, Mikiseetee went off with Ruben to catch a baby seal. My little son forgot all about the dog in his excitement to go hunting with his father. Meanwhile, I skinned the dog and buried the body under a pile of snow.

When I went into the tent to make tea, I heard a strange thrumming, buzzing sound approaching the roof of the tent and then stop. There it was again, that same sound, except now it was leaving. I was curious what made this sound I had never heard before. I stepped out of the tent and I saw two large black ravens picking at where I had buried the dog carcass. I shooed them away and put our wooden grub box over it. The ravens could have the dead dog's body after we left, I thought. When I turned to go back into the tent, I saw another raven perched on the tent roof pole. Then it dawned on me. What I had heard was the air vibrating against the tent roof from the wingbeats of approaching and departing ravens.

Mikiseetee and Ruben soon came back with two dead baby seals and the three ravens flew off to line up on the edge of the iceberg. After drinking tea and eating some biscuits, we packed up our camp, tied the seals and dog skin to the qamutik with the rest of our gear. Ruben cried a little more about his dead dog and I promised to get him another one soon.

When Ruben and I went on the exchange trip to Qaanaq, I saw that most Inughuit people had dog fur as nuilak on their parka hoods rather than the white fox fur we used here. The Qaanaq women told me that dog fur was as good as wolf and did not wear out as quickly as fox fur usually does. When we arrived home, I flensed the dog skin, washed it and stretched it out on a piece of plywood to dry. A few days later, I worked the skin, cleaned and combed the fur and cut it into wide strips. I sewed these around Ruben's parka hood as nuilak. My little son was so happy to wear a bit of his dog on his clothing. We did eventually get him another dog, too.

❋

One day Ruben complained about having a toothache. I took him along with me to the new dental office at the nursing station where the new dental technician had opened his practice at the nursing station. This young Qallunaq had been a former HBC clerk who had married a local Inuit girl and had gone out for training to get his certification to be able to work as a dental technician in Mittimatalik. He examined and cleaned my teeth while Ruben sat on the floor playing with the toys I had brought along. After he was finished with my teeth, the dental technician looked at Ruben's teeth as well. Ruben was quite relaxed and unafraid. The dental therapist said that one of Ruben's teeth had a cavity, that it was the hole in his tooth causing him pain.

I said to Ruben, "We're going to let the dentist to fix your tooth."

Ruben nodded and sat up in the dentist chair without a worry. The dental technician asked him if he could fill the cavity for him. Ruben agreed and the technician went to work. It did not take long. When the dental technician had finished, he had to wake up Ruben. He had fallen asleep in the dentist chair while having his tooth filled, amazingly enough. I was so glad he did not fear dental work.

When I got home with Ruben, my Sakialuk telephoned. She had heard that I had taken him to the dentist. Word got around fast. She wanted me to bring him over to her house as soon as possible to comfort the poor little thing. I suppose she imagined that he had been made to suffer. I did as she asked.

When I entered the house with Ruben, she demanded, "Why did you take him to the dentist?"

I said, "He had a hole in his tooth that was causing him pain and needed fixing."

"You made him suffer more. What kind of mother makes her child suffer?" she went on.

"He would not get such holes in his teeth if he did not eat so many sugary treats, candy, chocolate, and soda pop. I would like him to have good strong teeth in order to eat our land foods, not like his cousins who have lost their teeth by the time they are three years old," said I.

There was a moment of silence.

Then I said, "I know you want to give him treats to show how much you love your little grandson. Maybe it would be better to give him fruit, like apples, oranges or bananas. Eating real fruit does not do so much damage to teeth."

I could see my Sakikuluk thinking.

Finally. she said, "Yes, you are right. And fruit is so much more expensive to get here than candy and pop. That is a perfect way to show everyone how much I love him."

I was happy that my Sakikuluk stopped being angry with me, especially when Ruben said he had not been hurt. He proudly showed her the shiny new filling on his tooth. And, she no longer gave Ruben candy, chocolate and soda pop. Instead, she gave him expensive fruit. Years later, Ruben told me that he used to trade his fruit for his cousins' candy and pop that he craved.

Twenty-three

When Ruben was three years old, we were living in our own little house. After more new houses had been completed, the local housing association board chose from all the applications to whom they would grant housing that previous fall. It felt like a competition, like a lottery, and the whole community paid attention. There was a definite lack of housing and many homes were severely overcrowded. In spite of that, I did so hope that we would get our own little house.

My hope at the time was that Mikiseetee would, in a home of his own without the constant sniping of his Qallunaq brother-in-law and his mother's criticisms, become more independent, self-reliant and self-confident. He now had a well-paying job that he said he enjoyed and he was showing signs of responsibility, I thought. And I thought, too, that I would be happier without having my every move monitored, commented upon and broadcast to the community by my Sakikuluk.

In November, three months before our son turned three years old, we heard that the Housing Association decided to award us that broken-down, two-room house down next to the crossroads on the way to my Papa's house. Mikiseetee and I were overjoyed. We could finally have a home of our own where Mikiseetee and I could live with our little son and become a family. I did not mind that there were no amenities, no running water, no flush toilet and no real bathroom. It had just an old fridge, the old diesel cook stove. I had experienced doing without already and knew what to expect. Luckily, we had kept the apartment-sized washer and dryer when we had moved to the new house up on the cemetery hill. These now eased my existence in our new little place.

But then our elation over this good fortune was severely dampened

Ruben and friend on my small snowmobile in front of our little house 1978.

by news of the suicide of a young local Inuit man while he was in Frobisher Bay. He had applied for a local house in the hope of being able to marry his girlfriend. She had told him he must have a house before she would marry him. When he heard that the Housing Association chose Mikiseetee instead of him for the next available house, he must have despaired. The poor guy killed himself. I tried to shrug off oppressive feelings. I tried my best to look forward to making a home for my little family in that little house.

Of course, now there was the problem of taking little Ruben up to see my Sakikuluk and Sakialuk every day, so we bought a little snow-mobile for me to use while Mikiseetee was at work with his, taking ice samples and changing weather charts for Papa's laboratory.

Of the young men trainees working for Papa, Quviq was the brightest learner. He was very resourceful and had single-handedly built a house for himself and his wife, Hannah, very modern and well-built. But the local government authorities, ever conscious of following the letter of the law in representing the Canadian federal government, had it torn down because it did not meet the exacting standards of the nationwide Canadian Building Code. Quviq was terribly upset and Papa tried to help him.

This was in vain because the Canadian Federal government now claimed ownership of all the land that Inuit had occupied for millennia. It had gradually established ownership of Inuit homelands during the time of the arctic explorers who had mapped and charted the land and sea using Inuit as their servants. Canadian government authority and control had been firmly established in Mittimatalik during that infamous Robert Janes trial.

Quviq's little self-built house had been state of the art: insulated and fully electrically wired, a model of ingenuity and applied building skills Quviq had picked up from constructing the administrator's and teacher's houses in Mittimatalik. Sadly, Quviq and Hannah were compelled to apply to the local Housing Association to be assigned a tiny, broken-down, un-insulated, two-room shack of a house, like so many of us.

In spite of this, Quviq and Hannah remained undaunted. As soon as they moved into their little rented hovel, they held their wedding. Quviq had sent away for a mail-order wedding ring for Hannah, but the ring's arrival had been delayed and he feared he would not have a ring for the wedding ceremony. When he told me about this, I lent him the plain gold ring inscribed with *gaudeamus igitur* (Latin: let us therefore rejoice) that I had used for my first marriage to Michael. When Mikiseetee and I married, we replaced that old ring and Mikiseetee was happy to see the other one gone. The wedding was held as planned. A few seasons passed but the new mail-order ring never did arrive, and we all forgot about it.

A year later, Hannah gave birth to twins, which proved to be a great challenge since they wanted to keep them both. According to Inuit custom, twins were usually separated at birth with only one staying with the birth mother while the other was custom-adopted out to relatives. Just before Christmas, Quviq and Hannah decided to travel to Arctic Bay to visit relatives. They brought along one child and left its twin with Hannah's mother. The little Twin Otter plane carrying them flew from Mittimatalik to Nanisivik, the new lead-zinc mining community that served as the airport for Arctic Bay.

By this time of year, there was no actual daylight. By all reports, there was a sudden white-out, strong winds whipping up blowing snow that obscured visibility and buffeted the little plane on that fateful December 21, 1977. Somehow, the pilot lost control of his plane while attempting to land and it crashed on the runway. Everyone, including the pilot, was killed as the plane exploded. We learned later that it was impossible to assemble bodies, so all human remains were buried in Nanisivik in a mass grave. Hannah's surviving baby, the twin she left behind, was raised by her mother.

We can often lose things, little valued keepsakes, and not know what became of them. But my first wedding ring, the one used when I married the first love of my life, was not lost or misplaced. I know it is buried in that mass grave in Nanisivk.

Quviq, Hannah, and their baby were not the only ones who died in Nanisivik that sad day. Also on that flight was Annie, the beloved daughter of Stephen Koonark.

Koonark was Mikiseetee's uncle and a lay minister at the Anglican Church. He also worked for my Papa. He was an older man so he functioned not only as Papa's building supervisor, but as a supervisor of trainees as well. He had learned carpentry when he was away from Mittimatalik at a mental hospital. He had been sent there with a diagnosis of schizophrenia. This diagnosis had been an error, it turned out, after a few years. He actually had epilepsy which was now easily controlled with medication, and he was sent home to his wife and children.

His wife had proven to be a superb hunter while her husband was away. She was also excellent in her sewing skills. At her side, I saw a sewing style of caribou kamiks that local people usually did not use anymore, as caribou kamiks here were only for those who had chronically sweaty feet and could not wear watertight sealskin kamiks.

The family had already weathered many serious setbacks.

The Nanisivik accident happened just a few days before Koonark's birthday, December 26, St. Stephen's Day, the day after Christmas Day, known today as Boxing Day. Instead of withdrawing from everyone to grieve the loss of his daughter, Koonark participated in celebrating his birthday at Papa's house and also attended the games, dances, and feasts held annually for Christmas week at the new community hall. He did not show his mourning, but I knew that he was suffering.

Once, during this time, when we were alone, I asked him, "I know you must be sad about losing your beloved daughter. Why do you put yourself through this?"

"It is Christmas. I am Christian and I am happy that my daughter is now in heaven with Jesus, born at this time. I must show other people that the death of my daughter does not change my beliefs, that I am still able to enjoy the most joyous Christian holiday of the year." He was, as ever, so patient with my ignorance.

The rest of the community affected by the deaths mourned more openly. The Anglican missionary's wife, Sheena, did not take the Nanisivik air crash disaster in stride. She quit her part-time job as air expeditor for Kenn Borek Airlines. It was on her watch that the crash took place and she had followed the pilot's words on the two-way radio at the Anglican manse just before the crash.

The following summer, she and her husband, Laurie, moved to Arctic Bay, and a new missionary came with his wife to serve the Anglican Church in Mittimatalik.

In the spring after the air accident, Mama asked me, during a visit, if I would work for them at the laboratory as an instructor for their trainees. She said she was worried about Mikiseetee's relationship with Papa, that often Mikiseetee did not seem to understand what Papa wanted him to do, and perhaps, my being there would help. I thought it over and finally agreed. Since Mikiseetee and I were challenged to support ourselves as a little family, I thought working at the lab would be better than the part-time jobs I was doing for the sewing group Sanaugataarvik, my occasional tutoring, and doing skins for sale. Also, I knew that a local group of women had received funding and a house to operate a new daycare centre. I could leave Ruben there while I went to work, I thought. That sounded reasonable to me as it was what I would have done, were I living in southern Canada, the accepted way of a working woman.

I arranged a spot for Ruben at the daycare centre, left him there, and went to work at Papa's laboratory, happy that everything was working out so well. It was then a great revelation when I went to pick up Ruben after work a few days later. No one noticed me when I entered the house. I saw, and heard, a group of women gathered around little Ruben, playing with him and laughing, while all the other little children were ignored, some crying and unhappy. I understood immediately that my little son was being preferred and spoiled by these women who adored him as a little "half-breed". I could not allow that, I knew. And, then, later that day when I took him up to see his grandmother, she scolded me for putting him into daycare while I worked.

"I put him into daycare because I knew you have been suffering with your health," I said.

"Never mind about my health," she said. "Bring him to stay with me when you go to work."

Sarahme and I in the lab with our children 1979.

The next day, I arranged with my parents that I work only half-days at the lab so I could leave my son with my Sakikuluk for only a few hours each day. That arrangement worked well for a few days until my sister-in-law Joanna, decided to scold me for "nearly killing" my mother-in-law by burdening her with the care of my son while I worked. I had not yet experienced an Inuit scolding session.

Joanna did not speak English so her words were translated for me as she spoke her scolding words. I tried to explain but I was shushed. I had to wait until Joanna finished her rant which took about an hour. I was dismayed because Joanna and I had been such good friends and had often laughed together. She was obviously convinced that I needed to be shown the error of my ways and had to be set right.

When she finished, I told her that my Sakikuluk had demanded that I bring Ruben to her while I worked and that I could not refuse my mother-in-law. I told her I had tried to put him into the new local daycare while I worked, but the women who worked there only spoiled him while ignoring the other children. Joanna agreed that the daycare was not good for Ruben. We visited my Sakikuluk together and heard her mother declare that she did really want to have Ruben with her as much as possible, regardless of her health. It took a while, but Joanna and I resumed our friendship. It was a lesson in the customary Inuktitut scolding that deeply impressed me.

At the weather station in 1974, all the trainees, including me, were trained to use the commercial band of two-way radio and Morse code for air traffic control. At the end of training, we all received our official commercial radio licences. I found it difficult to hear, but everyone had problems hearing using the radio with all the radio static and other noise disruptions. What helped me the most was that radio transmissions were usually kept short. Somehow, by judicious guessing and spelling out incomprehensible words using the "Alpha, Beta, Charlie" alphabet system, I got by all right, almost as well as did the others. My parents used commercial two-way radio with their home office in St. Catharines to save on the cost of long-distance telephone charges. Now, as part of my work duties, I took on the weekly radio transmissions to transfer payroll information to Papa's secretary in St. Catharines.

My work duties in the laboratory were to show trainees how to use the new, vastly expensive, auto-salinometer, the AutoSal. We sawed the cylindrical ice cores into uniform sample disks, placing them in clean beakers to melt, and, after melting, placing a drop of the melt water on a slide for the handheld salinometer, reading the results three times and manually recording the salinities of water samples. We compared the

Papa teaching Sarahme in the lab 1979.

Koonark shaving on an extended hunting/sampling trip 1979.

results using the handheld salinometer and the AutoSal. I also showed trainees the proper cleaning of lab glassware as well as how to do titrations and other technical water testing procedures.

Papa's lab was the first place in Mittimatalik to use the new personal computer that had been recently made available to the public in southern Canada. The personal computer at that time was still quite complicated to use. Because I knew nothing about using the new computers, Papa and Mama trained two of the young women trainees how to use the computer to log the raw sea-ice information data into the computer.

I held information sessions on basic ocean science, like why the sea is salt, how the phases of the moon affect the tides, how ocean currents work, and so on. I actually enjoyed the work and made a friend of Sarahme with whom I worked every day.

While working in the lab, I discovered the reason for the misunderstandings between Mikiseetee and Papa. I observed how Papa would tell Mikiseetee what to do in English. Usually Koonark, his uncle, with whom he normally went to collect the ice cores, was beside them. Koonark did not understand English fluently. After Papa had left them, I overheard as Koonark asked Mikiseetee what the Sikulirijit, the person in charge of the sea-ice, as my Papa was called, had told him to do. Mikiseetee told Koonark and he responded that Mikiseetee should not do it the way the Sikulirijit had said. Koonark proceeded to tell him how he thought the task should be done. Later, there was unhappiness because Mikiseetee had not done the task the way Sikulirijit had instructed. At home, I asked Mikiseetee why he followed Koonark's instructions and not those of Sikulirijit.

"Koonark is my uncle, older than my father-in-law, so he is the elder to whom I must listen," he said.

I reported this to my parents. They could hardly believe what they heard from me and asked Ataata Mari if this could be true. Ataata Mari said that what I had told them was the traditional Inuit way. From then on, when Papa wanted Mikiseetee to do anything at all, he made sure that he told Koonark, with Mikiseetee translating his English to Inuktitut, and then Koonark repeated these same instructions to Mikiseetee in Inuktitut. That way, Koonark would always agree with Sikulirijit on how things were to be done. It was a simple way of compromising and saving face.

Mikiseetee's first polar bear, with Koonark 1979.

Before Mikiseetee and I moved into our own house, I had read a notice in an edition of *Inuktitut* magazine, at that time an English and Inuktitut publication provided by the Indian and Northern Affairs Canada, that called for submissions to Things That Make Us Beautiful jewellery-making competition conducted in Ottawa by the Inuit Art Section of the Museum of Man. I thought that, together, Mikiseetee and I could make a necklace for submission. He carved a pair of tiny ivory seals and a larger centre pendant ivory owl. I prepared and polished seal claws and Mikiseetee pierced them. I strung the claws and pendants symmetrically interspersed with red glass beads on waxed nylon thread, finishing the necklace with a commercially made clasp. We were pleased with the necklace we had made together and sent it in to the contest.

A few months went by before news about the contest reached us. We were by then living in our little house and both employed. We received a letter written in Inuktitut syllabics as well as in English, which I read very carefully, saying that our entry had not won or even placed in the contest. The people who ran the contest gave a thorough critique of our submitted necklace. I drew several conclusions from the information. Although they liked the little pendants and the use of seal claws, we should not have used glass beads, nylon thread or commercial fittings. Another criticism was the way the seal claws were placed on the necklace, with their points digging into the skin if heavy clothing were worn over the necklace. The end of the letter invited us to make another submission to this contest. Because there had been such a low response to the first contest, they were running it again and gave a new deadline. Mikiseetee by this time had lost interest in making another necklace and said I could do the next one by myself if I wanted to.

I tried my hand at carving tiny seals, but they did not turn out very well. I thought out a new design that did not use any animal figures, using instead, oblong lozenges carved from caribou antler that polished up in a muted pink colour. I made ivory beads from the tiny tusks found embedded in narwhal skulls that Mikiseetee had given me. This ivory was much softer and easier to carve. Rather than using waxed nylon thread for my necklace, I decided I would use narwhal sinew thread that I had made.

Out on the floe edge on Baffin Bay where we had gone narwhal hunting that June, I cut away narwhal sinew from the back of a narwhal carcass, scraped it, rinsed it in sea water to remove the blood and dried it. Then I twisted the sinew into sewing thread. I'd had some practice at twisting sinew thread for the women who were sewing a walrus hide umiak, women's boat, and a sealskin kayak, the previous summer. These women told me that braided sinew thread would tear the skin as it dried on waterproof skin boats while the twisted sinew would not. Twisted sinew looked like a miniature version of modern rope and would not wear the beads I made, unlike braided sinew with its saw-tooth edges.

I collected discarded seal paws left behind when women flensed their skins and carefully skinned the paws. I then boiled them down to get a few sets of curved seal claws. I pierced each claw through the front of the claw at the top so that the claw would lie sideways, like a comma shape against the skin. This was a definite challenge as often the claw would split while I made the piercing. I finally had two sets of five matching black seal claws that I hand polished to a high gloss.

I was almost all set to build my necklace. I had the twisted sinew, beads, seal claws, but now that left the problem of how to close the necklace artfully without using a commercially made clasp. I experimented around a bit and finally settled on a loop at one end of the necklace and lozenge at the other end, both carved from pinkish caribou antler. The lozenge fitted through the loop and sat crosswise against it, closing the necklace. I finally finished this novel catch and assembled the new necklace. Mikiseetee was away on a hunt, so I showed my new necklace to my Sakikuluk.

"No one wants a necklace made of Inuit material. I think you are just wasting your time," she said.

Mikiseetee and I had given our glass bead necklace to Mama. She knew how disappointed Mikiseetee was that it had been criticized and rejected by the contest judges. When she saw my new necklace of all Inuit materials, she praised it, especially the catch.

"I just followed their recommendations," I said, and sent it off by registered mail.

A few months later, I received a letter from The Things That Make Us Beautiful contest. I had won the prize for design. I was overjoyed. They sent me a glossy, letter-sized photograph of my winning necklace and a cheque for seven hundred and fifty dollars as prize money. I really appreciated the money with which I bought a synthetic insulated sleeping bag for low temperatures and a new parka also with synthetic insulation. It was a relief to have these things without feathers to which I am so allergic. Up to then, I just had to suffer itching and sneezing and now I could be warm in comfort while camping or travelling over the ice.

Mikiseetee and my Sakikuluk were astonished that my necklace actually won this contest. My Sakialuk just smiled around his pipe. My Papa was truly impressed. I was a little nervous about being not Inuit born, but the contest organizers assured me that I was considered Inuit by law because I was legally married to an Inuk, thereby taking on my husband's ethnic status. The meant that I could sell my artwork under

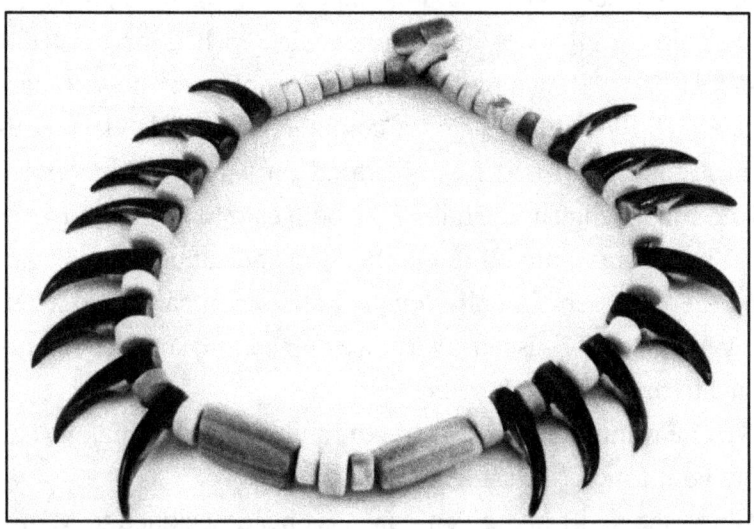

My necklace, 1979, now in the Canadian Museum of History.

my own "Inuit tag", a government trademark designator of authentic Inuit-made art. The contest-winning necklace was lodged in the Inuit art section of the Museum of Man in Ottawa, and later moved to the Museum of Civilization in Hull, Quebec, just across the Ottawa River. Today, this museum is known as the Canadian Museum of History and they still have it in their collection. I was told in 2004 that it is an important "transition piece" of Inuit artwork. I suppose this referred to the changes in Inuit art from traditional to modern and that my piece was poised somewhere between them.

I thought it was wonderful that a thing I had made would be purchased by a museum. This is the dream of every artist, I think. I had wanted to become an artist since I was a little girl and there I was, an artist/craftsperson with an actual piece in a museum. In my elation, I could not resist bragging a little to my first husband, Michael, the artist who replaced me with another woman. I still had the telephone number of his studio and I dialed the telephone.

"Hello," said Michael. I was surprised at how good it was to hear his voice.

I told him my news and he congratulated me. I told him I now had a little three-year-old son, that I was now the mother I had wanted to be. I asked if he was still with that woman with whom he had replaced me.

"No," he said. "I left her in the Yukon. She wanted to stay north, but that did not work for me."

He then told me that he'd had an awakening. Two people he loved had recently died: his beloved grandfather and his best friend, Ray. Ray had been murdered, he said, shot in Nova Scotia a few months past.

I could hear that he was crying when he said, "I made such a bad mistake in setting you aside. I'm so sorry for hurting you."

He said that he wanted me back, he would pay the airfare, and he would even accept my son. How heart-wrenching for me to hear these words.

I said, "It's too late. I cannot. I made promises, not only to Mikiseetee, but also to his mother and my son. I cannot break these promises. I must see this new life of mine to its end. I am so sorry."

By this time, I was also in tears because I had to deny him, he whom I had loved so long. We sadly ended the conversation. My elation at winning the contest and getting my work into the museum was spent.

That's what I get for trying to brag, I thought.

Twenty-four

Life with Mikiseetee at this time was better in some ways but not all perfect. He allowed himself to relax and be himself at home, went hunting regularly for our meat and generally seemed more self-confident. But, since moving away from my Sakikuluk's house into our own little home, Mikiseetee also became more liberated in drinking alcohol at home, something he never did at his mother's house. Binge-drinking became Mikiseetee's way. He would order liquor through the local alcohol committee that controlled incoming alcohol. He had friends on that committee, I later learned. His liquor order arrived by airplane the same time that all the other liquor orders arrived. For two days or so, the entire town had drunken men and women staggering around until all the liquor had been consumed. I was always so relieved after the alcohol had all been drunk and things got back to normal.

While we still lived with my parents-in-law, it had been my practice at my Sakikuluk's urging to follow Mikiseetee to wherever he went when he was drinking. It was often very unpleasant because I did not drink and did not share in the drinkers' sense of fun. Still, I knew that Ruben was being cared for by his grandparents while I was away from home. Now that we had our own little house, I found it very difficult to protect my husband as well as my son at the same time at all hours of the day and night.

Since Mikiseetee and I were now both working for Papa, I was now often too tired to do good work the next day because I had been up most of the night before. And, it was so difficult to tell Papa that Mikiseetee would not go to work that day or the next and not be able to tell him why. It was during his drunken bouts that Mikiseetee complained to me about working for his Qallunaq father-in-law. It did no good, my reminding him that I had tried to stop him from taking the job. He would get angry and say that he had no choice because he was forced by Inuit custom to obey his father-in-law, his son's grandfather, as well as his mother, and uncle Koonark,

I usually discouraged drunken visitors, but sometimes that did not work. So it happened that I was often grabbed and manhandled by Mikiseetee's friends. I had to rely on Mikiseetee to protect me and that often put me in danger when he passed out. Somehow, I managed but I do not know how.

At Christmas time that first year in our own home, Mikiseetee had spent a few days and nights in a drunken uproar and I had followed him around from place to place as he searched out his drinking buddies, looking for more booze. I was concerned about my Sakikuluk caring for my little son at a time when she was really not in good health. It was my task to prepare the annual family Christmas feast at my Sakikuluk's house, turkey and all the trimmings. I was exhausted from lack of sleep and emotional uproar for the last few days and nights. When the feast was ready, I went to lie down and put my feet up for a few minutes, but dropped into a deep sleep. I awoke with Ruben trying to wake me. And then Mikiseetee came into the room, grabbed me by the shoulders, and shook me hard. My Sakikuluk heard Ruben's crying and stopped

Mikiseetee from waking me. She chased him from the room. She knew how exhausted I was and let me drop back to sleep. The family had the Christmas feast I had prepared without me.

One evening a few months later in our new home, I had just put Ruben to sleep when my Sakikuluk called me, asking me why I had not gone along with Mikiseetee who, she heard, was out and about drinking.

"I must go to work tomorrow and I need my sleep," I said.

"You should be with your husband. What if he gets hurt or killed?"

"Then that will happen with or without me," I said. I paused, then continued, "You do believe in God, don't you?"

"Yes," she said, "Of course, I do."

"I do, too. I must leave Mikiseetee in God's hands and maybe you can, too?" I asked.

"Yes," she said sadly and hung up the telephone.

During that summer, my parents asked Mikiseetee and me to stay at their house, to house-sit, while they travelled to southern Canada. The house-sitting went well until a few days before their return. A large liquor order had just arrived and Mikiseetee went off drinking with his buddies.

I went to sleep with my son beside me on my parents' bed and the room was dark. I was awakened during the night. Mikiseetee was on top of me, forcing himself on me. I could not see his face but I could smell the alcohol on him. But something was not right. I felt the T-shirt against my breasts, and thought it odd that Mikiseetee would be wearing his clothes in bed as he usually slept naked or in his shorts. And he did not kiss me and that also felt strange to me. Was this really Mikiseetee? And then, suddenly, he was gone.

I jumped off the bed and ran out after him but he was already out the door. I could hear a snowmobile motor revving and watched as it disappeared over the hill. By this time, I was fully awake and went to drink some water to help me calm down. I wiped myself and this did not smell like my husband. I was suddenly very certain this had not been Mikiseetee at all. I knew that some of his buddies wanted a turn at me and I was afraid that I had been traded off for booze. A few moments later, there was Mikiseetee in his parka at the door, smiling from ear to ear and, of course, drunk. He was in a good mood for a change, unusual because he usually became angry with me when drunk.

"Were you just here?" I asked.

"Oh," he hesitated. "Well," he paused, "Yes." Another pause. "Why do you ask?"

He seemed to have a thought. "Yes. Yes, I was," he said.

I knew that he had gone to one of his uncles' places to drink the night before. The next day, this uncle came to visit at my parent's house while Mikiseetee was sleeping off his hangover. This uncle was an older man who regularly worked in the oil fields and was known as a big drinker. Many local women were afraid of him, I knew. He had never visited us at our home before, so I was surprised when he came into my parents' house.

"So how are you feeling today? Did you enjoy your husband last night?" he asked, grinning. "Is he at home?"

It had been this man, I knew. I was stunned and appalled.

"Mikiseetee is here, but I must ask you to leave," I said, barely controlling my anger. Thankfully he left right away.

My parents arrived a few days later and I talked it over with Mama. I told her I had been raped a few days before at her house and I even knew who did it. She advised me against going to the law. She reminded me that I was new to the community and new to Inuit culture, that I had volunteered to live among them, and I would find no sympathy among the Qallunaat police and government officials. And, the man who raped me would surely deny the accusation. My morals were already under scrutiny because I had chosen an Inuk for my husband. Drawing attention to myself by calling rape, would ruin what was left of my reputation. Mama said I should take as many showers as I needed to and pray that I was not pregnant. She also suggested going to the nursing station for a test of sexually transmitted diseases.

I did just that because I knew she was telling me the truth. I would not find sympathy and I would be hurt more than just by being raped. In those days, laying rape charges was very traumatic for the rape victim, and law courts did not deal well with such victims. It was just another of those things one had to accept and overcome. Ajurnaqmat. I had the sexually transmitted diseases test done at the nursing station. I had not caught anything and, thankfully, I did not become pregnant either.

Mikiseetee and I did not speak about this incident. I knew also that even if I were pregnant from the rape, he would just accept whatever child was produced as his own. Not a big deal for him, I knew, as every Inuit hunter wanted as many children as possible to validate his hunt.

The following spring, I had completed modifying my new, standard white, prospector's tent for use in our annual summer camp. I had inspected other tents that I admired while out camping. I wanted a tent in which I could stand upright. Because we used big rocks to hold down the sides, front, and back panels of the tent, a normal prospector's tent lost a few feet in height forcing those over five feet tall to stoop to clear the roof. I also wanted an area for storage at the back of my tent. I bought yards and yards of tent canvas and set to work with my sewing machine.

I first made a model out of paper to get an idea of what shapes I would need. I then measured the existing tent, unravelled the back roof and back panels. I then cut five long triangles and flat panels and sewed them onto that tent to form the rounded storage area when erected. After that, I sewed a long, two-way, heavy-duty zipper to the front flap opening that could be opened at both the top as well as the bottom. That would be handy to be able to look out without opening the tent altogether, letting in the cold air at ground level. Then I added a broad panel all around the bottom of my tent on which the rocks could be placed without shortening the height of the tent. Making these modifications to my tent made it the envy of all who saw it.

My Papa, in a generous mood, donated a large nylon rain fly which could be suspended over the tent. That was very handy because it often rained. The rain fly provided more protected space for outside storage and Mikiseetee kept his rifles and ammunition under it. I liked that better than having the rife and ammunition inside the tent. Mikiseetee was very proud of our wonderful modified tent, too.

Some summer nights in camp were quite cold and it was difficult to keep warm. I was against using a heater in the tent but, when we did use one, I made sure it was fuelled by naphtha fuel since my experience of diesel-fume poisoning. We used our propane fuel sparingly, only for cooking and making tea but generally not for heating the tent. So, it was with great pleasure that I accepted my new qulliq from my Sakikuluk. I was told that she had sacrificed the domed lid of her favourite large aluminum roaster pan from which Sakialuk made this qulliq. I was told it would give heat for an entire night provided one knew how to use it properly. It did not look like any other qulliq I had ever seen. They were usually quite flattened, like a half-moon shaped dish with a slight well to hold the seal oil. This qulliq had a very deep well. It was very light weight and I brought it along on our next camping trip. My Sakikuluk said her granddaughter, who was coming with us, would show me how to use it.

When we had set up our camp, I asked the young woman to help me set up my new qulliq. I already knew how to render seal fat to make seal oil and had some prepared. I poured some into the well. She showed me how to prop up the qulliq with a small rock so that the tilt was right. Then she showed me where to collect the willow fluff needed to make a loose mat as the wick. My young teacher said that was all she knew. I would have to figure out the rest for myself.

I had seen other qulliqs in use, so I had an idea of what to do. I laid the willow wick mat onto the oil and positioned it on the flat, straight edge along the front of my qulliq. Then it came to lighting the wick.

This was trickier and took some time. Whenever I started a flame by setting alight a thin wooden stick and putting it to the edge of the wick, it burned for a bit but then went out. I kept trying and had to replace my starter stick a few times until it occurred to me that the poor little flame was being drowned by oil. Using my stick, I folded over the edge of the wick and squeezed out the excess oil into the qulliq. Then I lifted up a bit of the almost dry edge of the matted wick and set the flame. By lifting and coaxing the flame along the edge of the wick from one end of the straight edge of the qulliq to the other, I finally figured out how it worked and how to control the height of the flame.

I experimented quite a bit with placing rocks to build a tripod to support my kettle and frying pan over the qulliq flame. I figured out how to boil water and even bake a frying-pan bannock over the qulliq. From then on, I was always warm in my tent at night and I never used candles for light again. I could even read by the light of the qulliq. Those who visited my tent for tea and baked bannock were surprised that I used a qulliq and soon word got back to my mother-in-law.

After we returned from camp that summer, I visited my Sakikuluk.

She said, "Ukuaq, I did not think you could use the qulliq, but people tell me they have seen you use yours and say you know how."

My Sakialuk just smiled. I knew he always had faith in me.

Working at Papa's laboratory had me walking to work along the road in front of the Catholic Mission and I often stopped in to visit Ataata Mari when he was in town. His missionary duties in Arctic Bay and Igloolik as well as the archaeological and other meetings elsewhere frequently kept him travelling. When he was home, we had wonderful conversations.

He told me about his archaeology work on digs in the area. He had received permission to pursue university archaeological studies by his superiors and he considered it his lifework to provide a record of traditional Inuit life of past ages. He had lived in the area for many decades and was able to speak Inuktitut so fluently that my parents-in-law both said he spoke it better than most living elders still alive at that time in Mittimatalik. During the 1940s, he started as writer/editor of *Eskimo Magazine*, published by the Catholic Arctic Diocese in Churchill, Manitoba, which began as *The Link* in the 1920s. In these, he published much of his research on Inuit history and culture along with his sketches, cartoons, and photographs. He was a gifted artist, I saw, from his drawings of Inuit children and string art figures to illustrate his articles.

I found his stories fascinating and vibrant with a keen sense of humour. He was very self-effacing and had a few charming eccentricities when speaking English. He was like a grandfather to me and I know he acted, aside from his priestly duties, in a fatherly way toward Papa, accepting him unconditionally. I know that he was Papa's confessor, too, so I was aware that he understood Papa well. I thought this important because my Papa had not had a good relationship as a youth with his own father. The main reason for this was that his father did not know him. My father had been sent as a baby to his maternal grandparents who raised him.

Ataata Mari had put up a large white crucifix on the hill overlooking the Catholic mission in Mittimatalik after he arrived in the late 1940s. It served as a landmark, like an inukshuk, to guide travellers to Mittimatalik. One day, when I stopped by, he was fuming with anger. He was sputtering on about those "cursed ravens having the audacity to defecate on head and shoulders of Christ on the Cross". He had just spent the morning removing old raven feces from the crucifix, using a long extension ladder borrowed from Papa, and a long-handled brush that he had to dip into soapy water. He said he had to brush hard to loosen the filth.

"I will shoot those blasted black birds, agents of the devil," he fumed. "They are such a nuisance, taking up my precious time for this cleaning."

He had often hunted game animals to supply meat for needy families in the days when he still ran a dog team. But those days were long over and he had put his rifle away in his advancing age. Now, I was surprised that he was seriously considering shooting the ravens. I reminded him that the Inuit I knew had a special relationship with ravens. My Sakikuluk said they are spirits and it was wrong to kill them. She told me how, in the winter, the raven is often the only living thing moving outside, the only sign of life, a comfort for those waiting for their hunters to return. At this, Ataata Mari gave me a hard look, shrugged, and then laughed.

"Of course, you are right," he said. "I cannot shoot the ravens. I am just getting too old and tired."

I suggested that he have one of the Catholic boys perform the crucifix cleaning for him.

"No one but me can clean this crucifix," he said, smiling lopsidedly. "I must perform my cleaning duties without complaint and be happy that I am still able to do it."

Later that year, after the new trailers that made up the Catholic mission church and living quarters had arrived on sea-lift and had been assembled, Ataata Mari took me inside the small missionary church where he had lived so long. He had spent months one winter just after his arrival painting a scene behind the old altar, showing a night sky lit by moon and stars, with a dominant star shining down on a scene of Inuit people and their snow houses. It was all done in various shades of blues and white. I had seen photos of beautiful famous religious paintings, but Ataata Mari's painting was, to me, the most beautiful I had ever seen. The painting was so serene. Just looking at it filled me with hope for my future.

Twenty-five

During the spring and summer of 1979, Mikiseetee and I were both working for my Papa, Mikiseetee as the sea-ice technician and I as the laboratory instructor. Mikiseetee went out on the sea ice daily until the mid-July breakup, collecting ice sample cores at designated points for Papa. In the lab, we had many sea-ice sample cores in the freezer that we were busy processing. We knew this research helped to shed light on northern ocean currents and their climates.

That summer, Papa received some new, very expensive, laboratory equipment. The microwave oven had become popular and Papa got one for the lab. Now we could thaw the ice core samples quickly which changed our order of procedures. There was also a new titration device that measured dissolved oxygen in water. But the AutoSal that measured salinity accurately in one reading of a single drop of seawater on a slide was the most valuable addition. Before using the AutoSal, we had to take a series of readings by hand-held salinometer, the device that reads salinity or the content of salt in a drop of water, and then had to average out the findings for the final reading. The precision of the AutoSal reduced technicians' errors and saved us a lot of time and effort.

After some time, Papa thought I should understand the principles and intricate interior workings of this new AutoSal. I was not a trained scientist and found his mathematical explanation baffling. When I asked him to explain something I did not understand, something that he probably felt I should have known, he lost his temper with me.

Without regard to our audience of Inuit lab trainees, he yelled at me. "How stupid you are! Any child can understand my explanations. You should be ashamed of yourself!" he bellowed. "At university you had to study something as useless as psychology, which is not a science." He continued raging.

I stood there unable to move, all this hostile noise washing over me. How had I triggered his anger?

The trainees ran off into the house to tell Mama that Papa was shouting at me. She came into the lab and Papa stopped yelling. I excused myself and started for home.

While I walked, I thought over what had just happened. It became clear to me that I could not continue working in the lab with Papa so prone to exploding in anger at me. I searched in my mind how I could possibly stop working for Papa in a way that would be acceptable to him. I did not want to insult him or harm his efforts at training Inuit and gathering vital scientific information. I wanted my quitting my work for Papa to be gentle, not retaliatory. It was a quandary, for sure, with my husband relying on continuing to work for Papa.

Then a new thought entered my mind. If I were pregnant, I could quit without Papa taking it personally. But, then, I had not become pregnant since I stopped using birth control when Ruben was six months old. He was now over three years old and still I had not become pregnant again.

Thinking about pregnancy, it occurred to me that Joanna, Mikiseetee's sister, was again pregnant, in fact, only a month or two away from giving birth. She had told me that if her new baby was a boy, she would give it to her older sister, Mary, and if it was a girl, she would give it to whoever wanted it. She suffered from an chronic heart condition and could not deal with a newborn, I knew.

I went straight to Joanna's house and asked her if she would consent to giving me her child, if it were a girl. She said she must ask her mother, my Sakikuluk, because it was she who made these decisions for our family. There was no way at that time of knowing what sex Joanna's baby would be. I was surprised and so happy my Sakikuluk agreed. This giving a baby away among Inuit is known as "custom adoption", a common way of dealing with unwanted babies. Usually, the baby was given to a relative and then registered with the local government that formalized the adoption. Now I just had to wait and see if Joanna's baby turned out to be a girl. I knew that if I presented my parents with the fact that I was adopting a baby, they would both agree that my ceasing work was the right thing to do. I did pray a little that this would work out to solve this delicate situation.

Joanna was sent out by air to the Frobisher Bay hospital to await the birth of her baby at the beginning of October. After work later, in mid-October, I received a telephone call. It was Joanna.

"Do you still want to have my baby?" she asked. "It's a girl."

"Yes. Yes, I do," I said.

Tears sprang to my eyes. Not only was I getting the daughter I had longed for, but this baby could help me out of the dilemma of wanting to quit my job without upsetting Papa. My prayers had been answered. This child would be mine, my Sakikuluk had told me. No one would be in charge of her except me, her adoptive mother. I could tell that she knew how difficult it was for me to take a back seat to her being in charge of my son, Ruben. I think agreeing to the custom adoption was her way of making it up to me for letting her do things in the traditional way as she was accustomed. How wonderful was the thought of having a child to myself, finally, to raise as I chose.

The next day I went to tell Papa about my new baby and how this was the reason I must quit my job. I thanked him for allowing me the chance to work for him, but now I wanted to devote myself to my new daughter. He took the news calmly and Mama was happy for me, knowing that I always had wanted a daughter and what prompted my decision to leave my job.

A few days later I was told to go to the airstrip, that my baby was arriving. Joanna had to remain in hospital for another week for treatment of her heart condition after giving birth. To receive my baby, I wore my old amautik, but it had the new outer cover I had sewn in anticipation of my next baby, cream-coloured with blue cuffs and border around the hood. My oldest sister-in-law, Elisabeth, helped me cut the pattern.

The plane landed and the passengers disembarked. Then a Qallunaq woman whom I did not know stepped out carrying a see-through plastic baby cot, the kind that infants are kept in at the hospital. The pilot helped carry the cot into the air terminal building. I saw that the baby's head was bare and that she was naked under her baby blanket. I grabbed her up with the blanket and asked my niece to put her directly into my amautik as I knelt down. The strange woman handed me a carton of mini-baby bottles with prepared formula.

"Why is the baby naked?" I asked her. I was upset because the baby was cold and crying.

She said, "The baby soiled herself and I did not have a change of clothes for her, so I just stripped her clothes off, threw them in the trash, and wrapped her in the blanket."

My guess was that this woman had no experience with babies in cold weather. Still, my new daughter seemed to be all right and had fallen asleep against my warm back. I took her home.

I named my new daughter Lilian-Ulayuk, with a hyphen between the Christian name and her Inuit name because I wanted her to be known as Ulayuk. My Sakikuluk told me her Inuit name was that of the last person in Mittimatalik who died, old Anaviapik's wife, Ulayuk. The practice at the local Anglican Church was to baptize a baby to its Christian name and this was then the child's official, legal name, the one that teachers would use for that child at school. My adopted child was the first Inuit baby to be baptized with her real Inuktitut name. It would be my daughter's choice which of the hyphenated names she wanted to be called in adulthood. The Anglican missionary agreed and performed the baptism.

I had noticed when I worked with the pre-school children during my first year in Mittimatalik, that most children had their Christian name, the one that appeared on the pre-school participant lists, but they

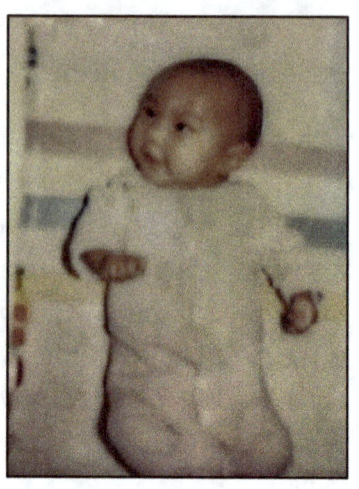

Ulayuk 1979.

did not respond when I read them out. It was hard for me to record attendance using their official school names. When these small children talked to each other, they called each other by the names they used at home, I also noted. The situation was this: at school, the children would be called by their Christian name and at home they would be called by their Inuktitut names. My Inuit assistant gave me the Inuktitut names of our pre-school children to write on the attendance form beside their Christian names and this solved the problem.

I felt that this confused identity of names could cause problems for any child. My daughter would be called Ulayuk, the same person at home and at school. I knew that the Lilian part of her name would soon be dropped by the teachers.

Now I had a baby daughter, a baby sister for Ruben. I was so pleased that I had been able to solve my problem of gently leaving Papa's employ while, at the same time, fulfilling my yearning for a daughter. I hoped she would become my best friend as she grew older, just like Mama and me.

With the newborn added to our household, the little two-room shack

Mikiseetee and I had been allotted by the local housing association when I began work for my Papa was now too small to accommodate us all. We petitioned the housing association for a bigger house with at least two bedrooms so we could have a children's room for Ruben and his little sister. We soon moved to the three-bedroom house on the corner of the street across from the nursing station. This was an ideal location because, by this time, my parents-in-law had moved from the old cemetery house to the house located beside the local Co-op store. This was now just around the corner from our new house. Both my parents-in-law by this time suffered from various health problems of old age and their house being closer to the nursing station made good sense to me. I could just walk to my Sakikuluk's house without the hassle of using my snowmobile.

As it happened, it was a very good thing that I no longer worked for Papa. My Sakikuluk was now no longer able to care for my son while I worked. Her health was declining and she was also losing her eye-

Ruben, his cousin Naaman, and me with Ulayuk in amautik before our "new" house 1980.

sight. She had spent a month almost blind before she was sent away to southern Canada to have her cataracts removed. She returned, and after a few weeks, she recovered some of her sight.

My Sakialuk had given up caring for those few sled dogs he had left of his former dog team. Now he spent time foraging in the local garbage dump for wood to build furniture, like chests of drawers, side tables and coffee tables. I was amazed at the beautiful coffee table he built for me for my new house. The old man was never without some project, carving stone or ivory, making ulus, knives and harpoon lines, or building something, but always with his beloved pipe clenched between his few remaining teeth. He often sang, too. Hearing him sing cheered me up when I felt down.

At this time, there were several adolescent grandchildren living with my parents-in-law, who were able, before and after school, to help the old people with their daily physical needs. The family's hunters supplied meat continuously, which my Sakikuluk still distributed among our households, including mine. Now I was happy to visit my Sakikuluk every day bringing along Ruben and baby Ulayuk, and help doing the daily household chores. It was good to live close by so we could just walk over.

During this time, my Sakialuk recorded many songs from memory onto audiotape for the CBC, Canadian Broadcasting Corporation, on a project to preserve local Inuit oral history as well as for Ataata Mari. Some of Sakialuk's songs are very old, said Mikiseetee. Some of his long stories were also recorded. It was our hope that these songs and stories would be preserved for coming generations of our family.

My Sakikuluk spoke to me about wanting to tell her own life stories so her children and grandchildren would know how she had lived and what challenges she had overcome. I thought this an excellent idea and purchased a supply of blank audio tapes and a small recorder.

Mikiseetee and I showed her how to use the little machine.

She tried it out and said she sounded strange to herself, hearing her voice speaking from the recorder. I would often ask her, when visiting, if she had made a recording. She always answered with some kind of excuse.

"I was not feeling well," or "I had too many visitors," she usually said.

I would ask, "Do you need help in making the recordings?" and she would reply, "I will do it by myself, thank you."

I suppose using the new technology was too strange for her and may have gotten in the way of her telling her stories. I found it difficult to picture her gazing through her glasses upon the audio recorder as she did when anyone listened while she told her stories to her visitors and grandchildren.

Living close to the nursing station was also a boon to me. When I received my baby Ulayuk from the hospital, she had been a sickly little thing and I was concerned when she did not gain weight. The nurse gave me a formula recipe for bottle feeding, Carnation brand evaporated canned milk, water and sugar. The formula she had been drinking from birth had been a commercial brand provided by the hospital. The supply she came with was used up in the first week after her arrival. Commercial baby formula was not available for sale at our HBC store during those days. Drinking this Carnation milk formula, Ulayuk developed digestion problems and even projectile vomiting. I was often at the nursing station with her and I became seriously concerned when she began to run fevers and to lose what little weight she'd had at birth. At that time, there were two nurses, a married couple. The male nurse told me that Ulayuk showed symptoms of chronic tonsillitis and that she needed to have them removed.

"Ulayuk is not even a chronic human being yet," I said. "How could she have a chronic health condition like tonsillitis at the age of less than a month?"

I argued with the male nurse, asking only for medication to reduce the fever but he refused. In frustration, I telephoned the pediatrician at the Frobisher Bay hospital. After listening to me, he said he would direct the nursing station to give me the fever-reducing medication and that I should bring the baby by MedEvac flight to Frobisher Bay hospital for observation. The nursing station grudgingly gave me the medication and arranged the transportation for us.

It was late November when baby Ulayuk and I left by plane. On arrival in Frobisher Bay, Ulayuk was whisked away into the hospital and I was taken to board with a local family. The next day, I visited Ulayuk at the hospital and saw that she had no more fever, and was very content. The staff, of course, was again feeding her the commercial prepared formula she was used to from birth. The pediatrician told me they wanted to keep her for a few days to see if she had suffered kidney, liver or other damage.

I spoke with this pediatrician about the formula recommended by the local nurse in Mittimatalik. He told me most children were reported to do well on powdered whole milk, water and sugar, but was not sure about the evaporated canned milk. It looked like my asking about evaporated milk was the first time anyone questioned about using this type of milk in formula for feeding Inuit babies. In the meantime, my Mama had telephoned the evaporated milk company, Carnation, and they told her that their product was definitely not to be used for infant formula because of the irregular temperatures at which their case lots were processed. I shared this information with the doctor.

I told him, "I think that the babies who were bottle fed locally on evaporated milk have had a lot of health problems including convulsions and chronic diarrhea."

He said, "You might have a good point there. I will look into the matter."

After observing Ulayuk a few more days and recording her daily increase in body weight and her general good condition, she was released from hospital and we flew home to Mittimatalik.

Now I had the problem of what to feed Ulayuk. The HBC store no longer supplied canned powdered whole milk. For a time, I had to import infant formula by air freight at great expense. Then the Anglican minister's wife came to the rescue. She had a few cases of powdered infant formula left over from her last child which she donated to us shortly before she and her husband left Mittimatalik.

That July, the HBC store received a shipment of cases of powdered infant formula as part of their sea-lift. This must have been the result of Iqaluit doctor's influence.

Part 3
1979–86

Twenty-six

Before long, the new housing project for refurbishing and insulating the older houses began in Mittimatalik, equipping older three- and four-bedroom houses with plumbing and running water and all appliances, reducing the number of rooms by one to make a proper bathroom.

Our house was, thankfully, on this project list. We moved temporarily to an empty house down the road overlooking Igarjuaq to the east of town while our house was being renovated. We would move back when the renovations were completed after a few months. Such construction work was usually done by imported Qallunaq work crews who worked long hours to get the outside work done in the summer months so that the fall and winter could be devoted to the interior renovations. I was looking forward to having a snug house with all amenities for my little family.

Mikiseetee continued working for Papa. He borrowed money from Mama and we were able to buy our own open boat and motor so that we would not have to depend on borrowing a boat to hunt at the floe edge or in ice-free waters or to go out to summer camp. Naturally, he made monthly payments to repay this loan which would take at least six months. What he did not know was that I had given Mama the money to lend him. I knew that he would repay Mama, his mother-in-law, but would not repay me, his wife. His stance was that whatever I had was his and whatever he had was none of my business, a stance I had seen before in other marriages. It had been my practice while working for Papa to put aside part of my pay to give to Mama. She put my money into a joint bank account I shared with her. That way, I had emergency funds should I ever need them. I continued to augment this joint account whenever I could.

Now, with the new baby, I again looked for ways to add to our family's income. I did not want to have to go back to doing all that physical and time-consuming labour doing sealskins for a measly twenty to thirty dollars per skin paid by the local Co-op store or the HBC store. I had given that up when I began to work at the laboratory. Of course, I still worked sealskins and other skins but only for our family clothing and foot-gear needs. I even experimented with preparing bleached hairless sealskin and flensing caribou skin which was quite different from the process used for sealskin.

After my traditional materials necklace had won the jewellery-making contest, I was eligible to sell any carved or handmade articles with my own official registered Inuit Art trademark tag on the things I made, showing them to be authentically handmade by Inuit. In the pursuit of a modest income from my artwork, I sewed wall-hangings that I designed with coloured felt applied onto a dark duffel background. I was able to sell them to the Co-op store but I found that the price I received for it was just a little over the amount I paid for the supplies. I was not paid for the all the hours I had worked. I did not make another one.

I made several necklaces that I left with the Co-op to sell on consignment. That meant I would be paid after they were sold with the

Co-op reserving their percentage. Some of the new necklaces I made looked different from the one that won the design contest. I found various ways of making beads out of bird bones and carving soapstone beads which sped up the production process.

I sent some of my necklaces to the Canadian Arctic Producers shop in Toronto through our Co-op Store. Mama visited that shop in Toronto on one of her trips south and reported back that my necklaces sold for ten times the money I received for them. I was used to our Co-op's take of between three to fifteen percent of what I was paid, usually around thirty or forty dollars, so I was a bit shocked. It was also a lesson in how Inuit art was being dealt with and why Inuit carvers found it so very difficult to make a decent living by making art.

My brother-in-law James, my Ulayuk's birth father, wanted to learn how to make these necklaces and I showed him the tricks I'd learned by trial and error, how to prepare the seal claws and sinew, as well as a few variations on bead making and the necklace clasps. He sold the necklaces he made under my registered Inuit Art tag. I was disappointed for both of us that we were not able to gain a decent income by our art and craft work.

Then it happened that the person who had worked as the local Pan Arctic Oils personnel expeditor had to move from the community, leaving that job vacant. At the same time, our Anglican missionary moved his family to Nanisivik where there was the iron mine, near Arctic Bay. The missionary's wife had served as the local Kenn Borek Air agent. So that job was vacant as well. I applied for the air agent's job and got that one right away because I had that commercial two-way radio license gained while working for Papa. I was happy that I could take the two-way radio to set up at home.

When I made my work application to Pan Arctic Oils, the local representative told me that they never hired women for the personnel expeditor's job because the local Inuit men were so rough. But, since no

Me as air agent and personnel expeditor 1980.

qualified man stepped forward to take this job and because I was already the local air agent possessing that valuable commercial radio licence, they gave me the job after all. Holding these two jobs together was perfect for me because Pan Arctic Oils chartered Kenn Borek Air planes for personnel transport to and from their arctic work sites. Holding these two jobs together, I now had a decent wage to help my husband support our growing family and afford the boat repayments, snowmobiles, hunting equipment, ammunition and fuel required for hunting food as well as to pay our living expenses. Pan Arctic Oils even paid me a generous retainer during the summer when the crews and I had our summer break.

I enjoyed my part-time air agent and personnel expeditor jobs. The air agent's job meant only two hours or so a week at the air terminal, newly built the year before, where I received and sent off passengers and freight. I did the passenger ticketing and writing of freight manifests at home and only called for the fuel truck after I had received the radio transmission confirming the plane's estimated time of arrival in

Mittimatalik. After that, I would go up to meet the flight, usually getting a ride in the fuel truck.

The Pan Arctic Oils work crew expeditor's job had me working once every six weeks, the length of time workers now spent at work sites. It was my job to alert the next outgoing team of workers and make a list of their names to give to the pilot, and to pass out pay cheques to returning workers the next day.

The same procedures were followed as for a regular Kenn Borek weekly flight except that the personnel flights usually arrived late at night. Sometimes, the police had to inspect the workers as they got off as well as those boarding the plane. Illicit drugs and alcohol were not permitted at the work sites but, still, there was a lot of smuggling. I was aware that homecoming work crews often carried illicit drugs but the police only clamped down on imported alcohol. The RCMP officer told me that it was alcohol that caused social problems for local Inuit, not the "other stuff".

Among the Pan Arctic Oils regular work crew was the man who had raped me the year before when I was house-sitting for my parents. He was aware that I had figured out that it had been him. He was worried that he would lose his high-paying job now that I was the new personnel expeditor. He expected me to take revenge on him. I had no intention of doing anything like that. I knew his wife and children and would not cause them harm by depriving him, their source of support, of income. Besides, he was related to Mikiseetee. This man was surprised when I called him up for his next tour of duty and passed him his pay cheque on his return. After that, he became my ally in smoothing over problems that arose from time to time with the other work crew members. He made a difficult job for me, still limited in my use of Inuktitut, much easier. For me, it was a case of "spilt milk", ajurnaqmat. There was no way to undo what had been done to me, but this sure helped a lot.

Both of my jobs, with Kenn Borek Air and Pan Arctic Oils, allowed me a month's holiday in the summer at the same time. Kenn Borek Air hired the local First Air agent to deal with passengers and freight in my absence. Pan Arctic Oils suspended their personnel needs for that period, but they continued to pay my monthly wage because, they said, they appreciated my good work and did not want to lose me. That was perfect for me. I could continue to enjoy spending time at our summer camp in Igarjuarq without losing needed income.

I had arranged with both my employers to take my annual holiday month starting the last week in July to the last week in August. The ice on Eclipse Sound usually broke up during mid-July and this arrangement allowed a leeway should the breakup be late. The ice breakup happened as expected. Mikiseetee did his daily hunts for seal, and during most of July, also for narwhal. We planned to go to Igarjuarq by boat as soon as my holiday began.

At the end of July, Mikiseetee was away on an overnight hunting trip. At home alone in the evening, I had put baby Ulayuk and Ruben to sleep and was flensing a sealskin, removing out the fat, when some sound caught my attention and I glanced away from what I was doing. I thought I had heard baby Ulayuk cry out. At that instant I sliced my left index finger with my very sharp ulu. It bled profusely, so I held it under running cold water, wiped it with a clean towel soaked in salty water and wrapped it tightly in a clean bandage. I checked on Ulayuk and found her fast asleep after all.

I could not just leave the sealskin I was working on with only a bit left to flense. So, I put my injured hand in a plastic bag to protect the bandage and finished flensing the skin. By this time, it was quite late, so I put the flensed skin in the electric freezer we kept outside until I had time to wash it and do all the rest of the work to get it up on my stretcher. After that I went to bed.

When I awoke the following morning, my injured hand was swollen double its normal size. I took my children to my sister-in-law Joanna's house a few houses down the road to wait there while I went to the nursing station.

The male nurse was on duty and said that it looked like I had a bacterial infection known as "seal finger". Apparently, he told me, many Inuit women lost their teeth to this disease when they chewed affected sealskin, almost as if it was their fault.

I said that I could not tell the sealskin was tainted. But now I could see that the cut was infected and that pus had formed beneath where the wound had closed over.

The nurse said he would lance the wound to release the pus. After that, he said, he would disinfect the wound, put on a new bandage, and give me a course of antibiotics to take to get rid of the infection.

The male nurse brought out a metal kidney-shaped bowl and scalpel, swabbed my wound with antiseptic, and began to cut into the wound. As the yellow pus began to ooze out, he suddenly collapsed.

As he folded, I was able to grab the scalpel. I could not believe that he had just passed out. I called for the other nurse, his wife. She came and saw him on the floor. I had just completed the lancing of the wound myself and was squeezing out the pus. She cleaned the wound for me and bound it, while her husband came to on the floor.

I took the first dose of antibiotic at the nursing station and put the rest in my pocket. I left the nursing station, stopping at Joanna's to pick up my children. I took Ruben up the road to spend some time with my Sakikuluk who was happy to help me out. I then went home and put Ulayuk down for her nap. By this time, the antibiotics, tetracycline, the strongest they had, the nurse said, was taking effect and I was suddenly very sleepy. I usually never lie on the couch, but this time I did and rested my sore hand across my chest. I must have fallen asleep.

The next thing I knew, something bumped my sore hand. Even before I opened my eyes, I pushed whatever it was away with my uninjured right hand. Then I saw that I had pushed Ruben. He fell and bumped his head against the coffee table and cried out. Ruben had never before seen me asleep on the couch, so it must have been a shock for him to see me sleeping where his father usually napped. Ruben must have tried to wake me, bumping my sore hand to which I reacted before being aware of what I was doing.

My Sakikuluk, standing in the doorway, saw me push Ruben, her favourite grandchild, and reacted. She hurried into the children's bedroom, grabbed baby Ulayuk and hobbled out the door with her. In my sleep-addled state, I hardly knew what was happening. I looked out the window and saw which direction she went, so I knew she was taking Ulayuk to her daughter Joanna's house. I put on my amautik, careful of my sore hand, took Ruben, who had already stopped crying, by the hand, and walked to Joanna's house. When we got there, my Sakikuluk was beside herself, shouting at me that I was an unfit mother, that Ulayuk should go back to her birth mother, Joanna, that I was not good enough to be Ulayuk's mother.

I told my Sakikuluk, "Please stop." To my amazement, she did.

I could see Joanna, holding Ulayuk, amazed and baffled. She did not comprehend what was going on. I took Ulayuk from her, knelt down, and asked her to put her into my amautik. I then went home with Ulayuk on my back, leaving Ruben with his cousins. I was sure that my Sakikuluk would explain to her daughter her version of what had happened.

In a little while, I saw my Sakikuluk walk past my house on her way home, holding Ruben's hand. After about an hour, I put Ulayuk into my amautik again, careful of my sore hand, and began to walk to my Sakikuluk's house to pick up Ruben. I knew that my son could tire out the old woman these days. As I went around the corner of the street on the way to her house, I glanced up and spotted my Sakikuluk on the hill up behind her house sitting on that big rock with Ruben playing at her feet. I just walked up and down the road at the side of the hill until Ruben saw me. He waved to me and then ran down to me. I saw how my Sakikuluk's body slumped as she sat on the rock, almost as if she realized that my son loved me, his mother, as well as her, his grandmother. I saw her get off the rock and walk slowly down to her house. I was sad and sorry that I had been so careless as to hurt my hand which led to this problem between us.

When Mikiseetee returned that evening from hunting, I told him what had happened, how I had hurt my hand and how his mother was furious with me for having more or less accidentally pushed Ruben. He could see our son was playing happily on the carpet beside his little

Me, baking Bannock on my qulliq in camp 1980.

sister on her blanket. I said I wanted us to leave for our summer camp at Igarjuaq that very night and, for once, he did not argue. The weather was calm and nothing prevented us from making the crossing by water.

Although my hand was still throbbing and painful, I felt much better when we arrived at our camp. We set up my newly adapted tent, of which I was so proud, facing the shore. In the cooking area to the left of the tent entrance, we placed the propane camp cook stove. We got a pail of water from the creek to set beside it. I set up and lit my qulliq before the sleeping platform on the right, my side of the tent warmed by the morning sun. I used vegetable cooking oil in my qulliq for the first night out, as Mikiseetee had not yet caught a seal. My children played happily on the quilted bed platform lined with caribou skins. I took my prescribed medicine and after supper we all took a walk along the beach. When the sun had moved behind the mountains and put our tent in shadow, it was nighttime and we all went to sleep, the sun slowly circling the sky.

Me, flensing a seal skin at Igarjuarq 1980.

The next day, Mikiseetee went off in the boat to hunt seal and narwhal. I decided I would bake bannock in my frying pan over my qulliq. I put the flour, salt and baking powder into my mixing bowl, measured in the cooking oil and added water. I placed a plastic bag over my injured hand to protect it from getting wet so I was able to knead the bannock. I formed and placed the bannock in the frying pan and positioned it over the metal tripod I had devised along with a rock to keep the pan balanced over the qulliq flame. Ruben burst into the rent, gleefully shouting that his grandmother and his older cousins had just arrived by boat.

His grandmother? My Mama? No. It was my Sakikuluk, his ningiu, who had stopped going out to summer camp many years before I arrived in Mittimatalik. She directed her older grandchildren to erect a small blue nylon tent. I turned over my bannock in the frying pan over my qulliq to bake the other side. Then walked over and greeted her and invited her into my tent. I knew she must be tired out from the boat ride. She came in and sat on the edge of my sleeping platform. The sun lit up the inside of my tent. I gave her a mug of tea with sugar and a biscuit. My bannock continued baking over my qulliq showing its golden top.

My Sakikuluk looked about my tent approvingly and said, "I like your tent. I can see now that you really do know how to use your qulliq."

She took a long pause, sighed and then said, "Ukuaq, I was so bad to you. I got angry at you. I thought you were trying to hurt Ruben, my beloved grandchild. I was wrong. I want to apologize." I was amazed to hear these words.

I did not respond right away. I could see that she was sincere, that she meant what she said to me.

Then I said, "You are my mother-in-law, my saki, and our family's elder. You can speak to me any way you choose. I was wrong to have stopped you scolding me at Joanna's house. It is I who should apologize to you for that. I am your daughter-in-law, your ukuaq, and I must do as you tell me."

Tears ran from my Sakikuluk's eyes and she removed her glasses, placed her open hands before her face to wipe her eyes with the back of her thumbs. She took a deep breath, smiled at me, stood up and gave me a hug. She felt so fragile and small.

Then she called out to the older grandchildren who had brought her, "Take down that little tent. I will not spend the night here." They obeyed, took down the tent, and started packing everything up again.

To me she said, "As soon as your bannock has finished baking, I want all of us to go berry picking near the river. Then I will go home and

Our tent at camp 1980.

your little family will come back here. Everything is now good between us again."

By this time, Mikiseetee had already come back to camp with our boat and had drunk some tea. He had seen his mother arriving while out on the water and decided to find out what the problem could be that made her come all the way to our camp. He was relieved to see his mother smiling. He helped his nieces and nephews stow his mother's things in the boat.

The boat carrying my Sakikuluk and her grandchildren helpers led the way while our boat followed carrying Mikiseetee, Ruben, and me with Ulayuk in my amautik. We spent the warm sunny afternoon picking berries beside the Janes River. The children ate more than they picked and played together when they got tired of picking berries.

In the early evening, my Sakikuluk said she was tired now and wanted to go home. We all got into our boats. My Sakikuluk's boat went off toward Mittimatalik that we could see away across the water to the west. Mikiseetee drove our boat in the opposite direction to our camp at Igarjuaq.

Later that night, we picked up the Mittimatalik community program

Ulayuk playing in the flowers 1980.

Mikiseetee caught a double-tusked narwhal 1980.

on our camp radio. We heard the voice of my Sakikuluk announcing to everyone that her Qallunaq daughter-in-law married to Mikiseetee was a "real Inuk", Inummariit, and how happy she was to have me in her family. I felt so honoured because I had somehow, instinctively, done and spoken only what I thought was right. I was glad to be accepted by my Sakikuluk who must often have thought me so strange and foreign.

Twenty-seven

When we had my younger sister, Irmgard, a geologist by training, with her husband, John, camp beside us for a few days at summer camp, she, in all innocence, asked me why I did not bring fresh vegetables and fruit out to camp with us. I had to break it to her gently that such food items were not affordably available to us, and even if they were, they would not keep, might even get unintentionally frozen and would then quickly rot.

Good weather can be deceptive, especially since the sun just circles around the sky without actually setting for a few months. Often, warm summer days included snowfalls and overnight freezing temperatures. My sister was fortunate that our weather did not treat her holiday harshly and she could leave when she was ready. Sometimes, wind, ice and sea conditions prevented travel, locking us in with massed ice pans blocking our boats or the waves thundering on the shore. Through hard experience, I learned patience and to be prepared for extended stays.

My sister Irmgard visits 1980.

The previous year, the ice broke up as expected in late July and moved toward the south shore of Bylot Island, allowing us to travel by boat to Igarjuaq without hindrance or danger. There were a few other tents at our camp when we arrived and we set up our tent. After a few pleasant days, the weather turned and pushed all that broken sea ice from Bylot Island tightly against our shore. Our hunters could not use their boats. No one could come or go from Igarjuaq. It stayed like that for weeks while we began to run out of food.

The first thing we ran out of was sugar. Mikiseetee was definitely unhappy about having no sugar for his tea. He craved sweetness so much that he used up the small amount of jam we had left for his tea. But Mikiseetee had no problem eating the semi-rotted muktaaq from the old narwhal carcass that someone had caught a week before we arrived. I had a problem with that and made do with searching the land for long vetch roots and mushrooms which I fried up in my frying pan. I knew that there were no poisonous mushrooms or plants this far up on Baffin Island. My children enjoyed these unusual meals.

I tried to use the minimum of my staples such as flour, pasta and rice so they would last as long as possible. I stopped giving out handouts like I used to, and some people grumbled about my being such a Qallunaq, so stingy and ungenerous, but I just ignored them and eked out what I had. My first priority was keeping my little family and myself from going hungry. We had no idea how long this ice blockage would last.

After an overnight storm, we found kelp washed up onto the beach from under the ice pans. Mikiseetee brought some up and dumped a length into my teapot. The brown kelp turned bright green. He pulled it out, shared it out to our children and me, and began to chew. We did, too, because we were all hungry. It was crunchy, but quite tasty. It made our tea taste salty, though. To me, tea was already bad enough without sugar. From then on, I used a separate pot of water for boiling kelp.

We woke one morning to shouts that a boat was arriving. The sea ice pans that had blocked us in for weeks had disappeared. We could finally go home. There is nothing like being hungry and being prevented from going home from camp to make one appreciate our usual good fortune.

That fall in 1980, while we were waiting for the completion of our house renovation, my Sakialuk came down with serious breathing problems and was sent away to hospital. He returned with a diagnosis of lung cancer and was slated for surgery to take place the coming spring in Montreal. Somehow, he made it through the winter. In late March 1981, he was sent out again for his surgery. We heard that he'd had part of one lung removed. About a month later, he was returned but was kept at the nursing station. Because Sakialuk's cancer was spreading rapidly, and he had not healed from his first surgery, the doctors decided against further surgery and had sent him home to die. My Sakikuluk worried about him all this time as did the rest of our family. The nurses did their best to keep the old man comfortable as much as they could. We all knew that he did not have long left to live.

There were no records of births kept when Inuit still lived out in their camps before the missionaries came north to the Inuit. For this reason, the birth dates of my parents-in-law had to be estimated. My Sakialuk thought he was about seventy-five years old as he said he had been born, according to his mother, in the spring when the last whaling ship came to the Repulse Bay area on Hudson's Bay coast near Igloolik in 1916 during the Great War, that is, World War I. My Sakikuluk estimated that she was about year younger than her husband, so seventy-four. She was born at a camp north of Clyde River on the east coast of Baffin Island.

Smoking was usually forbidden at the nursing station. But because my Sakialuk was receiving palliative care, the nurses allowed him to smoke his beloved pipe. They knew it comforted him and they also knew he would last only a few more weeks, or less. They provided him with a colour television set so he could watch the nature programs that he enjoyed, those showing the strange animals of the world he had never seen before. I had collected a batch of old *National Geographic* magazines that had photos of strange lands, animals and people, and I turned the pages for him when he could no longer turn the pages himself, when I visited him at the nursing station. We brought him his favourite foods but he usually ate very little. I brought him a tanned sheep skin donated by my parents to lay under him to prevent pressure bedsores.

My Sakikuluk was herself not in good health, but managed to visit her husband every day for long hours. The nurses urged her to go home to eat and rest after Sakialuk had fallen asleep, which he did more often as time went on. We all knew that the old man was slipping away but, still, it came as a shock to me when I heard that the old hunter had finally died that first day of May 1981. Of course, it was a release from agony for him, but it was the beginning of the great mourning for our family, the loss of our beloved and respected family elder.

Mikiseetee was in a stupor of bereavement. He moaned and cried with his mother, his brothers and sisters and their spouses at my Sakikuluk's house. The Anglican church minister came to pray with them and an Inuit lay-minister stayed with the family after he left.

I saw that no one took care of the small children. Their mothers were fully occupied with their grief, so I took on that chore, making sure that they were fed and that those too young to understand what was going on had the opportunity to get away and play at my house. I mourned deeply for my Sakialuk, but I could not openly grieve like Mikiseetee and his family. Instead, to show my grief, I took scissors and cut off my long hair. I had read somewhere that certain First Nations women did this to show their grief when a loved one died. It was at least a token of the loss I felt.

A few days after my Sakialuk died, the funeral was held at the Anglican church and the burial took place up in the new cemetery to the west above Mittimatalik. I went to the funeral at the church but did not go up for the burial. I stayed at home with Ulayuk and a few of her small cousins. Ruben went along with Mikiseetee, his nungiu, aunts, uncles and older cousins. The day after the funeral, the family was sad but they no longer grieved as openly as before. After all, my Sakialuk was now safe in heaven, they said. Life returned to a semblance of normal, but a much sadder normal than before. Mikiseetee tried hard to find solace in binge-drinking, but it usually ended in heightened grief, crying and weeping until he passed out. I did my best to provide some comfort, but often failed.

Ulayuk was progressing well, growing into a sweet little girl. One day, I made her several dresses out of Mikiseetee's old worn-out plaid work shirts. When I tried to put a dress on her, she absolutely refused, taking it right off again.

I asked her, "Why don't you like the dress I made for you?"

"I don't like dresses. I want to wear long pants like Ruben," she said. She simply adored her older brother.

Ruben liked her as much as any small boy can like a baby, but his father said she was a nuisance. Mikiseetee had been upset that I spent so much time and care on Ulayuk when she had been so sick as a new baby and even complained to his mother, my Sakikuluk, about this. My Sakikuluk, perhaps frustrated with these complaints from her son and with the sick baby she had given me in good faith, told me I should just let this one die, that she would get me another one, a healthier one, to replace her. I ignored this advice and persisted caring for her and getting the medical help Ulayuk needed to grow. It was still my habit to watch

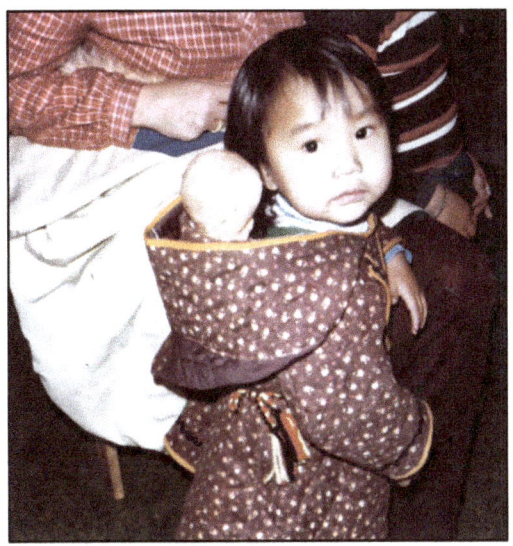

Ulayuk in her amautik 1980.

over her health at the time my Sakialuk, her grandfather, died. She was then about two and a half years old.

A few weeks after the funeral, Mikiseetee and I moved with our children back to our house, now newly refurbished, insulated and equipped. At last, we would enjoy running hot and cold water, a real bathroom with bathtub, shower and flush toilet, new full-sized washer and dryer, refrigerator and electric stove. The move cheered us up a bit. It was so much closer to my Sakikuluk's house, too. My Sakikuluk was fading in her grief, we could see, when we visited her every day with our children. She was so lost without her husband, her life's companion. That loss took away her appetite and her usual good cheer. She stayed in bed more often these days.

That summer, my little Sakikuluk was sent to the Frobisher Bay hospital for a doctor's examination and tests. After her return, she told us that she, too, had lung cancer like her late husband. She was told that she was scheduled for the same procedure he had undergone, surgery to remove the cancerous lobe of her lung. She really did not want to go and have this done, she said.

"My poor husband had this surgery

Ulayuk would not wear a dress, but loved her amautik 1980.

and it did not do him any good. I want to tell the nurse that I will not have this surgery. But I know that if I don't do as the nurse instructs, the police will take me away like they did when they sent me away to sanatorium."

I said, "That was when you had tuberculosis. That is an infectious disease that spreads to other people. That is against the law. But this is cancer. Cancer is not infectious. It cannot spread to other people. No one can catch cancer from you. I think you can refuse the cancer surgery and the police will do nothing."

Satisfied that I was telling her the truth, she said, "I will tell the nurse that I will not sign the paper that she needs that says I agree to the surgery."

The nurse became angry with me because my Sakikuluk told her that I had given her the information that she could refuse surgery.

That nurse said, "Everyone knows that you had a falling out with your mother-in-law when you hurt your hand. Is this perhaps your revenge?"

I was shocked by her words. I most certainly did not wish my Sakikuluk dead. I had just lost my Sakialuk, my father-in-law, and saw how that had devastated the whole family. I truly believed that my Sakikuluk should have the right to refuse surgery if that was what she wished. I also knew that it was just a matter of a few months before she also died. She, herself, was well aware of this and often spoke about how she did not wish to live without her husband. She also said she wanted to get to heaven before my Sakialuk's first wife got there so she could spend eternity with her beloved husband. She refused to sign the surgery consent form. The cancer spread rapidly through my Sakikuluk's body as predicted. She told the nurse that she did not wish to die in Mittimatalik, but rather at the Frobisher Bay hospital. The nurse granted my Sakikuluk's wish and made arrangements to have her sent there to die.

On an afternoon at the end of August, the day before my Sakikuluk was to be taken to the airstrip for her flight out to hospital, she had called Mikiseetee and me to her sickroom. We brought our children, Ruben and Ulayuk, to say goodbye. After kissing her beloved little grandson, she asked that the children be taken out of the room, that she had something to say to me.

"Ukuaq, I worry about you, about what will happen to you and your children after I die. I want you to leave this man, my son. He is not good. I know he will make you cry. I want you to take your children and go live down south."

I could not believe my ears. How could she say such things to me in front of her son, my husband? I noticed Mikiseetee's face tighten. I knew that he thought that I had replaced him in his mother's affections. Other family members were in the room and heard my Sakikuluk speaking these harsh words as well. They heard her wish me gone with my children. I saw Mikiseetee's body slump. I felt so sorry for him. He was already suffering so much grief over the death of his father and now his dying mother was rejecting him.

"I cannot do what you want me to do. I made him a promise when I married him," I said.

She sighed heavily and just nodded. She was too tired to argue, I thought. A few hours later she was taken to the airstrip. A little over a week later we received news that she died on September 7, 1981, at the Frobisher Bay hospital.

My brother-in-law Josepee was determined to have his mother's body shipped home to be buried near his father's grave here in Mittimatalik even though she had said she did not wish to be buried here. She had not given a reason for this. Mikiseetee and I not could understand why she would want to be buried in Frobisher Bay. Josepee succeeded in getting his way, but my sister-in-law Joanna did not agree with him. She felt that her mother's wishes should have been honoured.

So it happened that there was a funeral for my Sakikuluk in Mittimatalik after all. I attended, Ulayuk in my amautik, with Mikiseetee. In protest, Joanna had her husband take her away on the boat with her children taking along our son Ruben to avoid the funeral. Again, I did not attend the burial at the cemetery.

Mikiseetee, already grieving his dead father, was further crushed by his mother's death. The last words he heard from her were those telling me he was not a good man and that I and my children should leave him. I was so sorry that he had heard them. Inconsolable and full of bitterness, he told me his mother had loved me more than him.

He gathered our tent and camping equipment, took the boat and left for Igarjuaq. He stayed there until about the middle of October when the snows came in earnest and it became too cold to tent. Back in Mittimatalik for the winter, he began to spend most of his waking hours with his drinking buddies and staying drunk. I carried on as best I could with Ruben mourning both his grandparents. Ruben now spent most of his time with me and Ulayuk when not playing away with his cousins.

Twenty-eight

A few months after the death of my mother-in law, Papa urged Mikiseetee to return to work and he did go back again during the winter and spring. In the first weeks of the following summer, Papa helped us arrange for a trip out to visit my sister Ursula and her family in Tofino on Vancouver Island to give us a break from Mittimatalik. Kenn Borek Air gave us a free flight to Resolute Bay and Pan Arctic Oils flew us to Edmonton. Papa paid for our flight from Edmonton to Victoria. We took along Natanai, Ruben's cousin. He was Joanna's son, Ukayuk's birth brother, who had always lived with my Sakikuluk. He was to help me with the children. On the trip, Mikiseetee took every opportunity to drink alcohol which made travel and staying in motels difficult. He controlled himself better when we arrived at my sister's little cabin on Beck Island off Tofino harbour.

Ursula and her husband, Carl, did their best to show us around Tofino and the tiny Beck Island on which they had enlarged the original one-room log cabin. They were perfect hosts, feeding us local seafood,

With my sister Ursula in Tofino BC 1982.

and supplying Mikiseetee with alcohol and weed to smoke. This distracted him somewhat from his mourning giving him some relief from grief. The children and I enjoyed the beaches. It was wonderful to visit with my sister face to face. All too soon, it was time for us to leave.

On the trip back to Mittimatalik, we had to spend a few days at a motel in Edmonton waiting for the weather to improve for our return flights to Resolute Bay and on home. I was carrying our money, by now barely enough to pay the motel and food for all of us. Mikiseetee began to threaten me into giving him all the money so he could get drunk. He frightened my children so I had Natanai take them out to a playground.

I gave Mikiseetee some money but not all of it. After he had left for the bar, I went to the motel office and had the manager put the rest of the money and our flight tickets into his safe. We were to leave the day after tomorrow. Late that night, Mikiseetee came to our motel room only to pass out without incident. To me, this was actually a relief.

When he awoke the next afternoon, he said, "You should leave me, like my mother said. I am obviously just no good, as you can see."

I was not going to give up on him that easily and told him so.

The next evening, I gave him a little more money and he went back to the bar. When the bar closed, he returned to our motel room and passed out again. Since we were to leave the next day, I went to the motel office to retrieve our flight tickets and the rest of our money. It was a chore to wake Mikiseetee the next day, but we did manage to get to the airport on time, board our flight and be on our way home to Mittimatalik.

I was relieved to be home again after all the return trip troubles. Mikiseetee went back to work for Papa who arranged for him to spend time at Siiralik, his remote iceberg-tracking station at the tip of Brodeur

On a Pacific Ocean beach near Tofino BC 1982.

Peninsula on Lancaster Sound. During the brief times when Mikiseetee was at home, he stayed with us, but he was still so very unhappy that I did not even mind him going off to drink with his buddies.

Occasionally, it happened that Mikiseetee would run out of booze and then he would trade for booze whatever the other person wanted: tools, gasoline, whatever. I discovered that he often received booze having made a deal with some hopeful Inuk who wanted to try his hand at seducing me. When such a person, usually quite drunk, showed up to collect on the bargain, I had the unwelcome task of getting rid of him without raising his anger. Usually, this was not too difficult, but some men were more insistent. I was aware that Mikiseetee usually waited outside at those times with the intent of acting the outraged husband. It seemed to me he was trying to make an excuse to break up our marriage with these tactics, to make me do what his dying mother had wished, to leave Mittimatalik.

That late summer, we packed up to go to camp after the ice had broken up and moved out. I knew Mikiseetee had not returned my special adapted tent the previous autumn when he had stayed away so long. Although Mikiseetee had been drinking all that day, we left that evening by boat to make the crossing to Igarqjuarq. We made it about halfway across the water when the boat motor quit working.

Mikiseetee pulled and pulled the starter cord, to no avail. The motor would not start up. He checked the fuel tank. He had filled it up before leaving and we had not used up much fuel. We sat in silence in our boat for a while bobbing on the waves. Then Mikiseetee began to paddle the long way to shore.

I stood up, Ulayuk in my amautik, with Ruben by my side and stepped back to the outboard motor. I pressed the bulb on the fuel line between the gas tank and the motor. I pulled the starter cord. The motor sprang to life.

Mikiseetee threw the paddle into the prow of the boat and made it back to the motor to steer us to camp. He was very angry with me for getting the motor started.

I kept quiet to avoid upsetting him further.

When we arrived at Igarjuaq, I went to our customary place where we usually put up our tent. I saw nothing that resembled my special tent, but I did see a heap of dirty dark orange canvas.

"Where's our tent?" I asked.

"Ah. Yes," he said. "It's not our tent anymore."

"Oh, and why not?"

Ursula's house on Beck Island 1982.

"I gave it to my buddy in trade for a forty-ouncer of vodka and that old tent there."

I supposed he wanted me to get angry, but I did not. It was just such a pity that Mikiseetee was so driven by his grief and need for alcohol.

I silently helped him put up the old tent that had been left there in a heap. It was a square orange-coloured canvas tourist tent that was quite dark inside. My tent had been a modified white prospector's tent, so my children and I found it much too dark for us inside this orange tent.

Then it began to rain so we had no choice but to spend our time inside to stay dry. The tent began to drip in spots. It had been left collapsed and uncovered over the winter and lemmings had used it as their winter home. That meant lemming urine had dissolved the tent's waterproofing. We soon began to notice a tart, acrid smell. The drips were actually diluted lemming urine. I clipped plastic garbage bags with wooden spring clothespins between the back tent seams to deflect the drips to the tent sides. I had set up my qulliq and that, at least, provided some light and comfort within the damp tent. We all went unhappily to sleep.

The next morning, I had made tea for us on the propane camp stove. Ruben and Ulayuk were crawling around on the sleeping platform while I tended my qulliq. Mikiseetee poured out some tea into a mug and yelled at me. I glanced away from what I was doing to see what was the matter with him. At that same instant, Ulayuk fell against my qulliq, burning her little leg against the hot edge. Mikiseetee now began to rage that I was trying to kill our daughter. I let him rage while Ruben looked on and even Ulayuk stopped crying to watch. The burn was slight but must have been painful. I put dissolved sugar on her burn. This is something I first learned from burns I had when I learned to bake bread. When the sugar solution had dried on her little burn, Ulayuk said it didn't hurt anymore.

Mikiseetee had left the tent. By now the rain had stopped and I found him sitting on the overturned wooden box beside the tent entrance.

"When you poured your tea, why did you yell?" I asked.

"Lemming shit, lemming turds, those tiny black things, had fallen into my mug," he said.

Luckily the weather was dry. We emptied the tent and collapsed it inside out. I washed the inside tent walls with the dish soap I had luckily brought along and water to remove the lemming urine and excrement. Mikiseetee helped me erect the tent again and it dried while he tried his luck at narwhal hunting or shooting a seal. Luck was with him, and he brought back a seal as a truce, of sorts, I guess. We put the bedding and everything back into the tent again. We stayed the rest of the week in a semblance of peace and then returned home. I felt that Mikiseetee's trading of my special tent for booze was a definite low point in our troubled marriage.

In spite of the ongoing tragedies in our lives, we still needed to earn money to pay our expenses and the rent. Mikiseetee had missed a lot of work at Papa's Arctic Research Establishment with the deaths of his parents in 1981. I still worked part-time for Kenn Borek Air and Pan Arctic Oils and my employers had been generous in allowing me time off and provided support during our family trials. I let it be known that I was looking for extra paid work while I waited for the fall season to begin for the oil company workers.

About a year after my Sakikuluk's death, I was hired by the local housing association on a short contract to clean up and reorganize their files because their office was short-staffed. By custom, after anyone in the community died in one of their houses, the housing association moved the family to another house as soon as they could to help the grieving family. This meant that I had to deal with the previous housing files of my parents-in-law, to review them, and then store them in the inactive archive.

When I opened my Sakialuk's house file folder, I found two letters written in Inuktitut syllabics. I knew enough syllabics to decipher that one was addressed to my sister-in-law Joanna, Sakikuluk's favourite daughter, birth mother of my Ulayuk and my good friend, and that the other one was addressed to Ruben, my son. I could see that my Sakikuluk had written both letters in shaky syllabics, possibly just before she passed away. I finished my work that day and went to my sister-in-law's house to deliver the letter to her and took the other one home to Mikiseetee to read to our son.

After reading his mother's letter to Ruben out loud, Mikiseetee went to his sister's house to find out what his mother had written to her. When he came back, his face was etched with even more anguish than he had shown on the day his mother left the community to die.

"Now I know why my mother did not want to be buried here in Mittimatalik," he said.

He told me that, in the letter to his sister Joanna, his mother had confessed to a murder. Mikiseetee had been named after the person who had been killed, who had gone insane. An insane person was his namesake and he now believed he carried her spirit all his life without knowing it. I knew that if anything could frighten Inuit, it was insanity. Mikiseetee was deathly frightened.

He told me the story so I could understand. I report here what I understood.

> In the summer of the year before Mikiseetee was born in 1951, my parents-in-law travelled with their children, adolescent Mary, Josepee and the young Joanna, to the east coast of Baffin Island south of Button Point, about halfway to Clyde River, to a summer camp that Mikiseetee called the "place of the flowers". They travelled with another family and were joined by some of my Sakikuluk's relatives who arrived from Clyde River, my mother-in-law's place of birth. The weather was good and the men left on foot on a trek toward the west where they knew there were caribou. The women and children remained behind in camp.

One afternoon, my Sakikuluk was in her tent when her female cousin came to visit and drink tea. This woman suddenly grasped my little Sakikuluk by the throat and began to choke her. Mary, outside the tent, heard the commotion and saw the women struggling together on the floor of the tent. My Sakikuluk caught sight of her daughter.

"Hit her on the head!" she cried.

Mary, in her panic, picked up a rock or other hard thing and hit the woman on the head with some force. The woman let go of my Sakikuluk and fell over clutching her bleeding head. My Sakikuluk did everything she could to stop the bleeding and nursed her wounded cousin for several days. But the injured woman developed a fever and soon it became plain that she would die. She was still able to speak and, just before she died, she predicted that my Sakikuluk would conceive a child and that it must be named after her. My Sakikuluk promised she would do that. At that time, my Sakikuluk had been convinced that Joanna had been her last child because her monthly bleeding had stopped, that she would bear no further children. She promised her cousin so that she could die in peace.

The men came back from a successful caribou hunt to find their camp in mourning and they buried the woman. Everyone was sworn to secrecy. They all knew that my Sakikuluk would be arrested and sent away to jail for the death of this woman. It was my Sakikuluk, after all, who urged her daughter Mary to strike the death blow. At about fourteen years of age, Mary was not responsible, but her mother was. The Inuit of North Baffin had learned about the power of the RCMP that cancelled out local Inuit customs and laws in 1923 during the trial of the Inuit who executed Robert Janes after that man had gone crazy. They knew about the edict "Thou shalt do no murder" as the trial judge admonished the Inuit attending that trial. They also knew that killing was against Christian beliefs which they professed to practise. Both my parents-in-law had a long, friendly association with the RCMP, both of them working for them off and on throughout the past decades and had lovingly raising my Sakikuluk's son fathered by an RCMP officer. This unfortunate incident most definitely had to be kept from becoming public knowledge.

After my parents-in-law returned that fall to their home camp at Igarjuaq, my Sakikuluk found that she was indeed pregnant just as her deceased cousin had predicted. The following year, in April, she gave birth to Mikiseetee. She did as she had promised and gave her baby son her dead cousin's name among the many other Inuit names the boy received. His baptismal name, Melchizedek, of Old Testament fame as foreshadowing the coming of Jesus, was pronounced Mikiseetee.

I can imagine the fear my parents-in-law must have felt, the threats of Canadian justice as well as the perils of breaking Inuit traditional taboos as well as the sin against their Christian beliefs.

From the stories I had heard from various family members, I was able to construct a view of Mikiseetee's childhood. About two years after Mikiseetee's birth, my Sakikuluk was taken away by ship to the Hamilton Tuberculosis Sanatorium for treatment in southern Canada. As was the custom to avoid unnecessary worry or brooding, no one talked about his mother to little Mikiseetee while his mother was away and so he forgot all about her. When she left, Mary, his oldest sister, took on the role of mother for him. By this time, Mary was already married to Issigaituk but was still without children. When my Sakikuluk was returned to Mittimatalik in 1958 Mikiseetee, did not know her as his mother.

All the children around Mikiseetee's age were his mother's grandchildren and called her ningiu, father's mother, or ananatsiaq, mother's mother. When he copied these children, his mother frightened him, demanding that he call her anaana, mother. In this way, he learned not only to respect her, but to be afraid of her as well. Mikiseetee had to leave Mary's house and move into his mother's house, onto her sleeping platform. Later, his mother adopted a child from her relatives in her birth community, Clyde River, who helped her with her young son. This was Apphia, whom Mikiseetee regarded as an older sister. Many of his mother's grandchildren were much older than Mikiseetee. This must have been thoroughly confusing for him as a little boy.

My Sakikuluk's letter with its confession helped to explain why the family treated Mikiseetee differently from other children. Everyone told me about how the family spoiled Mikiseetee while he was growing up, the youngest of my Sakikuluk's children. He was never allowed to become unhappy, and everyone was on their guard to prevent him from becoming angry or upset. The whole family ensured that he always got what he wanted. I can comprehend the family fearing Mikiseetee's likelihood to become insane, like his unfortunate namesake.

I have noted that there may be no greater fear among Inuit than fear of insanity or mental defects. In the old days, I knew, anyone suffering insanity or mental defects was seen as a threat and more than likely executed, just like those with physical defects. I knew of an old woman who had raised a mentally defective son to adolescence. We all watched him laboriously learning to ride a bicycle and he finally succeeded. A few days later, we heard that he had smothered to death while sleeping. I found this odd.

My Sakikuluk had said, "The boy showed how determined he was to ride a bicycle. That means that, should he put his mind to wanting something, or a woman, he could easily rape, or steal or cause damage. He would have been a threat because he had a mind of a young child. His mother was an old woman. It is better this way."

Not long after, the deceased adolescent's old mother died. Everyone seemed satisfied how these events had unfolded. This showed me that there was much that did not appear on the surface in our community, that there were deep secrets kept.

Some of the traditional family customs were not enforced for Mikiseetee when he was growing up. For instance, if a younger child had something that he wanted, the younger child had to give it to Mikiseetee. Usually, the older child must always defer to the younger child. Appeasing Mikiseetee did not become a problem while they still lived out at their camp at Igarjuaq, but when they were moved to Mittimatalik in the mid-1960s, things became more difficult. Only family and close extended family lived at the home camp at Igarjuaq, but in the new settlement of Mittimatalik, many different families, although generally related, were brought together from their outlying home camps.

At first, only the school-aged children were taken by the RCMP into town to attend the newly built school to comply with Canadian law. These children, including Mikiseetee, at first lived in tents throughout the academic year, near the school, which was uncomfortable at best and dangerous at worst. Later, after more buildings were built, the schoolchildren were boarded in a boarding home staffed by local Inuit house-parents. The families out in their home camps sorely missed their children and readily consented to the move into town when housing was provided. Each family was given a house that they helped build from imported prefabricated summer cottages shipped north by ship. At first, everyone was happy with the new homes as they began to live in them in the summer, but soon it was winter and they learned the drawbacks of living in uninsulated houses. The glaring difference between the superior houses provided for the schoolteachers and government officials and what had been provided for the Inuit population, became painfully apparent. Luckily, Mikiseetee's parents were very resourceful and succeeded in making their home as comfortable as they could.

Growing up in Mittimatalik, Mikiseetee told me, he had become good friends with Samuel, son of the alleged shaman Kautainuk, who had been his father's rival. His father approved as was the Inuit way of forgiveness. Both boys were viewed with suspicion by the other children their age, the one because he had been so spoiled and the other because of his father's dark reputation.

At school, Mikiseetee proved to be a good student, he told me, and he learned to speak English fluently, as well as to read and write. At home, he learned to read and write in the Inuktitut syllabics his mother taught him from the Anglican prayer book and portions of the Old Testament Bible translated into Inuktitut syllabics. He told me he loved going to school and actually looked forward to leaving Mittimatalik to go to high school in Frobisher Bay. But his mother did not want him to leave her. He had no choice but to stay at home and go hunting with his father and older brothers, disappointed that other boys were allowed to continue their education away, but not him. He did not take well to being denied.

As an adolescent, Mikiseetee had styled himself at first as a hippie in colourful clothes and long hair, then as rebellious, like a biker gang member, and wore a black-leather biker jacket. He told me that some married older women introduced him to sex and gave him alcohol and illicit drugs. He was very popular with these women, he said. Alcohol was more readily available in town than out in the camps and was already becoming a problem disrupting families in town. Mikiseetee was known for his bad temper and people learned to avoid him, especially when he was drunk.

Anaviapik's oldest son, known as the "town fool", a designation of which he was proud, told me about how he, a grown man, walked beside Mikiseetee, then a teenager at about the age of sixteen. He said he was teasing Mikiseetee about something while they were walking when Mikiseetee suddenly lost his temper with him. Right there, on the road, Mikiseetee beat him up so badly he had to stay at the nursing station for a few days to recover. This man laughed when he told me this story. I asked why no one had scolded Mikiseetee about this.

The man said, "Everyone knows it was not Mikiseetee's fault," and shrugged his shoulders.

I found this difficult to understand, that it was just ajurnarnmat.

After this incident, his mother sent him to live in Arctic Bay for some years. When he returned, he got a job working in the kitchens of the transportation services in Resolute Bay. He did not stay long in this job because of homesickness, he said, and returned to Mittimatalik.

Home again, Mikiseetee soon became interested in adult education classes when a man named Douglas Green, called Asivak, spider, in Inuktitut, replaced the first local community adult educator, Fred Hunt, who went on to found the local Cooperative store and hotel. Spider Green, as he was known in English, introduced Mikiseetee to the microscope and fed Mikiseetee's natural squeamishness to insects by showing him, in high resolution, house fly legs with egg sacs attached. Mikiseetee, horrified but impressed, was permanently repulsed and began to fear houseflies. But it was through Spider Green's efforts that Mikiseetee became the candidate for running the planned local lending library out of the adult education centre. It was a year or so after Spider Green had left the community that I first met Mikiseetee and began my life with him.

After he had told me the contents of his mother's letter to his sister, all I could say to my distraught husband was, "You may be the namesake of a person who had lost her mind, but I think that your job is now to repair this name of yours so that it becomes a name worthy to give on to another human being when it comes time for you to pass on."

He said that he probably could not manage that.

My Sakikuluk's confession letter explained much of what had puzzled me about my husband. Now Mikiseetee's parents, my Sakialuk and Sakikuluk, were gone, leaving me alone to deal with my broken husband. From now on, I knew that our marriage would be put to its greatest tests.

Twenty-nine

One of the many things I missed after my Sakikuluk passed away was the daily contact I used to have with her. I used to visit her every day and, when I could not, I spoke with her on the telephone to let her know how we were doing. I was surprised how much the loss of this caring contact with my Sakikuluk affected me. I discovered that I was grieving for her but not nearly as openly as Mikiseetee. Having been our family elder, she had always been supplied with meat and fish by her hunter children and grandchildren and she used to make sure that I always had fresh country food: seal, caribou or char. I had relied on her for this, especially after Mikiseetee began to work as a wage earner. Because I had never before had a need for sea or land foods, I was ignorant of the fact that I was not to accept meat from hunters outside of our immediate family. The one time I unknowingly transgressed in this and accepted meat from a hunter who was not a member of our direct family, Mikiseetee reacted in anger.

He said, "You have, by accepting this meat, insulted me and our family hunters. You must only accept meat and fish from your sisters-in-law. Ask them."

I already knew that I was not to speak to my brothers-in-law in the presence of others. To approach my sisters-in-law if I wanted a share of their catch felt strange to me. Having to ask anyone for meat was new to me, but I had to get used to this new order of things. Often, by the time I was aware that any of my sisters-in-law had fresh meat, nothing was left for us. My Sakikuluk used to set some aside for me, but now, no one else in our extended family did this for me.

These days, Mikiseetee spent so much time away from the community, I could not count on him to provide meat for my children. There were months he spent away at the radar site or at the floe-edge at the junction of Eclipse Sound and Baffin Bay hunting narwhal and seals, while my children and I were left in town to fend for ourselves.

The year after we visited Tofino on Vancouver Island, my hardest tasks were to keep my children not only fed, but also reasonably content. Ruben had already been enrolled in school but was reluctant to go back to classes after the death of both his grandparents. It was a daily struggle to get him to go to school. Some days, he would go and then others he would refuse. I still needed to work part-time, and it was now difficult to find people to help me with my children. I had already lost the most important help, that of my mother-in-law. The whole family seemed to pull away from me as they grieved in their own ways.

Soon, I became friends with the new Home Management trainer at the local Adult Education Centre. She said she was surprised that I was a friendly person because my father had been so unfriendly to her when she met him a few months before. I suppose that she was as lonesome for company as I was since she was a trainer of adults and not part of the local schoolteacher clique. She had been provided with a government house near the beach, in which she lived alone. I found her generous to a fault and I was so happy to have a friend in whom I could confide. She was a full-figured woman and was sensitive about body image. Ruben liked her and it was she who corralled him and successfully dragged him off to school.

One day, my new friend said to me, "It must be wonderful for you to be nice looking."

I was surprised by her words. I had not thought about how I looked since my days as an artist's model in my former life in southern Canada.

"Is it? I wouldn't mind looking a bit uglier if I could just have a good relationship with my husband," I replied.

We discussed physical beauty and its downsides. How one looks — the cast of one's bone structure and skin tone, the entire physique — is more a product of chance in the lottery of life, I was sure. And I thought it more important how one wore oneself in spite of life's challenges. I always thought of my new friend as an attractive, confident woman in spite of what she saw as her shortcomings. I knew her as courageous with a wonderful sense of humour. We spent quite a bit of time laughing together during Mikiseetee's long absences.

That September, a teacher at the Joamie School in Iqaluit, our regional educational headquarters, came to Mittimatalik. She was committed to providing help to people with hearing problems in the small Baffin Island communities. She brought a portable hearing test machine to identify hearing problems among our schoolchildren. After she had tested them all, she opened the testing to Mittimatalik adults. I have always had problems hearing so I went for the test. Who knew what kind of changes had been made to hearing-test technology since my time at university? My local test results were such that I was included in the group of suspected hearing-impaired children and adults being sent out to Frobisher Bay's then new state-of-the-art audiology centre. At that time, it had an actual professional audiologist. As it happened, luckily, Mikiseetee was at home to stay with our children while I was away.

My audiology test result was a revelation. I was surprised to find my diagnosis as "borderline deaf". My hearing problem was identified as sensorineural hearing loss that we traced back to being the result of my severe bout of mumps when I was about two years old in Germany. At that time, I'd had a tracheotomy, an opening made to my throat, in order for me to breathe and survive. Now, ear molds were made for both of my ears, and I was given two hearing aids, one for each ear. The woman audiologist warned me that it would take about three months of headaches before I became accustomed to wearing them. She also warned me that they would only be of limited use with my kind of hearing loss, that they could only help a little and would not replace hearing. At that time, well before the new digital hearing aids I have now, managing the volume controls on those two aids to keep them in balance with each other was annoying and stressful. When they were out of balance they often squealed, which startled me, often making me jump while everyone near me was disturbed by the piercing screech my hearing aids made.

At the time of my diagnosis, the audiologist praised my ability to lip-read. Apparently, this ability is somewhat rare. I had not been aware, of course, how bad my hearing was growing up but I always knew that I had to see peoples' faces in order to make out what they were saying. She said that I had adapted to my hearing limitations from the time I had mumps as a toddler. I told her that a few years earlier, the doctors in southern Canada had said I had poor hearing because of "serous otitis media", blocked eustachian tubes, due to allergies. She told me, that since then, the technology for testing hearing had improved immeasurably. Lucky me.

When I returned to Mittimatalik, Mikiseetee said, "You can't hear. That's a disability. I can't have a disabled wife."

I thought at first that he was joking. But it turned out, he was not. Suddenly, I was required to be physically perfect with all senses intact to be his wife. I had heard that the blind, deaf or deformed in traditional Inuit life were at risk unless their family protected them. The only things different about me now was that I had been officially diagnosed and wore two hearing aids and was, of course, not Inuit born. And now I was no longer desirable to Mikiseetee, my husband, my protector and provider of meat for my children. He was ashamed of me. He now had a reason, valid to him, to set me aside. I wondered how this would play out.

That spring, I happened to read a magazine article, written by a psychology researcher, an expert on child psychology specializing in autism disorders in the United States, in which he claimed that Inuit children did not have "universal objects" as part of their early childhood development. A universal object is a soft toy or blanket, or similar, to which a toddler clings to help the child transition from the mother to other caregivers, for instance, a new babysitter or being left at daycare. I had graduated with a degree in psychology so this was of interest to me.

I wrote to this psychologist telling him that I thought he was wrong, that Inuit children did so have transitional objects but that they were not so obvious to outsiders. I wrote about the amautik, the carrying parka an Inuit mother wore in which to carry her child. It was the custom in our family to change the outer cover of the amautik whenever a new baby inhabits it. Whenever the baby or young child is given to someone for babysitting, this amautik would be what the babysitter wore to carry the child in. During long meetings or community gatherings, for instance, the child is often put to sleep on the floor ensconced in this amautik. The child recognizes it as belonging to him or her, a link to the mother. I would consider, I wrote, the amautik an important transitional object in Inuit child development.

I was gratified that the psychologist agreed. He made arrangements to visit Mittimatalik that winter so he could observe Inuit children in person. He asked if he could stay at my house, but I told him that was not possible. I said that my little family was definitely not traditional Inuit and, besides, I was having marital problems.

After his arrival in Mittimatalik, and having settled in at the new local Co-op hotel, the psychologist visited me and asked me how he could fast-track getting to know about Inuit traditional social and cultural life.

"I am in a hurry," he said. "I only have a week to spare from my clinical practice for this effort."

What could help this eager psychologist get the experience he wanted? I had recently heard about a local Inuit family who lived most of the year in their outpost camp away from town. The hunter/father had suddenly died leaving behind his widow and young children. The widow wanted to continue living away from town, but she needed income to be able to do that. I made arrangements for the psychologist to be a paying guest out in their camp.

Before he left for the outpost camp, I warned him that he would not be able to keep his normal hygiene habits because there were no amenities or facilities at all. I also warned him that he was to eat and drink what the family ate and drank, and if he brought any food items, he must share them with his host family. He was also not to complain about the smell or the cold or the lack of privacy. It was a tall order, I knew, but he agreed. He graciously endured the week, and returned to town grateful for the opportunity to observe a more-traditional Inuit family in outpost camp.

The psychologist must have gleaned from our conversations that I had some personal challenges aside from my marital difficulties and my hearing problems. After he arrived back at his clinic, he sent me some books about recovery from childhood sexual trauma and co-dependency. These books showed me how much the times had changed. Now it was possible to openly speak about such things without shame, and to be taken seriously by doctors and mental health workers. I read these books and thought over how I was leading my life.

Mama had spoken to me about how Papa had had a change of heart since the birth of his Inuit grandson. He now took his affiliation with local Inuit quite seriously and was looking for ways to leave a legacy for his Inuk grandson.

He had become quite close to Ataata Mari who heard his confessions with compassion and understanding. I have always been aware that Papa suffered mightily, physically and mentally, as a young German soldier on the eastern front during World War II. He had debilitating flashbacks and lingering health problems as a result of all his war wounds. I have always had a great respect for Papa's ability to teach himself what he needed when he was prevented by the war to complete university studies. I could almost picture Papa finally speaking his transgressions, hearing himself admit his compulsions, shame, and sorrows to Ataata Mari. It seemed to me that Ataata Mari filled the role of a loving accepting father that my Papa had not enjoyed in life.

I was aware that both my parents were aging and would eventually retire and leave Mittimatalik. I am sure that Papa had hoped I would take over his work here and carry it on with Mikiseetee. But he had, unfortunately, cancelled all hopes for that when he shouted at me in front of his Inuit trainees on that fateful day in the lab.

One summer, probably in 1983, Papa travelled from Mittimatalik, leaving Mama in charge of the Arctic Research Establishment. During his absence, Mama came to visit me more often and I continued to visit on Sundays with my children as was my habit. One Thursday afternoon, one of the laboratory trainees called me on the telephone, saying that she had not seen my mother for two days. My Mama always had coffee ready for the lab trainees and other employees for morning and afternoon coffee breaks.

I hurried down to my parent's house. I entered and called out, but there was no reply. I checked the washroom, radio room, visitor's room and finally my parent's bedroom. Mama's side of the bed was unmade but she was not there. How very strange.

Then I thought I heard a faint whimper. I found Mama on the floor wedged between the bed and the wall. She must have fallen out of the bed. I helped her up.

"The trainees said they haven't seen you for two days. What's wrong? Why didn't you call out to them to come and help you?" I asked.

"I didn't want to upset or alarm them," she said.

The next day, I took her to the nursing station to see the nurse. Mama may have suffered an ischemic stroke, sometimes known as a mini-stroke when a blood clot interferes with the brain, according to the nurse. Mama seemed not to have suffered permanent damage, she said.

After Papa returned and Mama told him about this, she left for southern Canada in order to see her doctor. Mama was worried that Papa would not be able to take care of himself. Papa said he would be fine and would cook for himself. I said I would come to vacuum, do his laundry once a week and at that time bake him a week's supply of home-baked bread.

Mama then left, satisfied that her beloved husband, her life's companion, would be able to cope without her.

I usually brought my children when I did the housework and baking at Papa's house. But one time I went without them. I would not be housekeeping this time. Having read the books sent me by the visiting psychologist, I had come to the decision that I should confront Papa about the childhood sexual abuse. I do not know what I expected. I knew I could not have done this if Mama were here to protect him from me.

"I need to discuss with you some things from my childhood," I said.

By this he knew that this time I had not come to do housework. We sat down at the table after I had made coffee for us. He nodded at me to start.

"I have been keeping secret our sexual relationship for a long time and now I need to tell you how much keeping this secret has bothered me and made me so ashamed of myself."

"But it was only for a few years and long ago," he began.

I interrupted, "I was nine years old and I believed what you told me then because you were my father and I loved you. Ever since my early adolescence I knew you lied to me. That hurt me very much."

I watched his eyes, his face. I could see his dawning understanding and could feel his sadness.

In a quiet voice he said, "I am so sorry if I have hurt you." I was happy to hear those words.

After a few moments of silence, he said, "You know ours was not the only secret I kept."

He tried to tell me of another secret, but I waved that off. His conscience was not my problem.

"I refuse to keep secrets for you and I am not sorry about that," I said, "but I am sorry that you need to keep these secrets at all."

I could see that he knew he had broken the ground between us regained by his apology, that I could not trust him again. Still, it was a partial reconciliation.

Thirty

I regularly visited Joanna, my sister-in-law and Ulayuk's birth mother, to take the place of my former routine of daily visits to my Sakikuluk. I tried to make sure that Ulayuk got to know both her birth parents, that they could be close with each other. James, her birth father, was at that time a lay minister at the Anglican church, a serious, devout man who suffered acute arthritis in his hands. I admired him for overcoming his alcohol habit and turning his life around. One day, James listened to the sorrowful complaints I made to his wife about Mikiseetee, how he spent so much time away from us, how he only came to town when liquor orders were expected, and how he seemed to avoid me as much as possible.

"As long as you keep secrets from your husband, you cannot expect him to improve," he said.

Somehow, James sensed that I was keeping a secret from my husband. He was right. It was true. I was. I decided to take a chance and reveal my secret to Mikiseetee. On one of the occasions that he was at home and seemed calm, I told him about my father, how it came about that he abused me from the age of nine until well into my adolescence, how it had hurt me, and how this is the reason there was such tension sometimes between my father and myself. I thought Mikiseetee understood. He seemed to hear me and looked sympathetic while I was speaking. After I finished telling him, he burst out laughing.

He said, "You think you are so different from the other women here? You're just like them. You're no different. All the women have been what you call 'sexually abused' by their fathers, uncles, brothers, brothers-in-law, grandfathers. That is how a girl traditionally becomes a woman. Why are you complaining?"

I was stunned. Obviously, I had been naive. How did I not actually know this already? I suddenly recalled when my Sakikuluk told me of the time she had her husband build a private room onto their qarmaq so that their adolescent daughter, Mary, would not be bothered by men while she was sleeping. I had not given this any particular attention at the time I heard it, but now it made perfect sense. Mikiseetee did not see me as "damaged goods" as would Qallunaat. To him, having a hearing problem far outweighed any other shortcomings I might have. I did not have the heart to tell my brother-in-law James that telling my secret to Mikiseetee did not have the desired effect of dispelling a long-held shameful secret thereby repairing our relationship.

Unfortunately, James was suddenly taken ill with viral pneumonia a few months later and was sent by air MedEvac to hospital. Before the plane landed in Frobisher Bay, he had already died. Mikiseetee had lost not only both his parents but now also the one person he could confide in. My little daughter, too, missed her birth father very much. We continued to visit Joanna every day, but she was in deep mourning for the husband whom she had loved, the man that she had chosen for herself, not someone chosen for her by her parents as had happened to her older sister Mary.

❄

After Ataata Mari completed his research for his book about the Greenlandic Inuit connection to the Inuit of Mittimatalik in May 1983, the community held another the exchange charter between Mittimatalik and Qaanaq, Greenland, like the one my son and I had gone on in 1978. This time, it was Mikiseetee's turn to visit Qaanaq on exchange and I paid for this trip. I hoped visiting his Qaanaq relatives would help divert him from his mourning and cheer him up a little.

The same plane that brought Mikiseetee back home to Mittimatalik took the Qaanaq visitors home again. One exchange visitor, Johannes, stayed behind, perhaps hoping to remain in Mittimatalik permanently. He had a local girlfriend and was living with her family. Mikiseetee was good friends with Johannes and his girlfriend and they often partied together. I was not invited, but I did not much mind. I was aware that Johannes had no chance of remaining in Canada because international visitors were only allowed to remain in this country for six months on a visitor's visa. Still, I was glad that Mikiseetee was actually happier after his trip to Qaanaq, but, sadly, he was just not happier with me. We just carried on as we had before.

That summer we went out to camp for a week at Nallua with Mikiseetee's oldest brother, Bethuel, and his family. I was a little surprised that Mikiseetee took our children and me along, but later I heard that Johannes and his girlfriend had already gone to her family's summer camp earlier that week.

I hoped this family camping trip would be a chance for Mikiseetee and I to come together again as a married couple so we could be a family again. At first, he acted like he was my husband and helped set up our tent, a canvas we had newly purchased at the HBC store to replace the one that had been traded away for booze. Our children were both happy to be out on the land together with their parents, like a real family. We brought along our adolescent nephew, Natanai, who had gone with us to Tofino.

Mikiseetee told Natanai to put up the small nylon pup tent and sleep there. Was Mikiseetee seeking privacy for us in our tent? I wondered. Was he was planning to have a private talk with me that he did not want Natanai to overhear? Mikiseetee and I had not been close or intimate for months. I knew he had slept around with other women when he was drunk, but I was willing to forgive him all that.

After we had eaten supper, and the children had gone outside to play, Mikiseetee told me that he was going to sleep in the pup tent with Natanai. Whatever I had hoped for this camping trip, was not about to happen. That became quite clear.

While at Nallua, our children and I did not see Mikiseetee much. It

Last family camp at Nallua 1983.

was an unusually bountiful seal hunt that summer and lots of beautiful silver jar seals were caught. That meant that Mikiseetee was away hunting most of the time with his brother and nephews. When we did see him, he only spoke to me when absolutely necessary as he delivered his catch. He still slept in the pup tent.

I kept busy flensing his sealskins, washing and pegging them out to dry with wooden stakes on the tundra edge of the beach. Ruben and Ulayuk often asked me why their father did not stay in our tent with us. I told them that he still missed his deceased parents and James so much and it would take a long time for him to get back to normal. I did not

Nallua camp 1983.

Mikiseetee and his sister-in-law Elisapee Ootoova 1983.

know if they would understand. I know they also sorely missed their grandparents, especially Ruben, who had been their favourite grandchild. Ulayuk was still very small but she did miss James, whom she knew as her birth father and remembered from our daily visits when he was still alive.

In spite of the estrangement between Mikiseetee and me, our last family camping trip at Nallua was enjoyable because the weather was good and we were so busy hunting and processing sealskins. It was a very good year for the summer seal hunt.

Then it happened that Mikiseetee sold our boat and outboard motor to pay for Birthe, who he said was his Qaanaq girlfriend, to fly to Mittimatalik from Nuuk, Greenland, via Iqaluit. When he told me

Flensing sealskins 1983.

what he was doing, I was at first surprised and then angry. He was actually replacing me, his wife, with this woman he hardly knew, using the boat I had helped him buy for his hunting. I knew then that I had to separate from him while he worked through this madness.

In the adult education library, I found a book that helped me draw up official separation agreement papers. I allowed Mikiseetee to keep whatever he wanted of what we jointly owned, but I did put in a clause

Me preparing a meal 1983.

about how he was to provide meat from his hunts for his children. Mikiseetee signed the papers and moved into his older sister Mary's house to await Birthe's arrival. I filed the signed papers with the local social worker for safekeeping. I knew he would try to find my copy to destroy it. The next time he was drunk, he trashed our house looking for these papers. I told him where my copy was and he finally left off bothering me.

When Birthe arrived, she lived with Mikiseetee at his sister Mary's house. He often came to visit our children during this time. On one such visit, he told me that Birthe had lost her parka and snow pants, possibly stolen, in Nuuk while she waited for the airplane to carry her to Canada. I found some cold weather clothes for her and Mikiseetee took them to her. On another visit, he said that she was bored and needed something to do. I knew that the women in Qaanaq were all so proud of their fancy beadwork. I gave him my supply of beads and beading needles. Perhaps, I said, that would occupy her.

One of my local Inuit women friends visited and we spoke about Birthe.

She said, "She is my friend, too, and so I can no longer visit you because Birthe is very jealous."

She apologized. I said it was all right. I thought of poor Birthe who did not speak the local dialect and

Sealskins drying at Nallua 1983.

Ruben caught a seal 1983.

actually had no other friends in town. I remembered how disoriented I had been when I first came to live in Mittimatalik. I knew she did not have an easy time at Mary's house. And I also knew that her days in Mittimatalik were numbered.

Then it was almost Christmas. Birthe's six months visitor's visa to Canada had expired. The RCMP officer came to Mary's house and escorted Birthe to the airstrip for her flights back to Nuuk, Greenland. Did Mikiseetee seriously think that an exception would be made for Birthe after he had witnessed Johannes forced the year before to leave

Mikiseetee visiting Ruben and Ulayuk 1984.

after his six months were over?

On Christmas Day, Mikiseetee came into the house drunk and announced that now that Birthe was gone he was moving back home again. I had to tell him that I needed a bit more time and there would have to be some changes before I could accept him back. I made arrangements with the Anglican church minister for Mikiseetee and me to meet with him at the church because I had something important to say that I did not want Mikiseetee to forget. I wanted the minister to be a witness to show Mikiseetee that I meant what I said.

"I will let you know my decision on your birthday in April. That will give you time to get used to not getting so drunk anymore."

I applied to the housing association for a house of my own so Mikiseetee could have his house back. That was how I discovered that Mikiseetee had not paid the rent owed to the housing association for the past six months, even though I had given him the rent money. The rental agreement was in his name. I confronted him with this and asked him what he had done with the money I had given him for the rent. He told me, since he had not been living at this house, he had spent it on liquor orders treating his drinking buddies and buying things at the store for Birthe and his sister.

In view of our marital separation, the housing association granted me an older, not yet refurbished, house. They would not allow Mikiseetee back into his house until the back rent was all paid up. Meanwhile, he continued to live at his sister's house. Mikiseetee went to work for a while for Papa in the face of his housing debt. I helped pay the back rent so he could live in it again because I knew that he was very unhappy living at his sister's house.

The house I was granted was located beside the old house my parents-in-law had lived in when I first arrived. It had a bathtub in one of the two bedrooms that had a drain to the outside. There was a water pipe system and pump connected to the indoor plastic water tank that worked most of the time, but there was no hot water. Still, I was happy to move.

In March, Mikiseetee told me that he had decided to not return to me and our children after all, that he now had a new girlfriend who would now live with him at his house.

"That is interesting, but I will make up my mind on your birthday in April, like I said at Christmas," I said.

On his birthday, he came to visit and asked me what I had decided. I said that since he already lived with his new girlfriend in our former house, he had made the decision for me. That seemed to settle things between us for a while.

Since the death of his mother, Mikiseetee had only worked for Papa on and off, only when he needed money. He stopped going with us when Ruben, Ulayuk,

Joanna, my sister-in-law, Ulayuk's birth mother 1984.

Mikiseetee at the Siraliq work camp, one last time 1984.

and I made our weekly Sunday visits to my parents after church.

Mama and Papa tried to console me, telling me that Mikiseetee would eventually recover from his grief, just as I had tried to tell my children. Papa said Mikiseetee's alcohol abuse would also lessen as he grew older. I was not convinced, but tried to keep myself together for the sake of my children. Papa and Mama even told me, one Sunday, that they had included my adopted Ulayuk, as my daughter, their granddaughter, in their wills. That did cheer me up. It was a sign of their acceptance of my daughter as they had accepted my son Ruben, their beloved grandson.

Finally, Papa became concerned about Mikiseetee's long absence from work and called me by telephone. He wanted me to talk to Mikiseetee, perhaps I could have him go to see him.

I said, "I will pass on the message to Mikiseetee when he makes his next visit to us."

I told Papa that Mikiseetee was no longer living with us, that we were officially separated, and that I thought he would probably not come to him. Papa said Mikiseetee could still work for him. It did not seem to bother Papa much that Mikiseetee and I were now officially separated.

He said, "What does Mikiseetee being separated from you have to do with him working for me?"

I tried to explain to him that Mikiseetee only worked for him because he felt compelled, that it is what his parents wanted him to do as a good Inuit son-in-law to him. Now that the old people were dead, he no longer felt so compelled. It had not always been all about the money for Mikiseetee until lately. I also reminded Papa that I actually made enough money with my air agent and personnel expeditor jobs to support me and my children, although these were considered part-time jobs. I passed on the message, but Papa waited in vain. Mikiseetee did not go back to work.

Life in my un-refurbished house that had seen use by a few of my extended family was a little different from the fully equipped and insulated house that I had to leave behind. It had been my brother-in-law Josepee who had at one point installed the full-sized, claw-foot bathtub and connected the electric pump that allowed cold water to flow into it from the oversized water tank. I also had cold running water for my kitchen sink. When we wanted to take a bath, we still needed to heat water on the stove and transfer it by bucket from the kitchen to the bathtub in the bedroom. It was a big improvement over the washtub "shower-stall" for a "pour-over" showers I used during the time

Ruben and Ulayuk in our new (old) house 1984.

Mikiseetee's house was being renovated. At that time I had improvised this by using a wire clothes hanger and a plastic shower curtain suspended from the ceiling of our little washroom. Just to have the bathtub in my own house was, I thought, pretty good, actually. When the tub was not in use, there was a fitted plywood cover to keep the children from playing in it. Ruben and Ulayuk soon accustomed themselves to our new home. Now I was a single mother on my own.

Thirty-one

In spite of the changes in our housing and home life after Mikiseetee and I separated in 1984, I still made an effort to keep a more or less normal rhythm to our seasons. Going camping without a husband, I knew, would be a great challenge. I approached some members of our extended family, and one of Mikiseetee's nephews finally promised to take us along in his boat to camp with his family. But, a few days later, he came and said he could not take us after all. He said it would not be right. I could not understand this. It occurred to me that perhaps he thought helping me would be taking my side against Mikiseetee, or something like that. Still, I had to accept what he said. And that left me on my own to come up with something as an alternative for our summer camping.

The Tununiq Sauniq Co-operative of Mittimatalik had, in the past, along with its store and hotel, operated a fishing camp for high-paying government officials, oil company executives and other guests at Qurluqtuq Bay out at Milne Inlet to the west of Mittimatalik. It was easily accessible by boat when the waters were ice-free, usually in late July, and it also had a broad and long gravel beach that had been used as a landing strip for Twin Otter aircraft in the past. The camp was not used that summer, I knew.

I approached the Co-op manager, Fred Hunt, with the idea of allowing me and my children access to the cookhouse so we could have a sheltered place in which to stay. It was my aim for my children and me to go camping by airplane that summer. He agreed for a modest amount of money. I made arrangements with Kenn Borek Air for time off as well as for chartering a plane from Mittimatalik to Qurluqtuq Bay and returning a week later. The Kenn Borek Air manager was happy to do this for me without charge as a thank you for my past service, for which I was grateful.

I gathered bedding, fishing gear and supplies and arranged for Natanai and his younger brother, Nonnie, to accompany Ruben, Ulayuk and me to Qurluqtuq Bay for a week. We really intended to fish. Papa loaned me a .22 rifle in case we needed it as well as a two-way field radio. Fred Hunt gave me the key for the cookhouse door. At that time, we had a small female dog, a Scottie mix, with mostly black fur. We called her Ginger. No one would care for our pet while we were gone, I knew, so we decided that she should come with us, too.

Papa's two-way VHF field radio was for daily transmissions. This was most important for the time of our return. I could give a local weather report to Papa to pass on to Kenn Borek personnel and for him to give me the estimated time of arrival of the airplane after it had left Mittimatalik for Qurluqtuq Bay.

So, on a cloudless beautiful day during the second week of August, the power plant manager's truck took our things and all of us, Ruben, Ulayuk, Natanai, Nonnie, Ginger the dog and me up to the Kenn Borek plane for takeoff.

The flight did not take long and soon we were descending to land at Qurluqtuq Bay. I had paper towels and garbage bag handy because I

Arrival at Qurluqtuq Bay fish camp 1984.

thought, perhaps, one of the children may get air sick. But, no, it was just our dog, Ginger, who threw up.

We landed without difficulty and taxied bumpily up the beach to the fish camp cookhouse. Arrayed behind it were rectangular wooden pads with frames that looked like skeletons without the tents that usually covered them.

After we unloaded our gear, I unlocked the cookhouse door and we dragged it all inside. It was all one big open area, a kitchen-dining room, with folded up tables and chairs arranged along one end. There were two great, black, restaurant-style stoves side by side along the back wall. The front wall across from it had a window that would open and close. Under it, I set up one folding table on which I put my small propane camp stove. We made a large bed of the foam mattresses and bedding farther along the floor into the corner and set up my qulliq on a large metal baking tray on the floor in front of the bed. I had brought fuel for the camp stove as well as a few gallons of cooking oil for the qulliq.

After we got our house in order, we took up some fish poles and went off to explore where we could catch the arctic char that Qurluqtuq Bay was so famous for.

It was an extremely long walk out to the river where I had been told we could catch fish and at last we got there. I had brought along a thermos of tea which we all drank from before heading back to the cookhouse. The older boys and Ruben would go back out there the next morning, we decided, while Ulayuk and I and Ginger would stay behind.

The next morning, after a good night's sleep, I gave the rifle to Natanai, he being the oldest, to take out with them to the fishing river. The boys carried the thermos and biscuits and disassembled fishing

Qurluqtuq Bay cookhouse 1984.

Ruben asleep at Qurluqtuq 1984.

poles and other gear. The weather was gloriously clear and we knew it would be a good day. The boys came back with two good-sized arctic char that night. I knew we would not go hungry. Fishing was good for the entire time we were there.

On my birthday, August 13, I baked a special birthday-cake bannock, sweet with mixed fruit. Natanai's brother Nonnie did not like the raisins, so I told him to pick them out after I cut him a portion. The others ate those raisins he left and were thankful for them.

Arctic char is a wonderful, tasty fish, my favourite, but after eating char for every meal day after day, it did lose its appeal somewhat. There were a lot of clam shells on the beach which showed me that there must be clams here, too. I knew nothing at all about clams and clam digging but hoped that, somehow, I would find some anyway. At low tide, Ulayuk and I were playing on the beach with Ginger, the dog, when I noticed a kind of hole in the wet sand that

Preparing my birthday dinner 1984.

seemed to exhale. Ginger ran up to it and began to bark furiously, like she was protecting us. There were many more of these exhaling holes, I saw. With a stick I dug down but I could not find even one clam. After their return to the cookhouse, the boys laughed when we told them about Ginger wanting to protect us from the dire threat of clams.

On the morning we were to leave, the weather became overcast with low thick clouds. I became anxious that we would be prevented from going home as scheduled. My radio exchange with Papa left me somewhat reassured that the pilot would do his best to come. They would check in later in the day to see if our weather had improved. There were a few hours yet to go, so we spent the time packing our things and putting the cookhouse back in the order that it was in when we arrived. Then I walked the beach runway to see that there were no obstructions that might hamper the landing of the plane. The children helped me pile up our things where we estimated the plane would pick us up.

Ulayuk and Ginger, our dog, at Qurluqtuq 1984.

The children and the dog played tag among the tent frames to pass the time. We had a quick lunch. The radio transmission went well after lunch and I reported that the sky had cleared, the clouds had lifted.

Papa said that the pilot would be landing the plane within the hour. While we waited, we walked around behind the camp that somehow now looked so abandoned. I looked through my binoculars and spotted a caribou standing alert, head up and alone, away in the distance at the foot of the mountain. The next instant, the caribou had vanished. I wondered if

Natanai with a big char at Qurluqtuq 1984..

I had just imagined it. Then I heard the sound of our plane.

We all helped to load the plane. Everyone was excited to be going home. Camp had been fun and the fishing had been good, but it had been lonely at times. Even Ginger the dog seemed happy to board the plane.

As the plane rose into the sky and turned to fly over the fish camp, I looked down. I saw two boats in the waters of Milne Inlet heading toward the camp. I wondered if they were coming to visit us.

This time, Ginger did not have motion sickness. The flight went well and we landed without any problems at the Mittimatalik airstrip. The power plant manager was there with his truck to take us and our gear home.

Later, I heard, that in the first boat going to the fish camp as we were leaving was a man who had often threatened me when he was drunk. In the second boat, following a way behind the first boat, was Koonark, Mikiseetee's uncle who worked for my Papa. He had been designated by my Sakikuluk as my caretaker before she died, I discovered later. Now that we were back in Mittimatalik, it dawned on me how dangerous my going to the fish camp with the children had been, a woman alone. I had no fear of bears or other animals, but I had not even considered the threat of predatory men.

Koonark, Mikiseetee's uncle, was in the habit of visiting me once a month, and drinking tea while I cut his grey hair. The person who used to cut hair had left Mittimatalik the year my Sakikuluk had passed away. Koonark liked his hair done in a buzz cut, short all over, flat on top, and that was easy enough to do with a sharp pair of scissors and clippers. I was happy to provide him this service.

That he was my designated caretaker appointed by my Sakikuluk

Playing tag waiting for the plane 1984.

Nonnie before take-off 1984.

before her death, I discovered when Koonark came to visit me at my new hillside house one afternoon with his wife. His wife had never visited me before, although I had visited her at her home a few times over the years. I set out the mugs of tea and waited for Koonark to begin speaking.

"Ukuaq, I know you are used to being married. You must miss having a man in your bed."

Oddly enough his wife smiled and nodded as he spoke.

He continued, "My wife and I have discussed your situation and, because I agreed to be your caretaker when your mother-in-law asked me to, I am now at your service as the man for your bed."

Well, this was awkward, I thought. I knew Koonark was a lay minister at the Anglican Church and very religious. What could I possibly say to deflect him without insulting him or his wife?

"I thank you and your wife for this kind offer," I said, "but does this

Koonark and his wife plus grandchild 1982.

not go against the rules of the Anglican Church?"

He nodded and said, "This has nothing to do with religion. This is about real life and my wife has agreed."

He is not making this any easier for me, I thought.

"As a lay minister of the Anglican Church, you will have trouble. You are such a good lay minister. It would be a shame if you had to stop your work for the church. Everyone watches who comes and goes at my house because I am a woman alone with children. Soon, someone would tell the Anglican church missionary. For sure, that would end your lay ministry. I really prefer to chose who it is that shares my bed. I am, after all, really just a Qallunaq. Thank you for wanting to take care of me."

"You are right, Ukuaq," he said. He must have been very nervous. He sighed, relaxed, and finished his tea.

Finally, they both rose from their chairs to go and Koonark's wife came to me and hugged me.

How complicated things can get, sometimes, I thought, without a husband.

I had looked over what men were currently unattached and available in Mittimatalik, both Inuit and Qallunaq. There was no one that I thought I could live with who would treat me well and who would accept my children. It was not so easy to replace what I had while my parents-in-law were still alive: a husband and a vibrant extended family. I had cut all ties with my former life in Ontario and had no wish to return there. I had no yearning to raise my children homesick for their Mittimatalik home, as aliens among southern Canadians from whom I now also felt alien. So far, I was able to support my little household on my two part-time jobs with Pan Arctic and Kenn Borek Air.

After the loss of my parents-in-law, I became friends with the new local school principal, Noel McDermott. I first met him in the summer of 1983 at the airstrip when he and his wife, Kate, and their two children arrived on one of the Ken Borek Air planes. On arrival, he was upset with me that his boxes of books had not been sent along with his baggage on this flight to Mittimatalik.

I inquired with my head office, and they said that people take precedence over freight and that the little plane had just been too full. Noel's boxes of books arrived in good order on the next scheduled flight and were delivered to his house. I went there to have him sign the freight manifest for the books and he apologized for having been so bad tempered with me. He told me of his love of books and I could fully understand that.

One afternoon, I visited Kate, Noel's wife. We sat and drank tea in her kitchen and she told me a bit about coming from Ireland and making friends in Mittimatalik. She asked me how I spent my free time.

"Are you reading any books?" she asked me.

"I'm reading Shakespeare's Sonnets, a book I brought north with me," I said.

She became excited and called, "Noel! Come here. This woman is reading Shakespeare!"

Noel came into the kitchen and sat at the table with us. He told me he was working on a dissertation about Shakespeare for his doctorate. That was why those books he brought were so important.

The McDermotts soon became part of our Mittimatalik community and heard all the gossip that included the doings of my husband, Mikiseetee, our marital status, his binge drinking, the story of both my parents-in-law dying in the same year, and all that.

Thirty-two

In the late summer of 1984, Pan Arctic officials arrived to hold a meeting of their local field workers. I arranged for the meeting to take place at the adult education centre and had the time and place announced on local radio. Pan Arctic Oils had suffered a serious business setback, the officials said, and they were forced to stop their northern operations. That meant that there would no longer be jobs for their Mittimatalik workers. The officials handed out bonus payments to all their former workers with their heartfelt apologies. The local men said they understood and thanked them for having provided them with jobs in the past. The officials also gave me a bonus. The former workers, in a little thank-you ceremony for my services to them, gave me a soapstone carving presented to me by the man who had, unknown to anyone else, raped me years ago while I was housesitting for my parents. He had become a good friend and helper over the years. It is so curious how things work, I thought, and accepted it graciously.

When no one was listening, that man said to me, "I have been looking forward to giving you this carving to thank you for forgiving me."

The Pan Arctic work stoppage meant that I not only lost my personnel expeditor's job. I also left my job as air agent for Kenn Borek Air because I knew what they paid was simply not enough to meet all my expenses. Now I had to find other ways to generate income to help support myself and my children. My Papa came to the rescue with a part-time job of payroll clerk for his employees at his Arctic Research Establishment while Mama was once again away in southern Canada for health reasons. That helped, but I could not picture a future in this.

With Noel McDermott's encouragement, I applied as a substitute teacher and taught social studies and geography while a regular teacher was away for a few months. That became interesting because in my class were a few of the children who had attended the pre-school in 1975 that I ran for a time while I was pregnant with Ruben. That I was not a stranger to these learners, helped to dispel any nervousness I felt because I lacked formal teaching skills. Substitute teaching paid well, but was, of course, only temporary, and I could not count on being rehired again until another teacher had to take an unforeseen a leave of absence. I looked into perhaps getting an elementary school teacher's license which, I knew, the local school principal could grant under certain conditions, but, unfortunately, Noel said, my university degree was not in any subject taught in northern schools, like English. Mine had been in psychology and German literature.

At the school, I became friends with Manik, a teaching assistant, who was beginning to take formal teacher's training in order to support her family. She was originally from Igloolik and was distantly related to Ruben. She lived with her husband and little family in the house next to us. I now had four new friends, the home management trainer, the McDermotts and Manik.

Through the home management trainer at the Adult Education Centre, I received a contract to prepare her local trainee, Mary, to take the General Education Development (GED) high school equivalency examinations. Mary wanted to attend the next summer's Train the

Trainer adult educator program at St. Francis Xavier University in Antigonish, Nova Scotia. The home management trainer was hoping to train her to become a fully qualified assistant in home management training. At the same time, I was also able to teach adults English literacy part time at the local adult education centre.

Even though I desperately needed income, I made a pact with myself that I would not take a job that local Inuit could do. I only took the jobs that no local could do. I did not want to deprive any Inuit of the opportunity to support their family. I needed to be able to feed my children, pay the rent and other bills for my household, but not at the expense of local Inuit.

At the time, Mama and Papa were trying to convince me to leave Mittimatalik with them, to do as my Sakikuluk had told me to do on her deathbed: take my children and leave. It sounded at times quite tempting, but I realized that this was not really something I wanted to do. I recalled all too well my own experience of being taken from my familiar home in Germany to come to Canada as an alien at the age of five. I wanted to spare my children such an experience. I also could not picture my children growing up in southern Canada, dreaming and longing for an idealized father. I needed them to know their father as a real person, not a fairy tale "my father, the great Inuit hunter".

Aside from that, I was leery of becoming financially trapped if my parents helped me to leave. Papa would finally be able to control me and my children. I could not do that to myself. After all, it had been Papa's attempt to control my life that had gotten me into this whole thing in Mittimatalik in the first place. It was his fear of my Sakikuluk's influence that made him careful and, of course, cunning enough to hire his son-in-law after my son was born. I was protected as long as my Sakikuluk was alive. Now that she was dead, I felt somewhat vulnerable. I simply could not trust Papa, in spite of his more-or-less apology.

On one visit to the McDermotts, Noel put a question to me, something like, "Why does a well-educated, fairly attractive, young woman throw her life away in this way?"

I did not have a ready answer on why I persisted. The reasons were complicated. But I did begin to think more deeply about how I could improve my life and that of my children. I had a home of my own, but now I needed a secure way to support us. As Noel pointed out, I was well-educated. Perhaps I could develop some kind of local career with that.

In the spring of 1985, the Mittimatalik community adult educator position had suddenly come open for competition. Could this be my job? The one that would allow me to support my children here in our home town? The home management trainer and I discussed my potential suitability for this job. I had an undergraduate university degree and experience in tutoring bookkeeping and training laboratory procedures as well as in substitute teaching at the local school, not to mention instructing local adults in English literacy. Noel, the school principal, also encouraged me. I submitted my application to the local education council along with letters of reference, feeling confident that this job was mine.

I thought that the local education council would choose me over other candidates because they were already familiar with me. I was sadly mistaken. They chose, as new adult educator, a young Qallunaq woman, the common-law wife of an Inuk formerly based in Igloolik, who had theatre experience, but did not have much in the way of academic qualifications. I had to swallow my disappointment and continued to work for this new adult educator as her part-time literacy instructor.

Then it occurred to me that I could also attend the Training for the Trainer program at St. Francis Xavier University (St. FX) in Antigonish, Nova Scotia, that the home management trainee, Mary, would attend that summer. Again, Noel encouraged me, as did the former local school principal, T. Bert Rose, who had relocated to Frobisher Bay. They served as my references for this adult educator training program. I had no idea if this would qualify me for other community adult educator positions on Baffin Island, but I felt it time to settle on a career in adult education anyway.

I had some money saved with Mama, so I was able to pay for the transportation, accommodation and course fees. My sisters-in-law said they would care for my children for these four weeks of training. I told my children I would call them every week by long distance telephone. Mama gave me a cheque from our joint bank account which I thought I could cash at the bank in Antigonish on arrival. This money was to pay for my meals and things I may need while away.

Finally, the day arrived when Mary and I boarded the plane for Nova Scotia. Mary and I were roommates at the St. FX residence. We settled into our room in the late afternoon and explored our floor of the residence. Classes were to begin the next day.

I had almost no cash money left after paying for my breakfast in the cafeteria. After class I went off to find the local branch of my bank to cash my cheque.

I had not used banking services in person since I went north a little over a decade earlier. The bank teller told me that they would take my cheque and process it, but they would not give me the money until the cheque had cleared. That, I was told, would take a week. Ouch! With the money I did have left, I bought a box of crackers which did the trick for a few days. Mary brought me whatever food for me she could smuggle out from the cafeteria where the program learners ate. Her meals had been prepaid as part of her Home Management training.

Having to rely on Mary to augment my meals this way, felt to me like I was homeless, recalling former times when I was hungry on the streets of Toronto as a young adult. I was embarrassed to have no money at all. Luckily, I was able to pay for my accommodation by cheque. After the week had passed, I received my money from the bank and was finally able to join the other learners in the cafeteria.

The four-week Training for the Trainer program was administered by the Adult Education Department of St. FX. Mary and I attended all the sessions and did well in all our learning tasks. There was only the final essay to write.

A few days before the end of classes, Rick Steele, our instructor, took me aside. I wondered if anything was wrong. Did he have bad news for me?

He said, "I see that you hold a Bachelor of Arts degree from Brock University in St. Catharines, Ontario. I think that your having completed my course so far is all you need to do. I will exempt you from writing the final essay and give you the Training for Trainers certificate if you go and see Dr. Marie Gillen, the administrator of the Distance Master of Adult Education program. I've already spoken to her about you."

I was dumbfounded, not fully comprehending.

"Go see Dr. Gillen now," he said.

I did that. I went to see Dr. Marie Gillen and had a long talk with her about my situation, my hearing problems, and what my future in adult education might include. She was fully convinced that I could actually do well in her Master's program. Finally, I completed the paperwork and wrote a cheque for the deposit. I was now enrolled in the St. FX Distance Adult Education Master Degree program. I could hardly believe it. Next summer, I was to come again for the six-week induction residency for the program.

Suddenly, I had a real future. I would become a professional adult educator. Whatever self-esteem I had lost during these past years, including the first challenging week of the Training for Trainers program, I had suddenly regained and even surpassed. With a Master's Degree, I would be more than eligible to work with Inuit adults on north Baffin Island, I thought.

Mary and I returned to Mittimatalik, both of us happily holding our Training for the Trainer Certificates.

At St. FX residence after my acceptance to the Master of Ad. Ed. Program 1985.

My reunion with my children should have been joyful. It was at first, but then I saw that little Ulayuk, who clung to me, was covered in suppurating sores. They were all over her body, I discovered. Ruben told me proudly that he had made sure that Ulayuk got something to eat every day. This puzzled me because I had assumed that her birth mother and her aunt, those with whom I had left Ulayuk, would have taken care of that. When I spoke to my mother about finding Ulayuk having actually suffered while I away, she apologized to me.

"I was so involved with your Papa's business for these weeks. I only remembered about checking on Ulayuk the last week before you came," she said. "When I finally did see Ulayuk, and the state she was in, I had your sister-in-law take her to the nursing station right away."

This was disappointing and upsetting. I suddenly realized that an adopted child, a tiguaq, was very often ignored or even mistreated, not usually cherished as I did my adopted Ulayuk. My son, Ruben, was treated much better even though the grandparents had passed away. I was grateful that my son had cared for his little sister while I was away. I had to make better, more reliable, arrangements for my children's care for the following summer when I was to leave again to start my Masters Degree, I promised myself as well as them.

I returned to work as part-time adult literacy instructor at the Community Adult Education Centre.

❋

Mikiseetee was in the meantime living in his house up the road from us with his girlfriend. He came to visit us every now and then. My children were overjoyed when he came. He and I did not talk much except about our children. One time, he came and surprised me. He said he was tired of being separated from me. He said he was now willing to try it my way and stop overdrinking. His girlfriend, I knew, was pregnant and he was not the father. I said that reconciling our separation was worth a try and that I, too, was weary of being without my husband. I wondered as I was telling him this if I were making a mistake.

Later that day, Ruben came and told me that his father had told him that he and I would be getting together again, that we would be a happy family once again. I had not seen Ruben so happy since his ningiu had died. Surely, everything would work out the way it should, I thought.

Then, a few weeks later, Mikiseetee came into our house very early in the morning. My children were still asleep. I knew that he was not usually awake at this hour, either. He was crying. Something must be wrong. Did someone die?

"Why are you crying?" I asked.

It took him a few tries before he could gather himself together enough to answer.

"We cannot get back together again. My girlfriend had her baby this morning at the nursing station."

This made no sense to me. I could not understand the connection between his girlfriend delivering her baby and his not being able to reconcile with me. I must have looked puzzled.

He continued, "The nurse thought I was the father and gave me the new baby to hold. Now I must be this baby girl's father, don't you see? I have no choice."

I dimly recalled something I had heard among my extended family about how the first person to hold the baby "belongs" to the baby; that is, that person must take care of that baby for life. This must be what this was about. I asked Mikiseetee, and he said that was it, an Inuit custom thing.

"Okay," I said. "You can stop crying. I understand and will not interfere. We will just remain separated then."

"That's the problem." he said. "I cannot tell my son. I cannot break my beloved son's heart. You must tell him."

He did not stay to face our children.

After breakfast, I told my children that their father and I, sadly, would not, after all, be getting back together as we had planned. Mikiseetee was right. This news broke Ruben's heart and he, in his uncomprehending childish way, blamed me. Ulayuk's heart was also broken in her quiet way, I saw. My own heart had been broken so many times before but now it broke all over again. We all cried together. And after we finished crying, we talked about how we need to be a family, just the three of us.

One afternoon, just after my literacy class had ended for the day, the new adult educator told me to call her supervisor in Frobisher Bay. She gave me the name and number and said to use the office telephone. I was puzzled but made the call. Apparently, the supervisor had been advised of the names of the people who had just graduated from the St. FX Training for the Trainers course, as well as the communities where they lived. She congratulated me on my successful completion of the course and said she needed a community adult educator for Arctic Bay, that a position had suddenly come open there. She said I should submit my application for this position, that the home management trainer would give me the form and all the information I needed to fill it out. I had never considered leaving Mittimatalik. Now, I thought that Arctic Bay was not really that far away, and Ruben had relatives there, too. This thought was enough to spur me on to making the application.

About a week after I applied, I received word that I had been accepted as the new community adult educator for Arctic Bay. I was overjoyed that I was now gainfully employed with the Northwest Territories Government and eligible for all the perks of my new position aside from proper pay and moving expenses, a decent house for my children and even paid vacations. The only trouble was that I would have to take my children away from Mittimatalik, their home. It was with a divided heart that I accepted this position.

After a week of frenzied packing and giving things away, Ruben, Ulayuk and I were taken by government truck to the airport for our departure. Kenn Borek Air flew us from Mittimatalik to Nanisivik where we disembarked. Nanisivik was a zinc-lead mining town and we noted the modern facilities and staff housing as we drove through the town in the government van on our way to Arctic Bay. The road was long and winding along the coast through the tundra and around mountain masses, now red and gold with autumn. Finally, we arrived at our staff house in Arctic Bay with its view over the bay. We were situated under the mountain that looked from a distance like a closed fist. The black sand covering the ground was the first thing we all noted that was different from Mittimatalik. This was now our new home.

I could imagine all those who cared about my deceased Sakikuluk's deathbed wish to have me and my children away from Mittimatalik, how they, and Mikiseetee, could now all relax. By taking this position in Arctic Bay, I had fulfilled her desire.

I realized that this was the end of the Mittimatalik chapter of my life. I may visit in future, but it would not be the home it had been for me. I felt this loss just as I had when I left my German home as a child.

From now on, I would have to find a way to further my education as well as my adult education career while raising my two unhappy, homesick children wherever that may be. I resolved to do my best.

Afterword

Our adventures were not over.

We did not find a real home in the small Baffin communities as I had hoped. No other place compared with Mittimatalik, our home of choice.

In 1988, my children and I moved from Arctic to Clyde River and in 1991 landed in Iqaluit, the former Frobisher Bay renamed in 1987. There, I facilitated adult literacy learning with Inuit and conducted evening programming as an adult educator at Nunavut Arctic College which was then known simply as Arctic College. I eventually even owned a house in Iqaluit, but a house is not a home, so even that could not make Iqaluit my home.

Papa donated all his holdings to the people of Mittimatalik after forming a local Inuit board of directors to oversee the property. My parents left Mittimatalik for good in 1988. Without my parents' direct involvement, the local board of directors finally faded to nothing.

In Iqaluit, Noel McDermott, then the principal of the Eastern Arctic Teacher Education Program at Arctic College, supported and mentored my higher education efforts. I did finally attain my Master of Adult Education from St. Francis Xavier University without the college's official consent in 1993. Gaining this credential did not enhance my position or employment security at the college as I had expected.

In 1994, a tragic fire consumed the Catholic mission/church in Mittimatalik and took Ataata Mari's life.

In 1995, my Papa died suddenly. To this day I feel ambivalent about him. I try to remember that he was just a flawed, damaged human being. The following year my son brought his ashes to Mittimatalik to rest near Ataata Mari's grave.

In 1996, funding for adult literacy was the first thing cut from the Arctic College budget when the Northwest Territories government downsized in preparation for the formation of the new Nunavut Territory and I was let go from the college. The college, in upheaval during its reorganization, was renamed Nunavut Arctic College.

From 1996 to 1999, I served the Nunatta Sunakkutaangit Museum as manager/curator which paid the barest minimum under the Northwest Territories pre-Nunavut budget cuts. I augmented my loss of income with part-time independent contracts, teaching life skills evening classes to prisoners at the correctional centre, conducting training workshops for personal counsellors, and writing adult literacy learning materials, and even working part-time for Nunavut Arctic College.

I was then, oddly enough, re-hired by the College in 1999 after the formation of the new Nunavut Territory. That same year, I felt compelled to turn down an administrative position offered to me because of my hearing challenges. I could control a classroom to accommodate my hearing needs but I knew I could not manage an administrative role with its interminable meetings. I was well aware that the College would be even more underfunded and that administration would be fraught with difficulties in its new iteration.

There were more challenges to come.

While I was visiting New Zealand in the summer of 2000, my daughter told me over long-distance telephone of her son's, my grandson's, sudden death. He was less than three months old. I immediately returned to Iqaluit. I found out that the RCMP had accused her of killing her child. I had an autopsy performed to exonerate my daughter. The baby had died of SIDS, Sudden Infant Death Syndrome. We held the funeral and then I took my daughter to my mother's house in St. Catharines on bereavement leave. By this time, though, my mother already showed signs of dementia.

I returned to Iqaluit and Nunavut Arctic College in December 2000 when Mama was placed in a long-term-care home. In January 2001, my Mama died. I went back to St. Catharines, again on bereavement leave. The following summer, my sister Irmgard brought Mama's ashes to Mittimatlaik to rest beside Papa's ashes near Ataata Mari's grave.

In the summer of 2001, after my supervisor at Nunavut Arctic College had gone on holiday, her replacement refused to allow me to extend my leave and demanded my immediate return to work. I was not ready, could not argue, so I quit. Later, my supervisor offered to reinstate my employment and I returned to Iqaluit for several months in 2002 but this did not work out. I had to conclude that my life on Baffin Island was at an end.

I moved away permanently from Iqaluit to Ottawa, Ontario, in May 2002.

In Ottawa, my first husband Michael and I became good friends all over again, both of us much wiser than when we parted in 1974.

Mikiseetee died in September 2014 in Ottawa. I visited him with my children in hospital shortly before he passed away.

I moved away from Ottawa in December 2014 to New Richmond, Quebec.

Michael died in February 2020 in Ottawa.

So, then, that leaves that question. Why did I, a "fairly decent-looking, well-educated young woman, throw her life away like this"? It was complicated. Even today, I have no clear response. But I am convinced it was all necessary. I did learn much about the lives of my

extended family in Mittimatalik, about myself and the vagaries of life.
 The memories of my Sakikuluk and my Sakialuk sustain me.
 I live and write on the beautiful south Gaspé coast.

Dorothee Komangapik
2022

Acknowledgements

I owe my deepest gratitude to my former mentor, Noel McDermott, who read portions of the first draft of this work before his declining health interfered. And I thank his wife, Kate McDermott, for her patience.

My friend and mentor, Sherrill Wark, provided me with invaluable support and encouragement throughout this project. How can I ever thank you, Sherrill?

I thank my readers, Catina Noble, my sister Ursula Banke, Cindy Cowan, Eliza von Baeyer, my daughter Lilian-Ulayuk Komangapik, and Kenn Harper who all provided me with thoughtful criticism and comments.

I thank Jeeteeta Ootoova Merkosak for allowing me to use her photo of Igarjuaq for the memoir cover, Gary Mills for my post-parachute jump photo in Chapter 2, and Norman Koonoo for the photo of Ataata Mari's crucifix in Chapter 4. Most of the photos in the text are from my personal collection.

I also thank Genvieve LeMoine of the Peary-MacMillan Arctic Museum, Bowdoin College, Brunswick, Maine, U. S. A., for permission to use their vintage photos located in Appendix 3, included as a memorial for my family.

Glossary

aglu — seal breathing hole in the sea ice
agvik — low platform for flensing seal skins
ajurnaqmat — cannot be helped (loosely translated)
akpa — murre, a white-breasted black seabird
amautik — women's baby-carrying parka
anaana — mother
aqiggiq — ptarmigan, a small white partridge-like bird
asivak — spider
iglu — house
igluvigaq — a snow house
igunaq — fermented walrus meat, an Inuit delicacy
ilisaiji — teacher
inaluaq — small intestines
inukshuk — a cairn-like structure made of stacked rocks to guide hunters, sometimes in human form

Inughuit — Greenland Inuit
Inuk — one person; Inuit — plural, people (formerly known as Eskimo(s))
Inuktitut — Inuit language
Iqaluit — Frobisher Bay, capital of Nunavut
kakivak — a trident-like leister or fish spear
kamik — boot made of animal skin
maktaaq — whale skin, usually narwhal or beluga, an Inuit delicacy
Mittimatalik — Pond Inlet
ningiu — paternal grandmother
nuilaq — fur trim around the parka hood
palaugaq — bannock, a type of quick bread
Qallunaq — a non-Inuit person; Qallunaat — plural
qamutik — sled pulled by snowmobile or dog team
qarmaq — sod house, old style Inuit house made of rock, sod and often whalebone
qulittaq — hunting parka, usually made of caribou skin
qulliq — seal oil lamp, usually shaped as a half moon open dish
saki — parent-in-law, used for both mother-in-law and father-in-law
silapaak — outer pants, made of animal skins
siqpi — white accumulations in the corner of an eye
siva — biscuit
Sivataarvik — Saturday, day when biscuits were distributed by visiting whalers
tiguaq — adopted child
tiigak — male seal in rutting season
ukaliq — arctic hare
ukuaq — daughter-in-law or female relative-in-law
ulu — half-moon-shaped women's knife
umiaq — skin boat

Appendix I

Qumangapik (aka Komangapik, at bottom) had a son by a woman in Iglulik before he married Inuujaq. His name was Piungnituk and married Kapik who died during the family's starvation ordeal at about the time that Inuuja's daughter by her former husband died of gangrene during the late 1940s.

(See, next page.)

364 | Dorothee Komangapik

From back cover insert of the book *Qitdlarssuaq: The Story of a Polar Migration*, Fr. Guy Mary-Rousselière, 1991, Wuerz Publishing Ltd., Winnipeg, Manitoba, Canada.

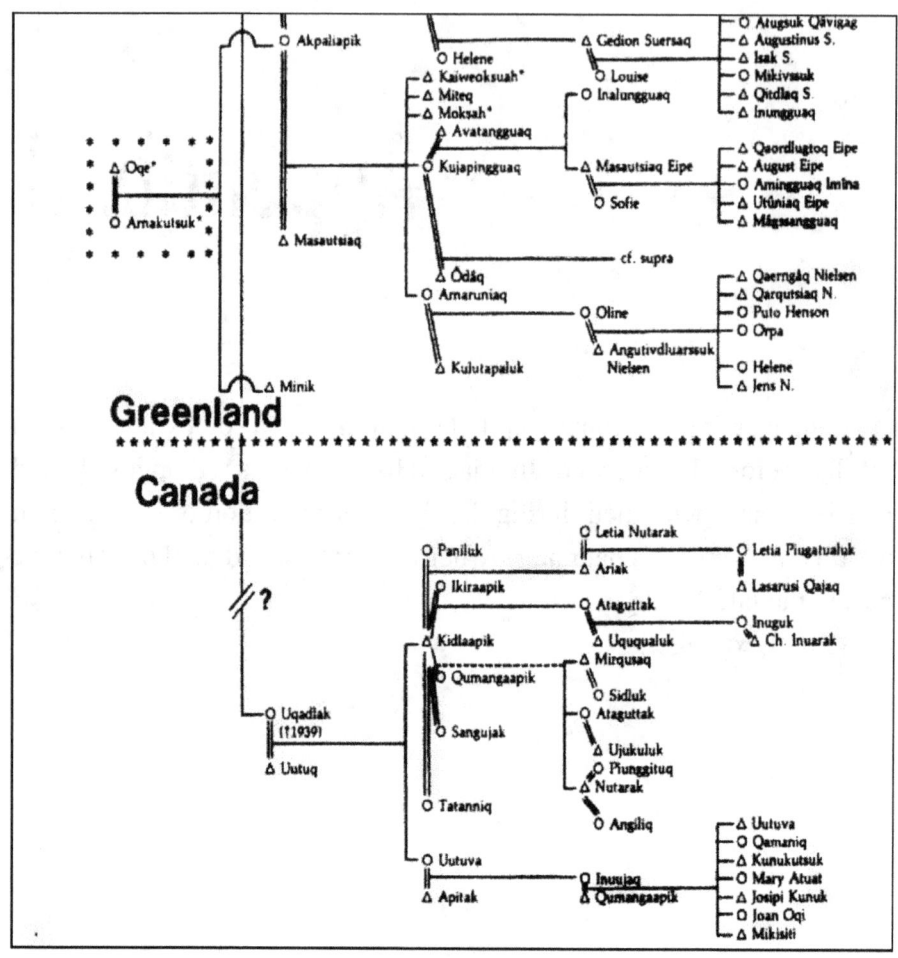

Genealogical chart including Qumangapik (Komangapik) family tree lower right.

Appendix 2

Portrait of my parents, Sophie D. and Hermann A. R. Steltner, 1993.

Appendix 3

Courtesy of The Peary-MacMillan Arctic Museum, Bowdoin College.

Pond Inlet (Mittimatalik) 1950 - 3000.33.5163.

Native (Joshua Komangapik) 1948-3000.33.4999.

Woman laughing (Inuuja, a.k.a. Miriam, Joshua Komangapik's wife) 1948-3000.33.5006.

Eskimo girl (Mary Issigaitoq, daughter of Inuuja) 1948-3000.33.5004.

Eskimo girl (Joanna Pewatualuk, Inuuja's daughter and my daughter's birth mother) 1948-3000.33.4997.

Eskimo boy (Kooneloosie Nutarak, my daughter's paternal grandfather) 1948-3000.33.4998.

Bi-racial woman with baby (Elisapee Ootova with Jayko, Elisapee is Jeeteetah's mother and my sister-in-law) 1948-3000.33.5002.

www.ingramcontent.com/pod-product-compliance
Lightning Source LLC
Chambersburg PA
CBHW060550230426
43670CB00011B/1766